THE AUTO REPAIR
PRIMER

Other Books by the Authors

Guy Alland, Miron Waskiw, and Tony Hiss:
*KNOW-HOW: The Fix-It Book for the
Clumsy But Pure of Heart*
Patricia D. Hemingway:
THE TRANSCENDENTAL MEDITATION PRIMER
THE WELL-DRESSED WOMAN

THE AUTO REPAIR PRIMER

Guy Alland

Patricia Drake Hemingway

Illustrations by Linda Lucero

LITTLE, BROWN AND COMPANY   BOSTON   TORONTO

FIRST EDITION
T 05/78

LIBRARY OF CONGRESS CATALOGING IN PUBLICATION DATA

Alland, Guy.
    The auto repair primer.

    Bibliography: p.
    Includes index.
    1. Automobiles — Maintenance and repair. I. Heming-
way, Patricia Drake, joint author. II. Title.
TL152.A274   629.28'8'22   77-18088
ISBN 0-316-35528-3

Designed by Susan Windheim

Published simultaneously in Canada
by Little, Brown & Company (Canada) Limited

PRINTED IN THE UNITED STATES OF AMERICA

I dedicate my contribution to this book to my dear departed dad, H. Gladstone Hemingway, from whom I inherited my lifelong love of cars and who instilled in me my mechanical curiosity and a high regard for precision tools as instruments of utility and enjoyment . . . and to Guy, my patient instructor.

P. D. H.
Bridgewater, Connecticut

I dedicate my contribution to this book to the enlightenment of all the fathers of the world who want their sons and daughters to become doctors, lawyers, and Indian chiefs, thereby denying said sons and daughters the pleasures of working with their hands on practical things, and to Rey Casella — a professional mechanic and my instructor, with whom I learned the meaning of the words "If it works don't mess with it."

G. A.
New York, New York

Acknowledgments

Special thanks for providing information and help in preparing this book to the following:

The Chrysler Corporation

Lucas Industries North America, Inc.

Delco-Remy Division of General Motors

E. I. Du Pont de Nemours & Company

Fiat Distributors, Inc.

Ford Marketing Corporation

Anthony Tung

Dale Pfeffer

Greg Alland

Contents

Preface

DATELINE — New York City, January 10, 1976

I have been driving an automobile for almost forty years, thirty-five of them legally. I grew up in Pennsylvania, where you had to be sixteen years old before you could take your driving test to obtain your driver's license. My father had taught me, with infinite pains and patience, to drive at the tender age of ten because I relentlessly bugged him until he did, and I was getting a bit large to be sitting on his lap while he let me steer. It was during the Depression when he was selling cars for my uncle, who owned the tenth oldest Ford garage in the world. Dad considered himself lucky to have the job. He had sold our own car, an Essex touring model with curtains on the windows and a bud vase on each side of the rear doors, not only because we needed the money but because part of the remuneration for his job was the twenty-four-hour use of a "demonstrator," that is, a new Ford that he took around the countryside to show his prospective buyers and let them drive for themselves the wonderful new product he was peddling.

Once I had prevailed upon him to teach me to drive, the next problem was where it would be safe and legal to enter upon the course of instruction. We were in luck . . . not three blocks from our house were the county fairgrounds, with a super racetrack upon which, one illustrious week of the year, drove such renowned drivers as Barney Oldfield, Indianapolis Speedway racer, and other luminaries of the racing world. If it was good enough for them, it was good enough for little Pat. Even as a small child I had a push-pedal car that was my favorite toy ("Very unlike a girl," my mother used to cluck disapprovingly). And, since my father worked for a garage and my uncle owned it, I hung around the place a lot. To the mechanics I was the Eloise of the grease monkeys. I learned through greasy osmosis some of the terminology of the trade, like gaskets, valve jobs, universal joints, the difference (in principle) between hydraulic and mechanical brakes, and so on. But I never learned how to fix anything. All that background taught me little, except that sometimes, just sometimes, it gave me a vague idea of what might be wrong with the multitude of automobiles I have owned during my lifetime. At least I knew I didn't need a valve job if I wasn't burning oil and I knew that every so often one should have the battery water checked . . . and even more obscure or remote things, but as far as any basic knowledge of the intricacies of an internal-combustion engine — forget it.

In 1949 I got my first automobile for fifty dollars cash. It was a fourthhand 1930 Ford Model A black coupe with a rumble seat. A great automobile. The automobile that made Henry Ford a multimillionaire. A superlative and simple motorcar, no frills, just good, sound mechanical structure. As I recall, it was the only car that would run one fine cold winter in New Hope, Pennsylvania, because it was the only car around that had a crank to turn the motor over in frigid weather. I was the envy of all for the three days the cold spell lasted. After driving it for over a trouble-free year, I sold it to a friend of mine for a hundred dollars cash, doubling my money.

My second car was a 1939 classic V-8 four-door Ford convertible phaeton with a Bermuda Bell on the floor; black with a black top and a thin red stripe around the midsection. Again fourthhand but a mint-condition stunner, genuine cowhide leather seats, white walls, and so on. As they say in the trade, a cream puff — trouble-free until I sliced the right side off on a steel guardrail late one evening. It was towed to my uncle's garage and repaired, and as far as looks were concerned was good as new. But when you drove it, it seemed to be heading toward Funston's — the wheels were headed straight but the car was veering left, like a Labrador on the run. Diagnosis: bent frame. Heartbroken, I parted with it, for the five hundred dollars I had originally paid for it, to the same friend who had bought the Model A.

My third car was a secondhand 1950 Nash Rambler convertible. A super little thing with only one fault — it wouldn't start when it rained without a lot of coaxing. That meant opening up the hood and drying everything in sight and sometimes applying heat in the form of an electric light bulb for a few hours to thoroughly dry everything out. But the mileage was superb. I could drive to Florida on two tanks of gas . . . if it didn't rain.

In 1952, I saw my way clear to trade it in to get my first *new* car, a Ford convertible, which I ordered from my uncle's son, my first cousin. I mean, if you can't trust your kin to give you a good deal, who can you trust?

With no little partum-pain I cleaned my personal things out of the trusty Nash Rambler and transferred them to the glove compartment of the new Ford. Kissed my kinfolk and Nellie (the Nash) good-bye, jumped into Ferguson the Third, and off I drove, back to New York, a three-and-a-half-hour jaunt from Bloomsburg, Pennsylvania, my hometown.

Before I got to New York the following things happened: the door on the driver's side flew open three times, the hood flew up in my face once, totally obliterating my forward vision. When I reached my destination I called my cousin. He said, "Oh, just a few minor adjustments. Those things always happen with a new car. Bring it back. It's under a three-month new-car guarantee."

Three times I drove the hell up there to have those identical things fixed. Three times I drove back to New York thinking they were fixed. Then the guarantee was up. In those days, pre–Ralph Nader, it was called tough titty. If you got a lemon, you were stuck with it. That car's problems started at the drawing board. A veritable onslaught of brilliant letters from me to Henry Ford II made no difference whatsoever. For the next eight years that I owned the car, I had the door and the hood wired shut to make certain I didn't fall out and to make sure the hood didn't pop up in my face at ninety miles per hour.

Then, fortune smiled upon me. It was 1959. I was going to Europe to pick up a brand-new Mercedes convertible, a 220 SE (SE standing for Super Einspritz —fuel injection), allegedly the best car Mercedes-Benz, the gods of the motor industry, had ever designed. I flew nonstop, New York to Paris, then took a Lufthansa from Paris to Stuttgart and a taxi direct to the Mercedes-Benz factory where my new baby, my dream come true, was waiting for me: cream yellow with black top, red leather bucket seats that you could push all the way back to make the most comfortable bed I had ever slept on, a polished mahogany dashboard that shone like a Rothschild antique, plush red carpeting, and when you slammed the door it sounded as though you had shut the door of the tomb of the Pharaohs, it was so solidly constructed. Men, women, and children stopped to look at that car as if it were Greta Garbo. I called her Millicent, the Mercedes. Elegant, I thought. And on her hood I replaced the Mercedes emblem with a nude Lalique goddess with flowing hair that captured the light from the headlamps at night for a magnificent effect. Nothing was too good for Milly, including the best mechanic in the world, the head mechanic of the Roosevelt racing team (who happened to live only a few miles from where I lived on Long Island). He was the cheapest, in the long run, because he only did what was right and necessary. He was a wonderful Irishman named McGee. He loved engines, his wife loved engines, and his daughter loved engines. (He once spoke to me about taking a course he was thinking of giving on how to repair engines. He said his wife and daughter were going to take it. I sadly had to decline because of lack of time and pressing obligations, but one day, I promised myself, I would do it, along with that photography course and agriculture course and a few others.)

Millicent also came with a three-month guarantee. Six months after I drove her out of the Mercedes factory she broke down on Fourteenth Street (a heavily trafficked two-way boulevard in Manhattan), the last shopping day before Christmas. *Something* snapped in the area of the steering column and I could not get the car into anything but the fourth forward gear, in which I barely managed to get it to the Mercedes garage many blocks away. In doing so I burned out the clutch. Several hundreds of dollars later I drove the car out of the garage and back to Long Island. In the course of owning that car for seven years I had three universal joints replaced (a few hundred dollars each time); it seems that model had a built-in penchant for chewing up universal joints. And the aforementioned break in the gear-linkage chain that caused the Fourteenth Street breakdown happened another couple of times. The second and third times I was sufficiently wise not to drive it home in fourth gear.

In those days, fuel injection was new to American mechanics. I drove the Mercedes to Pennsylvania for my father's funeral. A few miles from the funeral parlor the car stopped. It was Saturday afternoon and all garages were closed. My cousin (who had inherited the garage from my uncle) looked under the hood, saw the fuel injection unit and the huge motor, and said, "No one in this town can fix this. I'll have it towed up to Wilkes-Barre and call the guy up there to work overtime on it" (Wilkes-Barre was forty-two miles distant). After the funeral, at the wake, he came to me and said, "Your car's back." I said, "Super, what was wrong with it?" He looked at my brother as though they had something in common, then looked back at me and said flatly, "You were out of gas."

In the seven years I owned that car I spent over six thousand dollars in repairs and maintenance. I cannot say, even though it drove like nothing on this earth, *when* it drove, that I was reluctant to turn it in. It was similar to letting go a lover who has turned too expensive to keep up. In a way, I still miss her, because *when* she performed, nothing could touch her superiority on the open road.

I traded her in for a 1969 Mercury Cougar convertible, which was tantamount to trading an old glorious pure-Arabian stallion for a new crippled burro. I sold it on the open market six months later at a tremendous loss because it seemed to me the biggest travesty that had ever been perpetrated on an unsuspecting public since the peddlers of the defunct Comstock Lode. The center of gravity must have been somewhere in the front bumper, because the rest of the car headed skyward every time I went over an expansion crack in the pavement.

Then my financial fortunes took a turn for the worse. I hastily moved to Europe and purchased a fourthhand Berlin-bred Volkswagen-turned-into-camper by loving hands at home, that is, by two hippies who were on their way to India but had run out of money in Ibiza and were forced to sell it. It was seven years old when I bought it for eight hundred bucks cash. I named it Willie (short for Wilhelm, Kaiser Bill). I drove that rusty old bucket of bolts all over Europe, to Greece and back to Spain, where I pushed it over those Spanish goat trails called highways for over two years and never spent a peseta on it, before I resold it to an American for four hundred dollars. The only trouble I ever had with it was that once in a while it wouldn't start. The original owners had told me, when that happened, to open up the

back and give the battery a good kick . . . which I did and up it would start.

I loved that old bus so much that when I returned to the U.S.A. two years ago I purchased another — this time an honest-to-God proper VW Campmobile with a convertible bed, table, icebox, and sink-factory built in, and a top that went up and down to enable one to stand up when parked. (I was beginning to know how a hunchback feels, after three nonstop rainy days in Morocco stooped over in my old van.)

My Campmobile was purchased secondhand, only 8,000 miles on it. The salesman said, "This car was ordered and purchased by an Australian who took it from New York to California and back and traded it right back to us." I checked the owner's manual to see if he was lying. Sure enough, it had had itself stamped: Delivery Inspection, VW, Fifth Avenue, New York City, 4/9/73; 600-mile checkup — Roanoke, Virginia, 4/13/73 (that should have been my first clue; four days from New York City to Roanoke, Virginia?); 3,000-mile checkup, Modern Motors, Flagstaff, Arizona, 4/20/73 (whatever the problem was they must have fixed it in Roanoke, because seven days from Virginia to Flagstaff, Arizona, is not bad time); 6,000-mile checkup at Ray Powders VW, Casper, Wyoming, 5/11/73; then back to the original VW dealer in New York City for the 8,000-mile checkup, which is when I bought it. The car looked clean and beautiful . . . "Just nicely broken in," the salesman said, and I agreed with him. Nothing more boring than breaking in a new car properly.

We clinched the deal. I hopped into the driver's seat and gingerly started Wilhelm up. I smiled at the salesman and waved good-bye. As I pulled over the little hummock at the street entrance the motor stalled. I looked nervously at the salesman. "Oh," he laughed, "that's nothing. It always needs warming up first."

It was a warm May day. I started up again, gunned it over the hump, and off I toodled up Sixth Avenue . . . on the road again, high above the rest of the poor ordinary automobile drivers' heads, on my way to Connecticut. At every stoplight the car stalled. Oh well, once it warms up, I thought. At every tollbooth, from the Triborough Bridge to the Sawmill River Parkway, it stalled. Oh well, a minor adjustment to soup up the idle, I thought.

A few weeks later I took it back to the VW dealer whence it came and asked them to see to the adjustment. I spoke to the salesman from whom I had bought it. "Of course, just leave it to us. No problem."

No problem! When I went to pick up the car at five o'clock the salesman had "left for the day." I paid my money at the service desk for the oil and filter change (no charge for fixing the "problem") and was told the car would be delivered at the end of the ramp, which is located at the far end of the garage. Bear in mind it is closing time. The van came down the ramp and I noticed all the hubcaps were missing. I mentioned this to the driver. He said, "Are you sure you had them on?" As if I looked like the kind of person who would drive an automobile around with hubcaps missing.

"Yes, I'm sure," I said quietly, my eyes going up in their sockets.

"Oh," he said. "I'll go look for them."

A few minutes later he returned with my four hubcaps, his head shaking from side to side in wonderment.

"Must have forgotten to put them back on," he explained.

"Odd," I said, "since there was no reason to take them off in the first place."

No answer. I jumped into the driver's seat and drove off across town. At the first stoplight the car stalled. Furious, I drove back around the block. The garage was closed tighter than a drum.

It cost me almost ten dollars in taxi fares on top of the garage bill. On further examination I discovered they had also lifted a new five-dollar flashlight and a pair of fifteen-dollar sunglasses. A few weeks later I received a notice from the main distributor of Volkswagens in America stating that that particular garage had gone out of business. They referred me to another in Manhattan for future service.

That was the beginning of a long, expensive, and arduous series of attempts to have the stalling problem fixed. I tried in different garages, from Long Island to Key West and back again to Connecticut, to no avail. It was then that I decided to take the long-put-off course in auto mechanics to be able to fix the bloody thing myself. I checked the Yellow Pages and asked around town for the best beginner's course in auto mechanics. After extensive checking I came up with the answer — Guy Alland's Knowhow Workshop on Sixteenth Street, New York City.

The purpose of the course:

To be able to do things on your car that other people won't do properly for you, or if they do, charge you too much money for the services performed.

To learn about tools and motor-testing apparatuses.

To learn the basic makeup of an automobile and how it works.

To learn how to tune up your car.

To learn simple maintenance procedures to keep your car in shape.

To learn how to troubleshoot on the road or in the ditch.

Auto Repair,
the Great American Rip-off

In a comparative study done in 1972 by the Automobile Club of Missouri on 1,000 cars taken to garages for repairs, they discovered that 28.7 percent of all the work performed was done *unsatisfactorily* or NOT AT ALL (although charged for). Of that 28.7 percent the average bill was $127.

Now get this. They repeated the study two years later, in 1974, and the figure had jumped to 37.7 percent for work that was done unsatisfactorily or not at all, *and* the average bill for this travesty had risen to $148. If you care to extrapolate those figures (at a yearly growth rate of 4.5 percent and 8 percent respectively), by the time this book is in print (1977) those figures will have exploded to 51 percent of the repair work on your cars that will be done unsatisfactorily or *not at all*. And your average bill, circa 1977, for that will have soared to $186. (They didn't include in their study the garages that remove your good parts and replace them with worn-out parts.)

If one cares to go even further, multiply those amounts by well over 100,000,000 cars and trucks in the United States and see what an astonomical sum the rip-off amounts to.

Little wonder that practically every school system with evening adult education programs is instituting an auto mechanics course to at least explain the basics of how your car works so that you will be able to tell your carburetor from your distributor and have a vague conception of what the rip-off artists are talking about when they say, "Sorry, but you need a new muffler," when the trouble is in the electrical system.

Unfortunately, most of those courses do not come complete with textbook, and due to the limited time and the extensive amount of material they must cover they can barely scratch the surface of the many systems in your automobile. As an antidote we offer this book, which includes not only the famous New York New School's Complete Know-How Course of Auto Mechanics for the Beginner but also troubleshooting, the purpose and use of tools, gas-saving tips, maintenance instructions and procedures, and a simple to understand and follow motor tune-up for the beginner. The easily comprehensible text is accompanied by well thought out illustrations that further clarify the techniques, parts, and systems for the reader.

This book is written with the assumption that the reader is truly a novice and knows little or nothing about a car, its problems, or how to fix them.

DOING IT YOURSELF

One of the greatest recipes for living a happy life is to *enjoy the moment*. Enjoy *what* you are doing *when* you are doing it.

Tempus Fugit — The Bird Is on the Wing

Whether you are making bread, making love, or making repairs on your car, precious moments are consumed. Make each of those moments count by enjoying them to their fullest.

If you're worried about getting your hands soiled, turn your head around and think of the great painters who splattered in every color of the rainbow all their lives. It's just oil of another color. Remember all the fun you had making mud pies? Dress your mind as well as your body for the job at hand. Think of each drop of grease and oil as a lifesaver for your car (and perhaps yourself and your family).

It's your energy as well as your time that you are spending. Consciously transfer it into what you are doing — that's the secret of being happy at your work.

Think what it takes to have someone else do your work for you: (1) You have to make the appointment at the garage. (2) You have to remember to keep it. (3) You have to get the car there. (4) You have to wait to have the work done or make arrangements to be picked up by someone else. (5) Then you have to be dropped off when the car is ready. That all blows most of a day. (6) You have to pay for it.

(7) Then you hope that they did the work properly *if at all.*

We are not suggesting that the beginner start off by taking the car apart and putting it back together. We are not suggesting you attempt any *major* repair. We are hoping that after you have read this book and studied the procedures, you will attempt to do some of the simple maintenance, replacement, and repair yourself. Just these small, easy things can save you untold time, trouble, and money, and give you a tremendous sense of self-satisfaction that money cannot buy. And possibly some sly looks of envy and approval from your family, friends, and neighbors, who secretly wish they possessed your adventurous spirit.

If you are one of those who don't enjoy doing things alone, talk your spouse, child, friend, or neighbor into doing it with you. I promise you, you'll have many a laugh and good time that you wouldn't have had taking the car to the garage.

If you enjoy doing things solo, think of your car as a living, loving thing. As in your relationships with other people, for the most part your car will respond to your tender care or harsh treatment in kind. Lavish it with polish, grease, tune-ups, new parts (when needed), and it in turn will speed you in untroubled comfort in pursuit of other pleasures and endeavors.

Immerse yourself in the mechanism. Clear your brain of other thoughts and sounds and listen to the sounds of your engine on a cold morning, a hot day, a cool evening, a rainy afternoon. Get to know it under as many different circumstances as you would a friend. Recognize what the sounds are telling you every time it whines, purrs, coughs, moans, cries, squeals, thuds, thumps, sparks, flashes, rumbles — much as a mother recognizes her baby's needs. That is the only language you have between you, the only way you can communicate with each other. Let it become part of you, an extension of yourself, like your home. Your enjoyment of it will be enhanced.

We have all seen and admired antique cars twenty or thirty years old that looked as though they were just off the showroom floor. That doesn't just happen. Someone loved those cars and it shows.

When you are steering your car, submit to each movement as though you were part of the windstream, lean into the turns; it's all part of the total weight distribution. Know that every move you make when you are driving adds to or subtracts from the capabilities of your vehicle, just as surely as we know that every pebble moved changes the center of gravity of the whole earth. Let's face it, your car is *your* chariot of the gods, so *make the most of it*.

Nuts, Bolts, Tools, and Fear

It is the duty of the high priests of this world to keep us in ignorance lest they lose their power and control over us lesser mortals, be they priests of religion who incant ancient near-forgotten litanies, medical witch doctors who prognosticate our future (or death) in antique Latin jargon comprehensible only among themselves, or the high priests of technology who, moment to moment, progressively and systematically make our lives dependent upon their every whim. We, the uninitiated, are more and more at their mercy. It is time to call a halt.

The cost of labor goes up 10 to 20 percent a year. It will soon cost twenty dollars to change your windshield wipers. The more things we learn to do ourselves, the more independent and self-sufficient we become, the less we are under the power and spells of those high priests of technology, and the more satisfaction we have in doing it ourselves. By learning to do the simple repairs and maintenance you will have eliminated most of the work that will ever have to be done on your car and will have greatly increased your enjoyment of it as well.

As we learn to walk by crawling first, we learn to do the *simple* mechanical things first. There is nothing frightening about a screw and a screwdriver or a wrench and a nut. Your car is merely a lot of screws and nuts and bolts holding other pieces of metal together. They each in turn have a purpose and they all have a place in the scheme of things. There's a hole for every screw and bolt.

The most important tools you will need you already possess — your eyes, your hands, and last but not least, your common sense.

Many times our eyes are blinded from actually seeing what they rest upon by the fear of our seeming ignorant, to ourselves or others. We therefore subconsciously place a mental block that permits us to see the tapestry but not the threads that make it up, that is, the whole picture but not the component parts and linkages that, for instance, make up an automobile. Remember, an automobile is a logical machine. Look at it carefully and you will see the logic. When you put your foot on the gas pedal and depress it, a series of linkages cause more gasoline to flow, the logical extension of which is acceleration. The mystery of all those years of driving by rote can be wiped away. And so it is with all the other functions of all the other parts of your car. One look, a slight explanation and the mysteries will be gone and you will not be afraid of the unknown monster that lies under the hood and chassis of your car any longer. *You* will become its master and *it* your slave, for a change.

If you read this book and use your head, you will be able to figure out, by elimination and deduction processes, what certain noises, smells, and so forth, belong to what systems of your car. For instance, if you see steam escaping you will realize it has to do with the water cooling system. Even if you can't repair it yourself, it helps when you take the car to a mechanic to be able to say, "Something's wrong with the cooling system." Then he won't tell you you need a valve job because he will figure you are not a complete idiot since you know what system is malfunctioning. You will also know that a hose is an inexpensive item to replace and won't be taken in if a crooked mechanic wants to charge you fifty dollars for a hose.

If you are going to dismantle something, you will know that if it is complex you will have to have a schematic drawing or you will never get it back together by yourself; if it is simple you will have to take a good look before you rip it apart to see how you are going to get it back together. *You will need a system of work.* As you take off parts, line them up *in order* so you will know that they go back in the same order. That is using your noodle, your common sense. Get in the habit of laying out your parts from right to left or vice versa, whichever is easier for you — then stick to that way of working or you will get confused. Be neat in your work habits, have a place for your tools and keep them there. Then you'll be able to find them when you need them. Keep records; make diagrams if necessary. If you want to tackle a not-so-simple job and you're afraid of it, give your neighbor or the service station mechanic an hour's wages after his work hours or on his day off to help you the first time around. Then chances are the second time you will be able to do it yourself.

Get used to handling and working with your tools by doing simple jobs like tightening things, replacing bulbs, and so on, so you will feel at ease with them. Manual therapy is extremely gratifying and wonderful for the nerves, as any therapist will tell you, particularly for cerebral people — more so for them since they are giving the brain a rest, or at least a change, than for people who work with their hands all day long.

Use high-quality tools, for they are much better balanced than lesser tools; they actually feel better when you handle them. Take two wrenches of equal size, one of poor and one of excellent quality. Fondle them, weigh them in the palm of your hand, and you'll see what I mean. Since good tools are honed to a much finer degree of tolerance they do a better job, last longer, and cause you much less trouble than poor-quality tools.

And keep records, which can be fun if you turn your head to it. A "ship's log" not only keeps your mileage records but you'll have a record of all the repairs, their cost, and when they were done. Invaluable for tax purposes and your own amazement. I keep a fairly large diary with everything in it, including my trips and where I stayed, broke down, whatever. Even the names and addresses of the people I met on the road. I refer to it more times than I can tell you, even the weather and the sunsets. I even paste pictures in it of places that I have been. In other words, I enjoy it as it is a constant source of pleasurable memories every time I open it.

I suppose if there were one word to express the way to deal with your car it would be *awareness.* The more you work on your car the more aware of it and its foibles you will be; you will feel part of its life and obtain the unique pleasure that participating brings.

Happy Motoring . . . Bon Voyage. . . .

HOW IT WORKS

1. The Systems Approach

Way back when, Henry Ford, Horace Dodge, Walter Chrysler, and a few other fellows decided to get rid of the horse and install an internal-combustion engine on their old buggies. Eventually they got Harvey Firestone and a man named Goodyear to invent some inflatable rubber tires to put over the old hard-rubber wheels to make the "motor car" ride a little smoother over the rutted country roads. The difference between the horse and the internal-combustion engine is that the horse *pulled* the buggy and the engine *pushes* it via the rear wheels (or the front wheels in the case of front-wheel drive, which is gaining in use).

Then as the years went by they added things like power steering, automatic transmissions (instead of the old clutch-and-shift-gears method), air conditioning, new suspension systems, power brakes, power windows, fuel emission systems, and so forth. Each system considerably complicated maintenance and repair. A child could have repaired the old Model T Ford — a factory-trained mechanic today has difficulty fixing many of the things that go wrong with the ultrasophisticated equipment that is now being sold.

There are six basic systems that go into the making of an automobile: the power system (including the oil system, the fuel system, the exhaust system and pollution controls, and the cooling system), the electrical system, the drive-train system, the steering system, the suspension system, and the braking system.

The purpose of breaking the car down into separate systems is simple. Usually when a car breaks down it is because of a malfunction in *one* system, not all systems, or certainly not all at once. If several of your car's systems break down all at once yell RAPE and get rid of the car, because it will rape your bank account *and* your heartstrings if you keep throwing money and time and sweat into it. Many inexpensive cars simply weren't designed to last more than a given number of miles, regardless of the care you take of them. They have what is known in the trade as "built-in obsolescence." In other words, all the materials used were chosen to wear out at approximately the same time in all the systems.

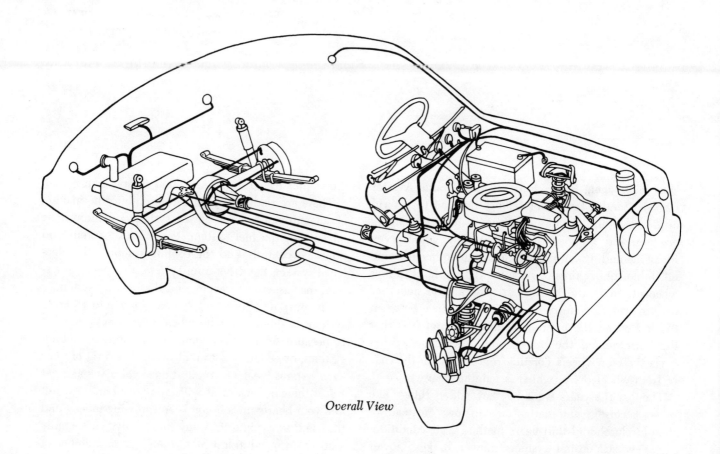

Overall View

THE POWER SYSTEM

The power system is the *raison d'être* of all the other systems. It consists of: the mechanical system, that is, the stationary and moving mechanical parts of the engine itself; the fuel system, for supplying gas and air to the combustion chamber; the exhaust system, for expelling burned gases; the oil system, for lubricating all the moving parts so as to reduce wear and friction; the cooling system, to keep operating temperature down and prevent welding of metal to metal; and finally emission controls, to reduce noxious gases and pollution. (At the time of this writing, the Honda Civic engine is the only automobile internal-combustion engine that does not require emission controls, because of its efficient combustion-chamber design.)

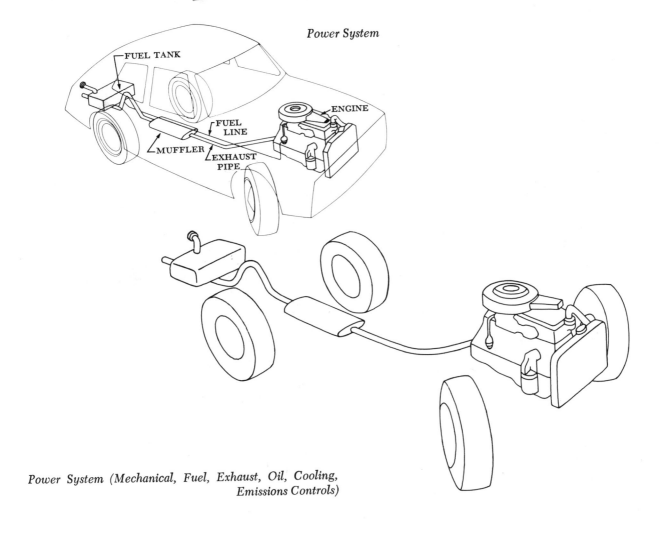

Power System

FUEL TANK

ENGINE

FUEL LINE

MUFFLER

EXHAUST PIPE

Power System (Mechanical, Fuel, Exhaust, Oil, Cooling, Emissions Controls)

THE ELECTRICAL SYSTEM

Most of the problems you will ever have with your car will be from the electrical system. Why? Because it is so omnipotent. Nothing can run without the electrical system. It powers the windshield wipers, the horn, the cigarette lighter, the lights, the battery, the alternator, the spark plugs that fire the fuel that makes the pistons go up and down, which makes the transmission revolve to make the wheels go around.

If you ever have a short in your electrical system, good luck in finding it. I know people who have had to trade in a car because no mechanic could find the short. By the way, a "short" means a short circuit, an incomplete electrical circuit. The electrical system and its baby systems will be discussed in greater detail later on.

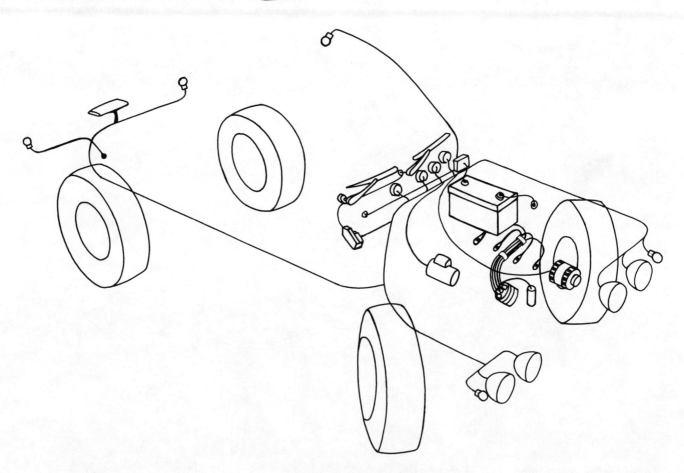

Electrical System

THE DRIVE-TRAIN SYSTEM

This system consists of:

(1) The *transmission*, the purpose of which is to enable the engine to cope with the variations of power and torque required to begin moving the car, climbing a hill, or traveling at high speed. This is done by selecting the proper gear ratio. A wide range of speed ratios between engine and wheels is thus made possible.

(2) A *front universal joint* and a *rear universal joint*, which allow the drive shaft to absorb shocks and turn the wheels smoothly.

(3) The *drive shaft*, which takes the energy from the transmission and directly powers the wheel axle.

(4) The rear-wheel *differential*, which helps the car around corners by allowing the outside wheel to revolve faster than the inside wheel.

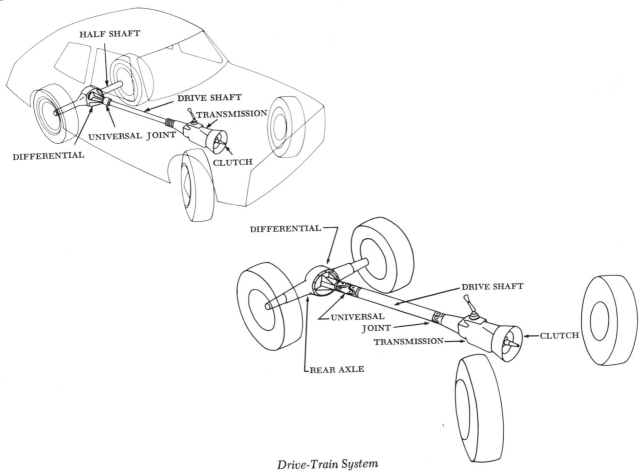

Drive-Train System

THE STEERING SYSTEM

There are two different types of steering systems: the *recirculating-ball* and the *rack-and-pinion*. The recirculating-ball type predominates, and can be power assisted. Power steering is merely a system that uses a hydraulically (meaning it uses a fluid) powered pump to assist the driver to turn the wheel with greater facility. Very handy for parking a large vehicle in a small space but cuts down considerably on muscle building. Since power-steering systems are hydraulic, a periodic check of the fluid level is required and is a must to put on your maintenance schedule.

Rack-and-pinion steering is found in many better sports cars. Why? Tighter response, less play in the wheels, allowing for finer control. It's the hard way to steer but it is more precise. If you move the steering wheel the tiniest bit, the front wheels move accordingly. For the racetrack it is the best type to have; for city streets it is the worst. (It's much harder with rack-and-pinion steering than it is with power steering to maneuver a car into a tight parking space.)

As for your repairing your own steering system — forget it. It takes a lot of expensive equipment to do it properly, thousands of dollars worth, not to mention the space needed for such equipment, which the average car-owner's garage could not accommodate.

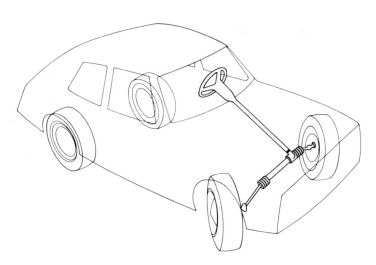

Steering System (Rack-and-Pinion)

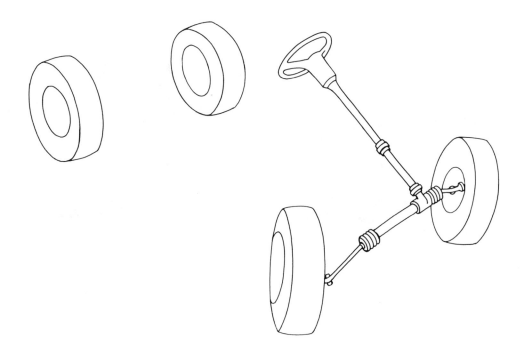

THE SUSPENSION SYSTEM

This system's function is to make the ride smooth, easy, and as "shockless" as possible. The major components of this system are thus the *shock absorbers,* the *springs,* both coil and leaf, and the *torsion bars,* which perform the same function as some coil springs.

On some cars, changing the "shocks" is the easiest job imaginable. On others it's not only difficult but dangerous. In some cases you have to compress the coil spring to get the old shock out. That takes not only strength but dexterity. If the spring ever got away from you, it could take your arm or a piece of your arm with it. We don't advise tackling this job unless you know what you are doing. You may even need special equipment, like sprocket holders, to replace shocks in some cars. So we won't encourage your saving money by doing this repair. Sears Roebuck and some other outfits run sales on shocks. Keep your eyes open if you think you're going to be in the market for a replacement.

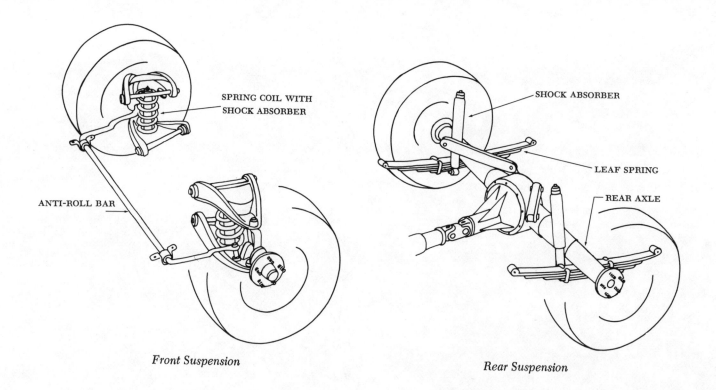

Front Suspension

Rear Suspension

THE BRAKING SYSTEM

There are two types of brakes: one is the _disc_ brake and the other the _drum_ brake. The function of both types is to stop the car or slow it down. There are few more important parts of an auto than the brakes. If they don't work at all or work erratically you could be in big trouble. On today's motorcars the brakes are hydraulically (fluid) powered. In the old days they were "mechanical," or activated by a shoe-spring mechanism instead of fluid.

Some cars today also have "power" brakes. They are usually optional on less expensive models. Like "power" steering, they draw power from the motor to assist in applying the brakes. Less foot thrust is required to achieve the same results.

We will discuss brakes in more detail later. Suffice it to say here that it is a major repair job to change brake linings and we don't recommend it for the beginner. We will, however, teach you how to maintain the proper brake-fluid level.

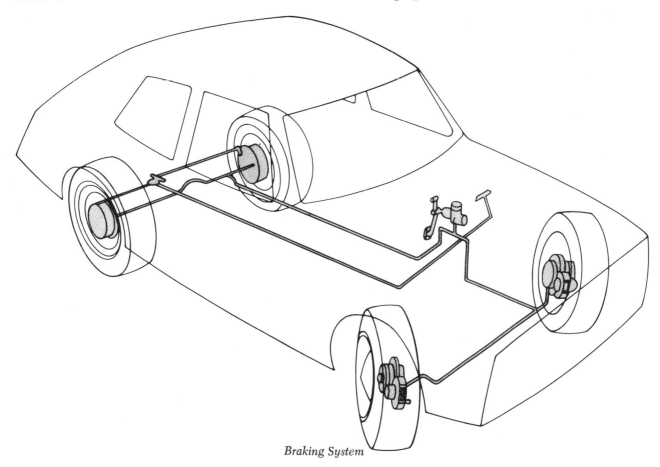

Braking System

THE BODY OF YOUR CAR

"Bodywork" refers to the repair of everything in the car that is external to the mechanics of the car, such as fenders, bumpers, grille, doors, steel beams, roof.

Outside of washing and waxing and polishing the car's body, I suggest you leave all bodywork to the craftsmen, because that's who it takes to do successful bodywork. It is an art best left to the artists. If you don't believe me, just try to patch up one tiny place on your fender and you'll see what I mean.

Taken as a whole, your automobile and its engine may seem incomprehensibly complicated, but, if you break it down into component systems and deal with each one step at a time, the seemingly unsolvable difficulties gradually disappear. Thus each of the following sections will be devoted to one system of the automobile and its potential problems.

2. The Power System

The Internal-Combustion Engine

Unless you are one of those rare old birds who own an electric car, you probably drive an automobile with an *internal-combustion engine*. Don't panic because of that technical-sounding terminology.

You *know* what an *engine* is. An engine is a device that converts heat energy into mechanical work.

You know what *combustion* means — burning.

You know what *internal* means — inside.

Voilà! An internal-combustion engine merely means that the fuel is burned *inside* the engine instead of *outside* the engine, which would make it an *external-combustion engine*, like a steam engine, for instance, which burns the fuel in a boiler that makes steam that is then *sent* to the engine.

The internal-combustion engine of today is not the most efficient way of making power, because only a small percentage (25 percent — 15 percent to drive the wheels and 10 percent for accessory power) of the fuel burned is translated into actual power — most

of it goes, shall we say, "up in smoke," polluting the atmosphere. However, it seems that we are stuck with it until such time as someone invents an improvement upon it that will make it as profitable for the auto manufacturers and gas producers as the internal-combustion engine is. Or, for those of us who live in hope, until such time as our ecosphere becomes more important to the world than monetary profit for the few. Unfortunately, we can't hold our breath for that moment to arrive.

Most automobiles today have four, six, or eight cylinders. In the old days, the big, expensive cars like Lincoln and Cadillac sometimes sported twelve cylinders. Needless to say, with the inefficient combustion, twelve cylinders burned a lot of gas. They used to get about six miles to a gallon, with luck.

The internal-combustion system is designed to do several things: it has to let the fuel in, let the fuel out, burn at very hot temperatures, and have a mechanism for firing the fuel. The problem is that instead of using 100 percent of that piston power to drive the wheels, it has to support all the other systems as well: the air conditioning, the lights, the radio, the gas pump, and so on. So, the more gadgets we add to the car the less power we have to run the wheels, the more parts to repair, and the more weight to carry.

HOW THE POWER SYSTEM WORKS

Initially, when you turn on your ignition key you electrically activate a *starter motor*, which engages a *flywheel*, which turns a *crankshaft*, which sets into motion the *intake stroke* of the *pistons*.

Our auto pistons have a four-stroke cycle: (1) *intake stroke*; (2) *compression stroke*; (3) *ignition and power stroke*; (4) *exhaust stroke*. The *intake stroke* of the piston creates a partial vacuum that sucks *fuel* (a mixture of gasoline and air) into the piston's *combustion chamber*, where the mixture is then compressed (in the *compression stroke*). In the *ignition and power stroke* the fuel mixture is ignited by a spark that forcibly expands the gas, creating an extreme pressure that forces the piston downward (in the power stroke). Attached to each piston is a *connecting rod*, which connects the piston to the

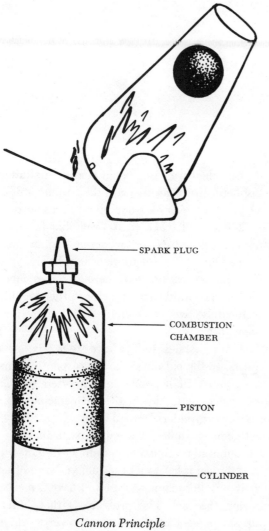

SPARK PLUG

COMBUSTION CHAMBER

PISTON

CYLINDER

Cannon Principle

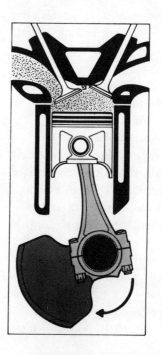

Intake

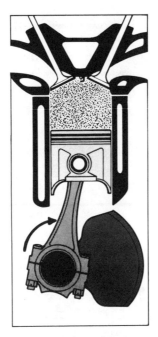

Compression

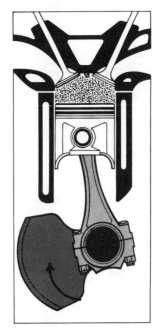

Power

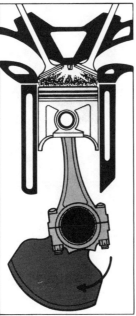

Ignition

Exhaust

crankshaft. It is at this juncture that the up-and-down motion of the piston (in some engines, as fast as 100 strokes a second) is transformed into rotary motion. As the crankshaft turns, or revolves, it delivers the power into the *transmission*, or *gearbox*. There, after you have decided at which gear speed you wish to travel, *low gear, second gear, third* or *high gear*, or *reverse*, the transmission sends, or transmits, this rotary power to the final *drive shaft* or *propeller shaft*, which ultimately delivers the power to the wheels.

The final stroke — the *exhaust stroke* — pushes the burned residue into the exhaust system.

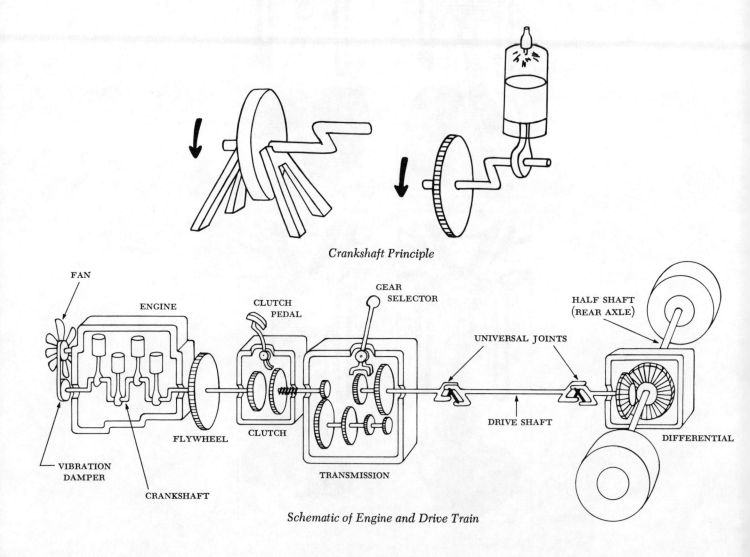

Crankshaft Principle

Schematic of Engine and Drive Train

PARTS OF THE ENGINE AND THEIR FUNCTION

Carburetor — part of the fuel system. It takes gasoline, atomizes it, and mixes it with air. This mixture is drawn into the combustion chamber of the engine's cylinders, where it will be ignited by the spark plugs.

Rocker arm — rocks open the intake valves, which let the fuel from the carburetor into the combustion chambers, and the exhaust valves, which let the exhausted fuel out of the combustion chambers into the exhaust pipe and then into the world.

Rocker cover — a metal pan that covers the rocker-arm assembly.

Valve spring — closes those same valves by spring action.

Pushrods — connected to the rocker arm. These operate by a nudge from the *eccentric lobe* on the camshaft that pushes on a valve lifter that connects with the bottom of the pushrod, to push the rocker arm to open the intake and exhaust valves.

Camshaft — a long cylindrical shaft that runs hori-

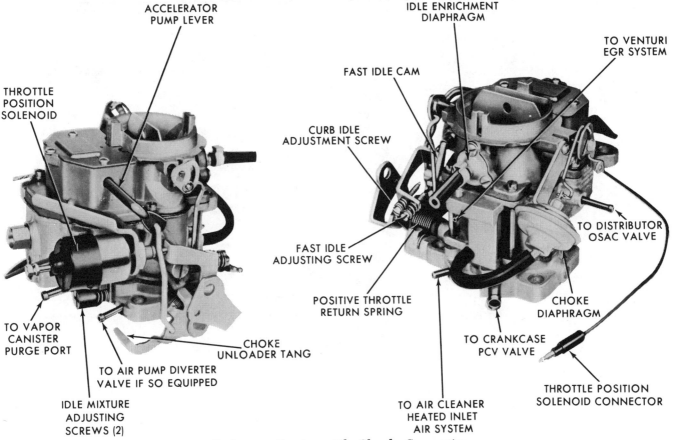

ACCELERATOR PUMP LEVER

THROTTLE POSITION SOLENOID

TO VAPOR CANISTER PURGE PORT

TO AIR PUMP DIVERTER VALVE IF SO EQUIPPED

IDLE MIXTURE ADJUSTING SCREWS (2)

CHOKE UNLOADER TANG

IDLE ENRICHMENT DIAPHRAGM

TO VENTURI EGR SYSTEM

FAST IDLE CAM

CURB IDLE ADJUSTMENT SCREW

FAST IDLE ADJUSTING SCREW

POSITIVE THROTTLE RETURN SPRING

TO AIR CLEANER HEATED INLET AIR SYSTEM

TO CRANKCASE PCV VALVE

TO DISTRIBUTOR OSAC VALVE

CHOKE DIAPHRAGM

THROTTLE POSITION SOLENOID CONNECTOR

Carburetor. Courtesy of the Chrysler Corporation

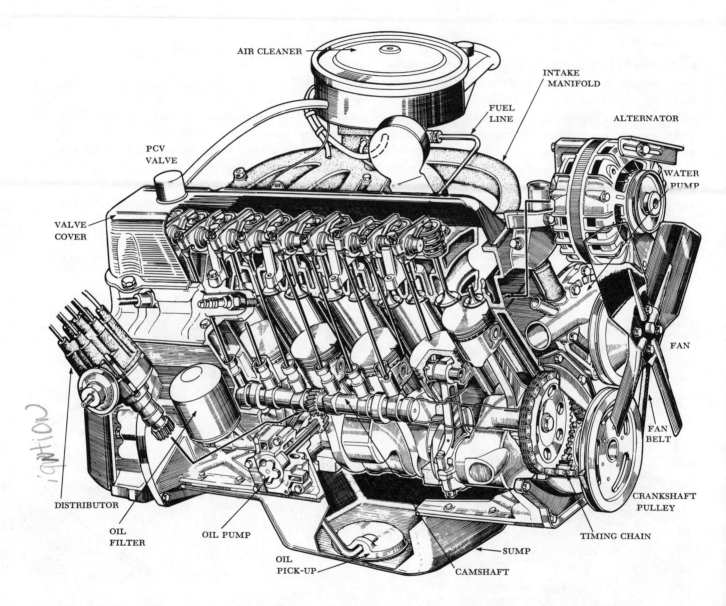

AIR CLEANER

INTAKE
MANIFOLD

FUEL
LINE

ALTERNATOR

PCV
VALVE

WATER
PUMP

VALVE
COVER

FAN

ignition

FAN
BELT

DISTRIBUTOR

CRANKSHAFT
PULLEY

OIL
FILTER

OIL PUMP

TIMING CHAIN

SUMP

OIL
PICK-UP

CAMSHAFT

Engine. Courtesy of the Chrysler Corporation

zontally the length of the piston assembly. It has eccentric (for our purposes, elliptical, like an egg) lobes; they are shaped to have a high and a low spot to activate the pushrods. The camshaft has an additional duty of rotating a vertical shaft that turns a rotor in the distributor (at the top) and turns rotors in the oil pump (at the bottom of the same shaft).

Valve lifter (or *tappet*) — a part of the pushrod–rocker arm assembly. It fits on the bottom end of the pushrod, and is the part that the eccentric lobe of the camshaft is in contact with.

Distributor — the brain or the commander in chief of the ignition system. When all goes according to plan, its rotor spins around, sending electrical charges to the spark plugs to ignite, in proper sequence, the compressed fuel mixture in the pistons' combustion chambers. You can always locate the distributor because it looks like Medusa, with long wires streaming from its top leading to each spark plug.

Intake valve — opens (and closes) a hole in the cylinder head that lets in the fuel from the carburetor at a given moment — the intake stroke of the four-stroke piston cycle. Intake valves belong to the valve-train family.

Exhaust valve — opens (and closes) another hole in the cylinder that lets the exhausted, or burned, fuel gases out of the cylinder. Exhaust valves also belong to the valve-train family.

Spark plug — the heavy-duty worker on the electrical system that delivers the spark from the distributor to each piston's combustion chamber. They get dirty, or fouled with oil or carbon, and have to be cleaned or replaced with every engine tune-up. You have one spark plug for each cylinder in your engine. They provide this spark at a given moment in the piston's four-stroke cycle, the ignition and power stroke.

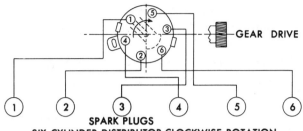

SPARK PLUGS
SIX CYLINDER DISTRIBUTOR-CLOCKWISE ROTATION
FOR 225 CUBIC INCH ENGINES
FIRING ORDER-1-5-3-6-2-4

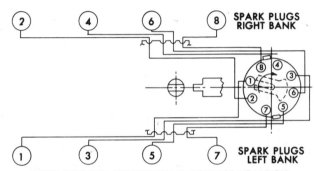

EIGHT CYLINDER DISTRIBUTOR-CLOCKWISE ROTATION
FOR 318 AND 360 CUBIC INCH ENGINES
FIRING ORDER-1-8-4-3-6-5-7-2

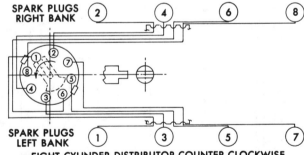

EIGHT CYLINDER DISTRIBUTOR-COUNTER-CLOCKWISE
ROTATION
FOR 400 AND 440 CUBIC INCH ENGINES
FIRING ORDER-1-8-4-3-6-5-7-2

Firing Order. Courtesy of the Chrysler Corporation

Spark-plug cover — a rubber or similarly flexible composition shield that protects the spark-plug top from moisture.

Cylinder — the number varies. Cars have either four, six, eight, or twelve cylinders in their engines. These cylindrical holes are cast into the engine block.

Piston — a disk or cylindrical part usually made of aluminum alloy fitting tightly within a cylinder. Each piston has the four-stroke duty to perform, and each at a given moment. This is called the *firing order*, similar to the pecking order of birds. Each piston is connected to the crankshaft by a connecting rod. The connecting rod is a very important item because it transforms the up-and-down power of the piston into rotary power that goes into the crankshaft, thereby providing the driving power. As the crankshaft turns,

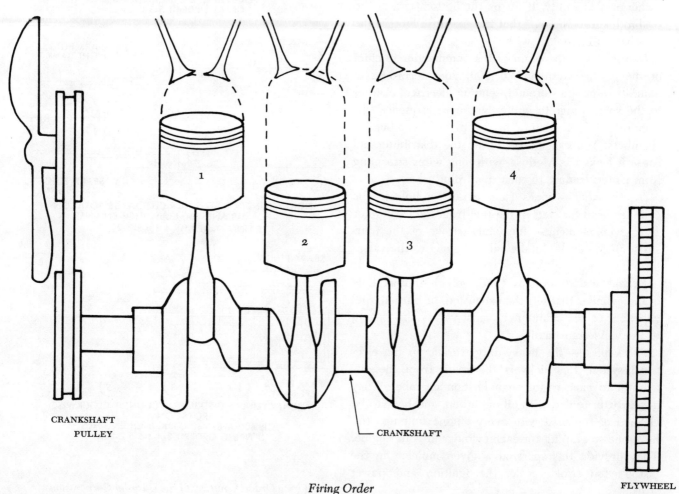

CRANKSHAFT
PULLEY

CRANKSHAFT

Firing Order

FLYWHEEL

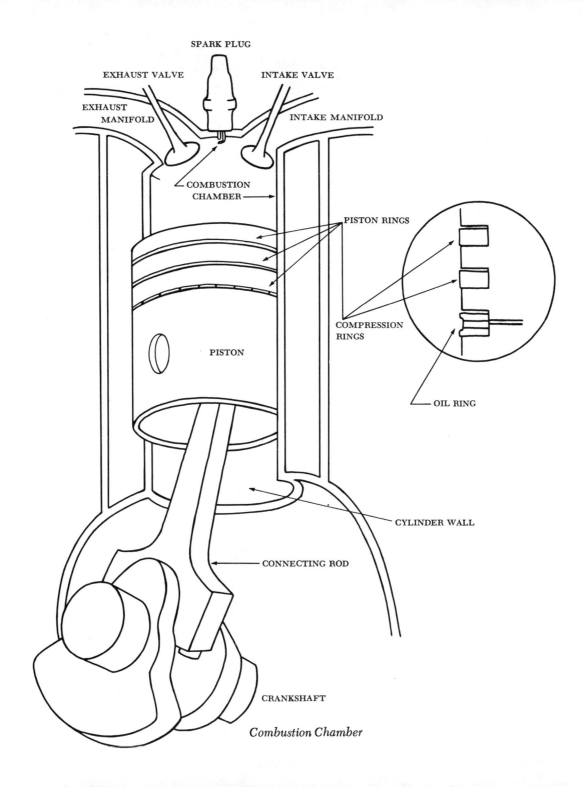

SPARK PLUG

EXHAUST VALVE

INTAKE VALVE

EXHAUST
MANIFOLD

INTAKE MANIFOLD

COMBUSTION
CHAMBER

PISTON RINGS

COMPRESSION
RINGS

OIL RING

PISTON

CYLINDER WALL

CONNECTING ROD

CRANKSHAFT

Combustion Chamber

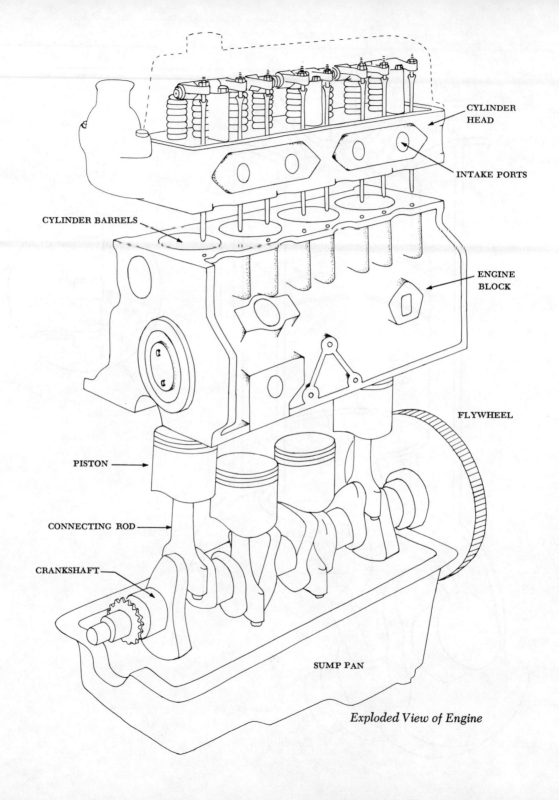

CYLINDER HEAD

INTAKE PORTS

CYLINDER BARRELS

ENGINE BLOCK

FLYWHEEL

PISTON

CONNECTING ROD

CRANKSHAFT

SUMP PAN

Exploded View of Engine

it moves each piston up or down in a differently timed stroke, which causes not one great explosion with all pistons firing at once but a continuous series of timed explosions, thereby yielding continuous power; otherwise your car would leapfrog along the highway.

Each piston has three rings encircling it. Two of these are called *compression rings* because they help to maintain the seal that enables the piston to compress the fuel. The other is called the *oil ring* because whenever you have metal parts rubbing against each other you need oil to reduce the friction (wear and tear). This ring allows oil to enter the chamber while the piston action is taking place.

When you hear the mechanic say, "Hey, lady, I hate to tell you this but you need a ring job," he's not proposing marriage but an expensive replacement of the rings on your pistons.

Another thing that each piston requires is a *counterweight* (located on the crankshaft), which acts on the same principle as when you pedal a bike — as the piston goes down, the counterweight goes up; when the counterweight goes down, the piston goes up. Checks and balances, you might say, like a self-powered assist on the old funicular style — the car coming down assists the other car back up the mountain.

Cylinder head and *cylinder block* — the cylinder head contains the combustion chamber, two valve ports, and two valve openings for each cylinder. Engines with this arrangement are called overhead valve engines. There is also a spark plug for each cylinder.

The cylinder block, or *engine block*, is the largest and heaviest part of the engine, usually cast iron except on some high-powered autos that use aluminum.

The engine block is the name given to the metal casing of the engine. The engine block itself looks like a huge chunk of swiss cheese gone wrong. There are large holes to house the cylinders; holes and channels for the water that cools your engine to flow through; different holes and channels (called *oil galleries*) for the oil that lubricates your engine; holes to attach various other parts, like the distributor, the fuel pump, sprockets, and so on. Engine blocks are durable and are made to withstand considerable amounts of heat, as much as 1,300 degrees Fahrenheit. What they cannot stand too well is *sudden change of temperature.* Many an engine block has been ruined when cold water has been poured into a hot engine that is not running. Then it is called a *cracked block* AND IT IS GOOD-BYE TO THAT ENGINE SO BE CAREFUL THAT YOUR MOTOR IS RUNNING WHEN YOU ADD COLD WATER TO A HOT ENGINE. That is one problem Volkswagen or other air-cooled-engine owners don't have to worry about since they don't use water to cool their motors. Another thing to be careful about is leaving your car parked in ultrafreezing temperatures — make sure you have enough antifreeze in your engine to withstand the cold because the water in the engine will freeze, expand, and your engine will crack like a milk bottle if it freezes solid, spilling your cylinders just like your milk. In the old days, before the development of ethylene glycol, or "permanent antifreeze," people used alcohol, which boiled over a lot. And if too much boiled out and you parked your car for too long on a cold night, your block cracked. Many people put newspapers and blankets over their engines to keep that from happening. Others left an electric light burning all night under the hood.

Another important part of your engine's makeup is the *head gasket.* This is a piece of fabricated material that slips between the cylinder head and the engine block and acts as a seal.

To avoid a sudden buildup of heat within the

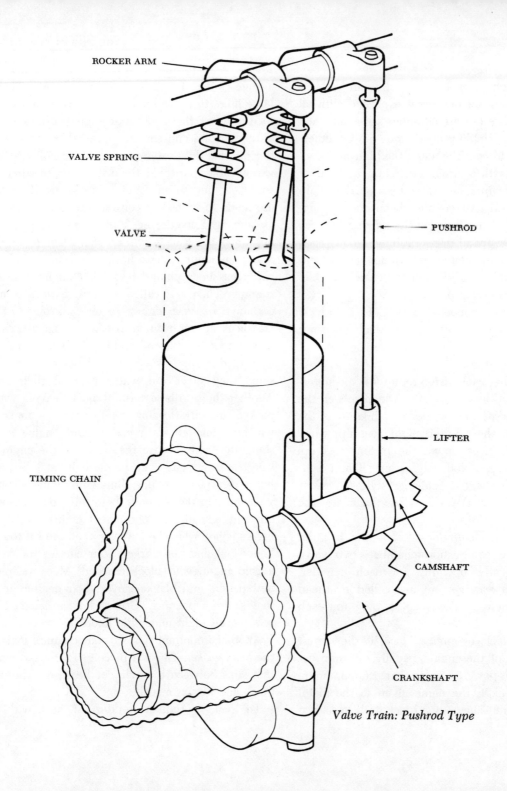

ROCKER ARM

VALVE SPRING

VALVE

PUSHROD

LIFTER

TIMING CHAIN

CAMSHAFT

CRANKSHAFT

Valve Train: Pushrod Type

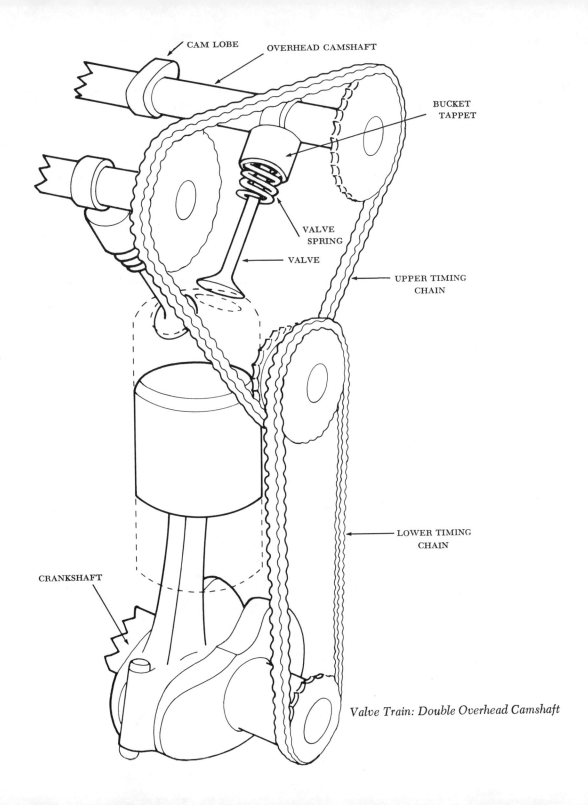

CAM LOBE

OVERHEAD CAMSHAFT

BUCKET
TAPPET

VALVE
SPRING

VALVE

UPPER TIMING
CHAIN

LOWER TIMING
CHAIN

CRANKSHAFT

Valve Train: Double Overhead Camshaft

engine block, a sleeve was designed that fits into the original cylinder wall so the friction created by the pistons going up and down is somewhat absorbed before it hits the engine block; otherwise it could crack it.

Whenever you have metal fitting to metal in your car you will usually find a gasket that fits between and seals in whatever there is to be sealed in, be it fuel, air, water, gas, or oil. Heat eventually destroys these gaskets, and they must be replaced every so often or you'll find you are losing whatever substance it was you used the gasket to seal in in the first place. Head gaskets have also been known to break when cold water is put into a warm engine or when the motor is run for long periods of time at very high speed. While gaskets themselves are relatively inex-

pensive, often the labor involved in replacing them is extensive and could cost you a bundle unless you can do it yourself.

The cylinder head is where all the action takes place. In that area the fuel gets fired up, the compression takes place, and the valves do their business.

A word about those intake and exhaust valves. It is extremely important that they open and close properly as well as *seat* themselves properly — that is, when they are in their return position they seal the cylinder chamber. One of the first things I can remember hearing about big trouble in a car was "a valve job." When the mechanic says those words to you he usually accompanies them with a tragic shake of the head signifying that it's going to be expensive and you'll be without your car for a few days.

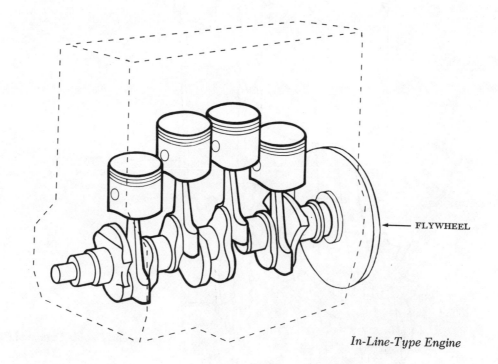

FLYWHEEL

In-Line-Type Engine

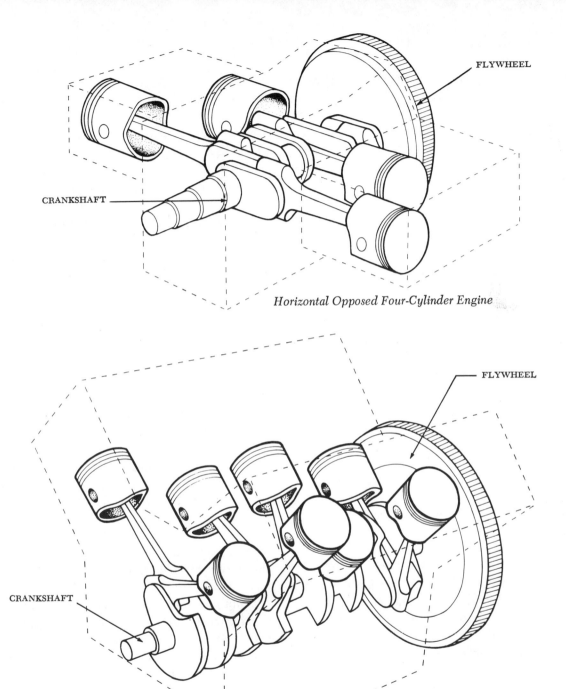

FLYWHEEL

CRANKSHAFT

Horizontal Opposed Four-Cylinder Engine

FLYWHEEL

CRANKSHAFT

V-Type (V-8) Engine

Sometimes if the valve doesn't open it's because you have sticky valves or maybe sticking rocker arms or a broken or bent lifter. If it doesn't close you might have a broken spring or maybe your valves aren't properly aligned in the valve guides. Sometimes these valves have to be sent off to a machine shop to be reground. Suffice it to say, a valve job is not for the beginner to tackle, as you will possess neither the tools nor the know-how for the task.

Valve lifters have holes through them to allow for a flow of lubricating oil, which keeps the lifters running cool so they do not bend or break due to excessive heat. Remember, excessive heat can ruin practically any part of your automobile, including your tires.

Hydraulic valve lifters are self-adjusting — but most foreign and small American cars with solid lifters do require adjustments to be made.

Just as shoe manufacturers use different lasts, automobile manufacturers use different methods of putting their cylinders together, such as *in-line* (like a *straight six* or a *straight eight* or a *straight twelve*).

The in-line system can be straight up and down or it can be slanted. Dodge had great success with their *slant six* engine. It was considered to be balanced extremely well.

Opposed — one cylinder opposite the other, as in a Volkswagen.

V-type — like the Ford V-8 or V-6 or a Triumph V-4 Spitfire.

Crankshaft — an irregular shaft that runs the length of the engine and is attached to the engine block by *main bearings*, which allow it to rotate, and is connected to the pistons by means of the connecting rods. The front end is attached to an assembly that drives the fan belt; the rear is attached to the flywheel. It supplies the driving-power link between the pistons and the transmission.

Flywheel — a large, heavy metal wheel that is mounted in the rear of the engine, attached to the crankshaft. It serves two functions: (1) it acts as a vibration damper to balance the vibrations of the engine; (2) it is the mounting for an encircling band of metal called the *starter ring gear*. When you turn your starter switch (ignition key), the starter motor sends out a small pinion gear that engages with the ring gear on the flywheel, turning the crankshaft, which activates the intake stroke of the pistons.

A nearly perfect engine is nearly perfectly balanced. If you don't balance an engine properly, it vibrates. If a piston doesn't work properly, it vibrates. Eight pistons not working properly vibrate like hell. The flywheel and counterweights also help balance the engine.

Combustion chamber — the cavity in the cylinder where the fuel is compressed, ignited, and expanded.

Exhaust manifold — the pipe that channels the exhausted gases from the combustion chamber to the outside world via the tail pipe.

Intake manifold — the pipe that channels the fuel from the carburetor to the combustion chamber.

Starter motor — the electric motor that, when activated by turning on the ignition key, engages the flywheel and turns the crankshaft, thereby moving the pistons up and down.

Sump — the metal pan located under the engine that serves to hold the oil supply while it is being recirculated.

Drain plug (oil) — plugs the hole in the sump until the time comes to drain the oil, when it is unplugged.

Oil filter — a replaceable canister that cleans the impurities and sludge from the oil before it gets to the engine. The filter must be changed periodically.

Oil pump — a pump that circulates the oil through the engine parts.

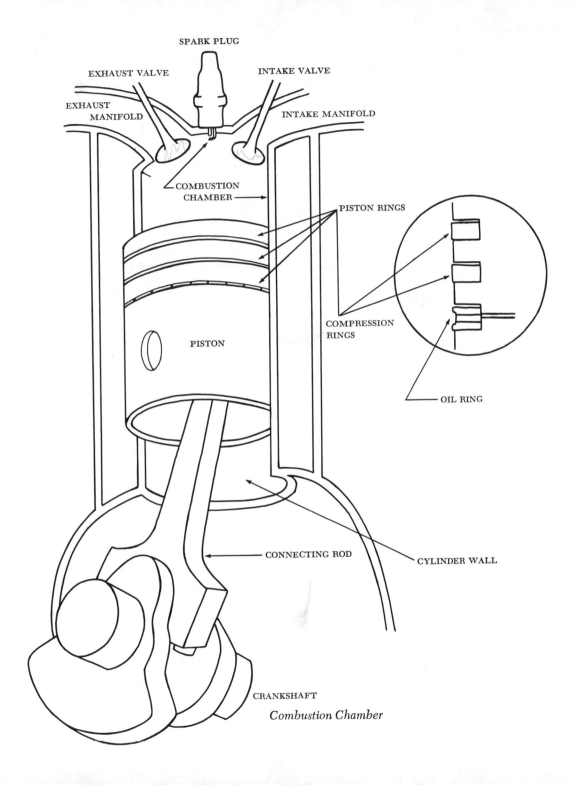

SPARK PLUG

EXHAUST VALVE

INTAKE VALVE

EXHAUST MANIFOLD

INTAKE MANIFOLD

COMBUSTION CHAMBER

PISTON RINGS

PISTON

COMPRESSION RINGS

OIL RING

CONNECTING ROD

CYLINDER WALL

CRANKSHAFT

Combustion Chamber

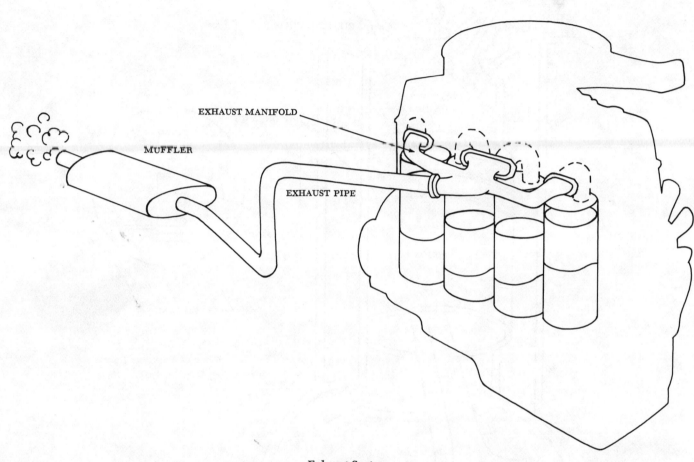

EXHAUST MANIFOLD

MUFFLER

EXHAUST PIPE

Exhaust System

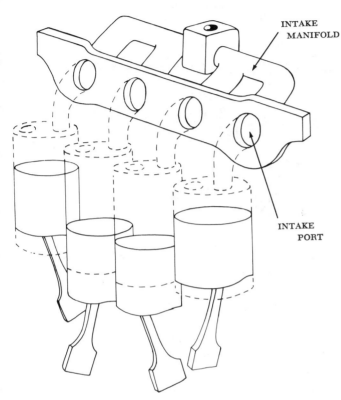

INTAKE
MANIFOLD

INTAKE
PORT

Intake Manifold

Oil suction filter — another oil filter, located in the sump.

Water pump — circulates water to cool the engine.

Fan — pulls cool air from outside to cool the radiator water.

Fan belt — attached to the crankshaft. Turns the fan to cool the engine and drives the alternator/generator and power steering and air conditioner.

Thermostat — also part of the cooling system. It governs the circulation of water into the engine.

Oil cap — covers the opening where you add oil to the engine.

Oil dipstick — a long, slim piece of metal with markings on it to indicate how full (or empty) of oil your crankcase is.

High-tension wires — channel the electricity from the distributor to the spark plugs.

Coil — a cylindrical metal part of the electrical system that transforms low voltage into high voltage (12 or 13 volts to 20,000 or 30,000 volts). It ignites the fuel in the combustion chamber.

Fuel pump — sends gasoline from the gas tank to the carburetor.

Alternator (generator) — serves as an electrical dynamo. It is driven by the crankshaft via the fan belt.

Vacuum advance — a metal muffin-shaped piece attached to the distributor. Its purpose is to change the timing for the most efficient engine operation at idle and low speeds.

Timing chain — a chain that connects the crankshaft and camshaft so they rotate in unison.

Air cleaner — a large circular metal pan that sits on top of the carburetor and houses a replaceable air filter that purifies the air of dust and dirt particles before it enters the carburetor.

Radiator hose — part of the cooling system that serves as a conduit for the water from the radiator to the engine and back again.

Radiator — part of the water cooling system. A large rectangular unit with many tiny tubes that utilize the onrushing air to cool the water, then send the cool water back through the engine compartments to cool the engine.

Battery — the heart and soul of the electrical system. Stores and manufactures electricity.

Throttle linkage — the mechanical tie-line from your gas pedal to the carburetor.

PCV (positive crankcase ventilation) valve — part

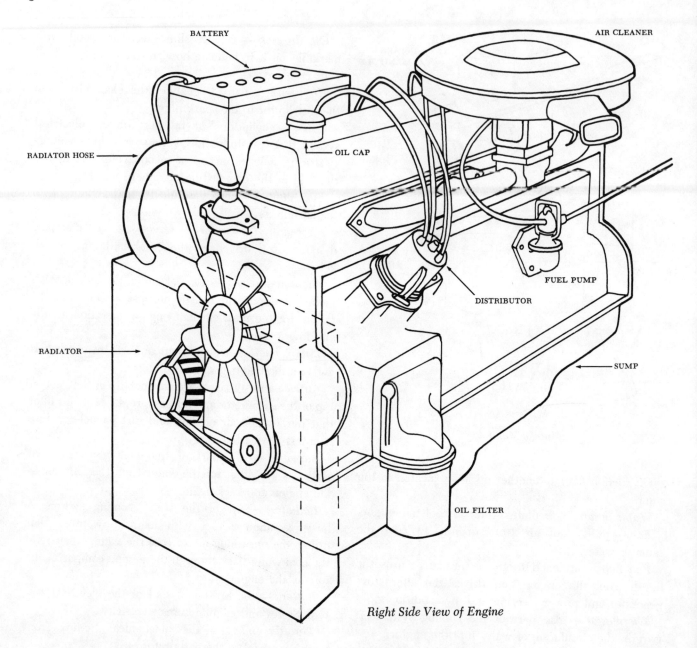

BATTERY

AIR CLEANER

RADIATOR HOSE

OIL CAP

FUEL PUMP

DISTRIBUTOR

RADIATOR

SUMP

OIL FILTER

Right Side View of Engine

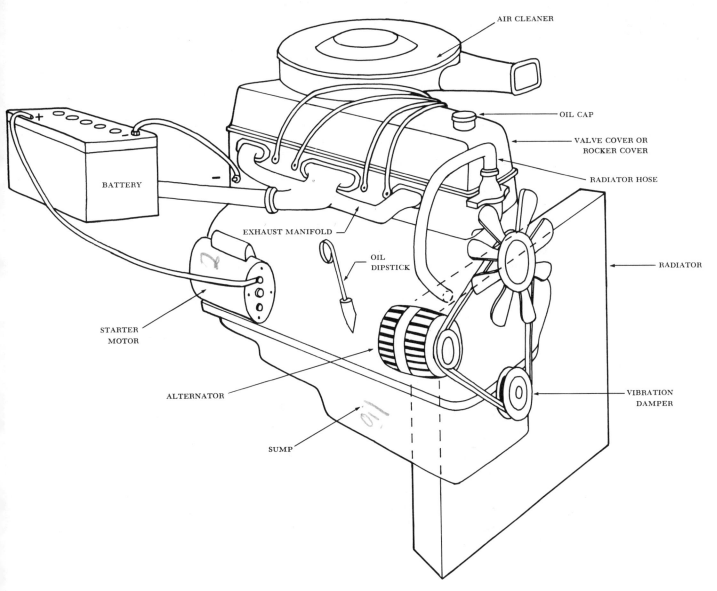

AIR CLEANER

OIL CAP

VALVE COVER OR
ROCKER COVER

RADIATOR HOSE

RADIATOR

VIBRATION
DAMPER

EXHAUST MANIFOLD

OIL
DIPSTICK

BATTERY

STARTER
MOTOR

ALTERNATOR

SUMP

Left Side View of Engine

of the emission-control system on your car. Needs replacing periodically when clogged.

Radiator cap — a turn-top that closes the hole in the top of the radiator where you add water to the cooling system.

Petcock — a small screw-type plug at the bottom of the radiator that allows for periodic drainage of the radiator. Not necessarily fitted on all cars.

Engine mountings — a series of rubber cushions that the engine rides upon, located between the engine and the frame of the car. It is a must that these be secure, or your engine can shift on its axis and all kinds of trouble can occur.

Vibration causes the screws or bolts holding these rubber cushions to work loose. Vibrations cause all sorts of things to work loose. Therefore, it is wise to look under your hood every once in a while when the engine is running. If you notice the entire engine jumping up and down or vibrating more than usual, have the mountings checked next time you have the car lubricated. If it's really hopping about, have it checked immediately.

THE FUEL SYSTEM

As even a rank amateur might imagine, the car doesn't go far without the fuel system. This system's component parts are: the *fuel tank* (*gas tank*); the *fuel lines*; the *fuel pump*; perhaps a *fuel vapor separator*; *fuel filters*; *fuel gauge*; *air cleaner*; and *carburetor.*

Fill'er up!

Let's start at the point where gasoline is ingested into the car . . . at the *fuel tank*. This is a large metal container usually located under the chassis at the opposite end of the car from the engine (in case of fire). Depending upon your car, the size and shape of these vary somewhat. Some tanks carry ten gallons, others forty gallons. I had a little Nash Rambler convertible that had a twenty-gallon fuel tank and I got thirty-some miles to a gallon, which meant I could drive from New York to Florida making only one gas stop. Then again, I have had cars that took me only from Bridgehampton, Long Island, to New York City and barely made it on a large tankful, a mere hundred miles.

There isn't much one has to know about a gas tank except to remember to put gas in it occasionally. It is true the less gas you carry in your tank, the greater the possibility of moisture collecting and condensing, putting water in with your gas, which can cause no end of troubles. Many therefore advise keeping a full tank instead of an almost empty one. Then there is the school of thought that likes to keep only a quarter-full tank because hauling all that extra gas around adds unnecessary weight, approximately eight pounds per gallon, reducing mileage commensurately.

I am of the school that keeps a full tank because nothing makes me madder than running out of gas. I've done it only a few times in my life but I still remember them because they were always in the middle of the night on a spooky highway. In my new Dodge van I always keep an extra five-gallon can for emergencies. I fill it with white Amoco gas that I can also use in my Coleman stove and lantern. The *fuel gauge* is on your dashboard. Heed it but don't rely 100 percent on it. When some fuel gauges say "empty" they mean it. Others leave you a gallon or three leeway.

The tank itself sometimes has a drain plug in the bottom in case you do get water or dirt in it.

The *fuel lines* leading from the tank to the carburetor are soft metal tubing that should be trouble-free

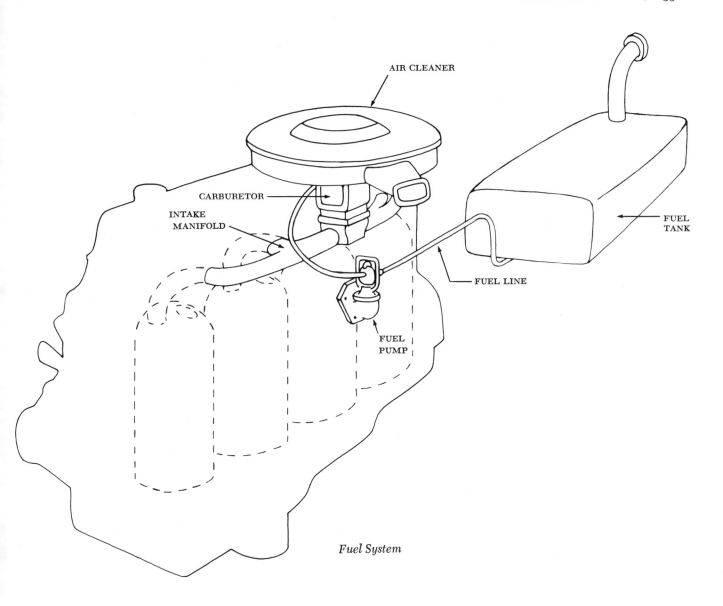

AIR CLEANER

CARBURETOR

INTAKE
MANIFOLD

FUEL
PUMP

FUEL
TANK

FUEL LINE

Fuel System

unless they are damaged by rocks flying up from the road or you run over something that cuts or bends them badly.

Because the gas tank is lower than the engine it requires a *fuel pump* to pump the gas to the engine. This does go bad occasionally. There are two kinds of fuel pumps, mechanical and electrical, the majority being mechanical. The mechanical pump is activated by the camshaft. The average pump *can* push about a pint of gas a minute, but it usually pushes a little less. While the mechanical pump must be located near the engine, the electric pump can be remotely mounted. Fuel pumps can be trouble-free for 100,000 miles or more if you're lucky. Replacement is usually not difficult, depending upon where the pump is located. Factory rebuilt ones are available as well as new ones, which naturally cost more.

In order to screen out particles of dirt and rust, there is a fine filter in the gas system, sometimes located on the line leading to the carburetor and sometimes built into the fuel pump. These always need cleaning or replacing at periodic intervals.

The *carburetor* is the most complicated part of the fuel system and always requires attention, if only at tune-up time. In the old days carburetors used to be called "mixing chambers." That is exactly what their function is — to mix the gas and air together into a properly proportioned mixture called fuel — so many parts gasoline and so many parts air. These proportions vary and are predetermined by the engine, the load, the speed, and the temperature. Parts of the carburetor are therefore, of necessity, constantly self-adjusting; others you adjust periodically.

The average mixture would be about 16 parts of air to 1 part gasoline. *Jets* (bolts with precisely calibrated lengthwise holes) are also in the carburetor picture. They control the amount of gasoline that mixes with the air in the carburetor.

A *choke*, or *butterfly valve*, controls the amount of air to be let in. This is located at the top of the carburetor. A choke is for adjusting the mixture for cold starting, say 1 part air to 3 parts gas. That is called a "rich" mixture.

Most of today's autos have "automatic" chokes. In my Dodge manual it says, "The automatic choke provides the richer fuel-air mixture required for starting and operating a cold engine." I hasten to add, when

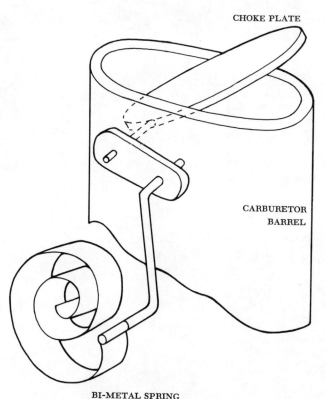

CHOKE PLATE

CARBURETOR
BARREL

BI-METAL SPRING

Diagram of Choke (Automatic)

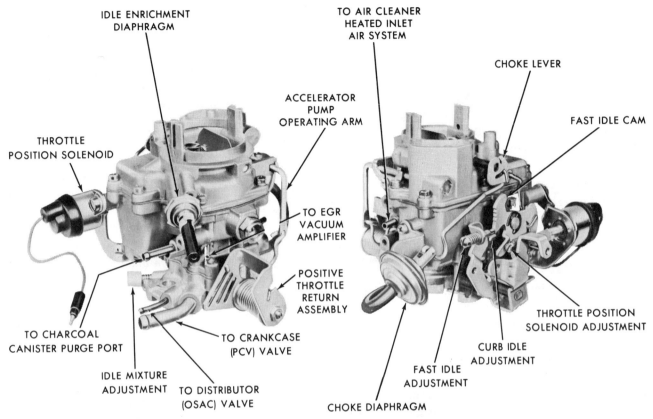

IDLE ENRICHMENT
DIAPHRAGM

TO AIR CLEANER
HEATED INLET
AIR SYSTEM

CHOKE LEVER

ACCELERATOR
PUMP
OPERATING ARM

FAST IDLE CAM

THROTTLE
POSITION SOLENOID

TO EGR
VACUUM
AMPLIFIER

POSITIVE
THROTTLE
RETURN
ASSEMBLY

THROTTLE POSITION
SOLENOID ADJUSTMENT

TO CHARCOAL
CANISTER PURGE PORT

TO CRANKCASE
(PCV) VALVE

CURB IDLE
ADJUSTMENT

IDLE MIXTURE
ADJUSTMENT

TO DISTRIBUTOR
(OSAC) VALVE

FAST IDLE
ADJUSTMENT

CHOKE DIAPHRAGM

Carburetor. Courtesy of the Chrysler Corporation

it works. The one on my VW van didn't work when it should have and did work when it shouldn't. In cold weather it would stick all the way open and when it was prudent to creep along an icy road the engine would race along on its own.

The _throttle_ is also a valve, but it controls the amount of air/gas that reaches the cylinders. Essentially, what you are doing when you press down on the gas pedal is to open the throttle plate, increasing the flow of air through the *venturi* (the narrowest opening in the carburetor barrel), which sucks more gas from the carburetor.

Carburetors can have a single barrel, two barrels, three or four barrels. (The barrel is where the mixture of gas and air takes place.) The more barrels, the higher-performance the car. If your car has *fuel injection*, you won't have a carburetor. You will have a computer that governs all the variables that determine how much fuel is required.

For the carburetor to meet all the idiosyncrasies of

the various needs of the engine it has what are called *carburetor circuits*. They are:

The *idle circuit* — a possible air/gas ratio of 12 to 1. After the car has started but is not yet going anywhere we say it is "idling," just as a person who is not doing anything is an "idler." Ideally, if the carburetor is adjusted properly, or, I should say, if the *idle screw* is set properly, the engine should be supplied with enough gas to idle without your pressing on the gas pedal.

In your idle circuit you have both a fast and a slow, or curb, idle. The fast idle is an adjustment (screw) that allows the engine to idle faster while it is warming up so it won't stall out. Once it has warmed up, it reverts to slow idle again. This also has an adjustment screw.

Low-speed circuit, or *part throttle* — at say 30 to 65 mph. A possible air/gas ratio of 16 to 1.

High-speed circuit, or *full throttle* — a possible air/gas ratio of 13 to 1.

Acceleration circuit — a possible air/gas ratio of 12 to 1. As you step on the gas to accelerate (particularly at speeds under 30 mph), you open up your throttle and allow a blast of air into the carburetor. The gas is slow in following. This circuit adjusts the gas flow to compensate for its slowness. Otherwise you would have some hesitation in the operation, or what is known as a "flat spot."

The *float circuit* — this governs the amount of gasoline that flows to the engine. Float settings are therefore extremely important lest your mixture be either too lean (not enough gas, too much air) or too rich (vice versa).

When the mechanic and I did a tune-up on my new Dodge van, we looked up in the manual what the proper curb idle speed was, that is, revolutions per minute with a warm engine. My car's specifications called for 750 rpm. He asked, "Do you have air conditioning?" I answered, "Affirmative." He then added 100 rpm to the setting, because it takes that much extra to run the air conditioner or the engine would stall out at idle when my air conditioner was in use.

The *choke circuit* — this has a possible air/gas ratio of about 8 to 1 because you need a rich mixture to start the car when the engine is cold. In the old days we had manual chokes, which were operated by a knob on the dashboard or perhaps on the floor beside you. On cold mornings you pulled the choke knob out before you pressed on the starter, then after the engine was started for a minute or so you pushed it halfway back in and drove off. Then, as your engine warmed up to normal running speed, you pushed it all the way back in, opening the valve again to let air in (leaning the mixture). What this did was to close off the air coming into the carburetor, enriching the mixture. As the engine warmed up, you opened up somewhat, allowing more air in to make the mixture leaner; the faster the engine goes, the leaner the mixture, to a point of no return, of course.

The only instruction the salesman gave me when I bought my Dodge van was: "Before you start the car, press down once on the accelerator and let up halfway. Then start the car." What he was telling me was that that would close off the air or shut the automatic choke valve, as well as shoot some gas into the carburetor. If I pumped the gas pedal more than a few times I would shoot too much gas and flood the engine.

The parking-lot attendant where I park my car in the city flooded the van the first time he tried to start it. I had to unscrew the motor lid, remove it, take off

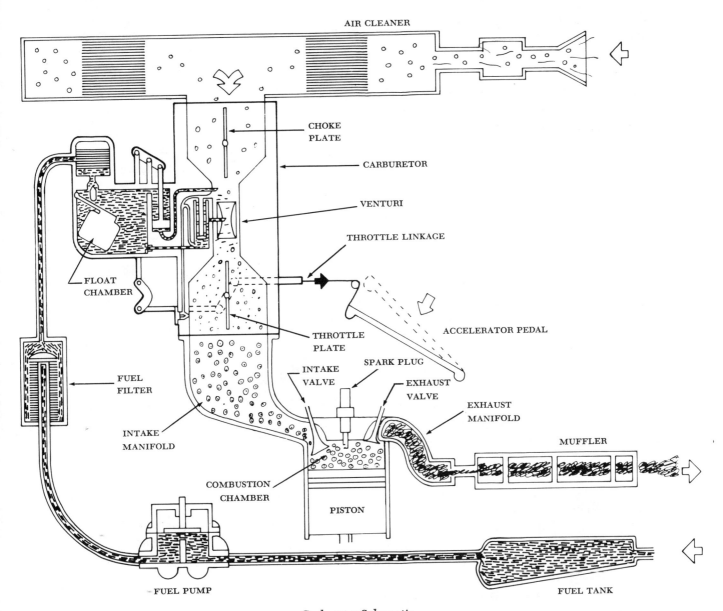

Carburetor Schematic

the air cleaner, and open the choke to let enough air into the carburetor so that it would start. Then he put a huge deep scratch in the dashboard when he replaced the motor cover.

Later my class instructor informed me that I could have saved myself a lot of time and trouble had I just held the accelerator pedal down for a full minute or so, allowing the excess fuel to evaporate. (Sometimes that works; sometimes it doesn't.)

The *air cleaner* is that sort of flying saucer–like large round metal attachment that sits on top of the carburetor, usually attached by a wing nut, inside of which is found the actual replaceable filter, sometimes made of paper filigree or cellulose. The *air filter* is a very important part of the system and is responsible for ensuring that the air that is being mixed with the gas is clean, free of as much dust and dirt as possible. Like the gas filters, it is the janitor of the air supply to the engine. Any fool can change an air filter. (See Maintenance, page 160.) The main premise to remember about the fuel system is that cleanliness is truly next to godliness. Keep it clean and keep the linkages that connect all the moving parts of the carburetor, the choke, and the throttle moving freely.

For any serious carburetor work I heartily suggest you take your car to an expert for, as you can see by the following views of a carburetor assembly, repairs can be quite complicated. You can more easily replace the entire unit but a new two-barrel carb can be quite expensive.

GASOLINE AND HOW TO SAVE IT Today, everyone, rich or poor, pedestrian or motorist, is faced with a common concern, gasoline. Whether it be the cost, the availability, or the pollution aspect, it concerns us all. Therefore it behooves us to use it wisely and well.

Naturally, high-speed, high-performance cars use

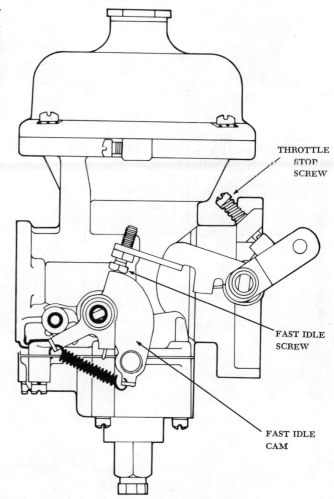

THROTTLE STOP SCREW

FAST IDLE SCREW

FAST IDLE CAM

Stromberg C D Carburetor. Courtesy of Lucas Industries, North America, Inc.

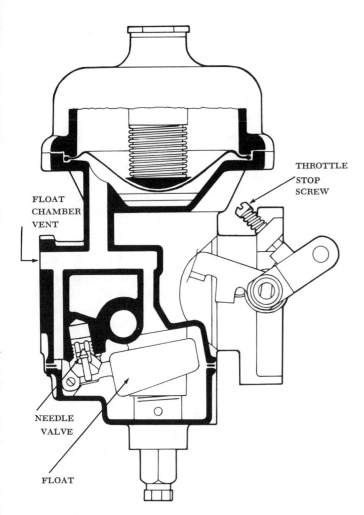

Stromberg C D Carburetor (Cross Section). Courtesy of Lucas Industries, North America, Inc.

THROTTLE
STOP
SCREW

FLOAT
CHAMBER
VENT

NEEDLE
VALVE

FLOAT

more gasoline than low-speed, low-performance cars, all other things being equal. But regardless of the size and power of your car, you can decrease the amount of gasoline consumed tremendously by (1) keeping your engine in tip-top shape by adhering to good tune-up and maintenance schedules, (2) having the right tires that are kept properly inflated, (3) watching your driving habits.

To determine how much gasoline and oil is costing you each mile, each year, you are going to have to keep some records. That can either be boring or it can be fun. Try for the latter. I keep an Auto Log, much like a ship's log, in which I record: date; number of gallons; type of gas — high-test or regular — and sometimes the brand if it is especially inexpensive or expensive; trip statistics; type of terrain if it is especially mountainous or curvy; traffic conditions; weather conditions; time it took me to get from place to place; and anything else that I think might make a difference in the mileage or remind me of the experience for any reason, such as that someone other than myself was driving and driving extremely badly. For instance, I travel back and forth to Florida every once in a while. I only have to refer to my diary to know how long it will take me to get from one place on the route to another because I always record what time I start out, where and how long for lunch — good food or terrible — cost, pit stops (if a major layover was involved), campsites and lodging, cost (great or horrible), and the time I arrived at my destination. If you're a traveler, an on-the-road type, and there are many of us, it is sometimes nice to compare notes. I record what and when repairs were made and the cost in time and money of same. I use a book with no dates on it. By writing in my own dates, I have made the book last for three years now, and it still has over half the pages left. It gives me and my car's relationship another dimension. Each time I stop for gas I fill the tank up and that way can tell exactly how much mileage I'm getting by subtracting the present mileage from the last. I know immediately if my car needs adjustment.

Since I've been checking my tires every other gas stop (with my own tire gauge) I am getting a mile or so better mileage than I did when I used to drive with them four or five pounds too low. Not to mention better tire wear.

There are so many variables to deal with that affect your gas mileage:

1. Speed — the faster you go, the less mileage you get after 35 or 40 miles per hour. Over 40 to 45 the mileage drops considerably each additional mile per hour you travel, that is, a car that gets 50 miles per gallon at 30 miles per hour could drop as low as 25 miles per gallon going 70 miles per hour. That's a 50 percent increase in gas consumption. Think it over if you're short on cash. Is the extra time saved worth the extra money?

2. Weight is another very important factor. It affects fuel consumption in almost direct proportion — if you double the weight you carry, you double the gas you use. So, as the old pilots used to do when they wanted to be sure of a good takeoff, jettison some of that junk you've been carting around in the trunk that adds weight and cuts down mileage.

3. Wind resistance is a big factor in mileage calculations. Wind resistance is greatly increased not only by increased speed but also by whatever you put on top of the roof or on the front of the car. It can cut your mileage in half easily. If you must carry stuff on the roof or on the front of your car, look into a spoiler that will reduce wind resistance. Taking a canoe on top on a very long trip may cost you more than renting one when you get there,

particularly if you're a fast driver or encounter heavy winds. At high speeds, open windows cause considerable air resistance. Just open the side vents or the regular windows a crack.

4. Accessories. Air conditioners cost you approximately 2 to 3 miles per gallon; heater fans cost you almost as much. Anything that puts a drag on your electrical system costs you in gas mileage, particularly at speeds *under* 70 miles per hour. Utilize the "air flow" system in your car instead of the heater fan or air conditioner whenever possible unless extreme heat or cold prevails.

5. Letting the engine idle for more than a minute cuts your mileage to practically nothing. Shut off your motor if you can; even if it's just for a minute, it pays. It also helps keep the environment free of pollution.

6. Avoid jackrabbit starts and stops. They both eat up gas. Drive as smoothly as possible, steady as you go, matey. Use your head to drive ahead. If you see that traffic ahead is stopped or slowing down, slack off the accelerator instead of zooming up and using your brake. Smooth and easy does it.

7. Use your brakes instead of your gearshift to stop.

8. Avoid speeding up hills. Try to maintain a steady pace. Take a tip from the truck drivers: if you're headed downhill and see an "up" hill approaching, get a good start on it. It takes less gas that way.

9. Options:

a. Radial tires cost more initially but they last longer and get much better gas mileage due to less drag. Wide- and deep-tread tires (snow, mud) take more gas to run.

b. Standard shifts get better mileage than automatic shifts.

c. Small cars get better mileage than big cars.

d. High gear takes less gas than second or low gear; overdrive takes less than high gear.

e. Smooth roads take less gas than bumpy roads.

f. Night driving takes more gas than daylight driving, all other things being equal, because of the power used by the headlights.

g. Cold-weather driving uses more gas than warm-weather driving.

h. Diesel engines get better mileage than gasoline engines.

10. Don't use a higher octane gasoline than your car needs. If it doesn't knock on low-test, use it. If it does, move up one notch on the octane ladder until it stops knocking and then stay there.

11. Don't fill your gas tank so full that gas runs out the overflow.

THE EXHAUST SYSTEM

This system of your car might be likened to your own pulmonary system. In the intake stroke of the pistons your engine is inhaling carbon, oxygen, hydrogen,

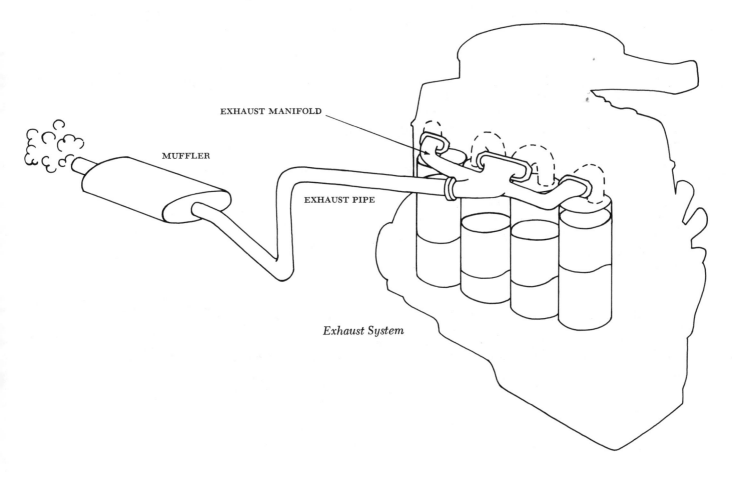

MUFFLER

EXHAUST MANIFOLD

EXHAUST PIPE

Exhaust System

and nitrogen; on the exhaust stroke your engine is exhaling lead oxide, carbon, resin, steam, nitrogen, carbon dioxide, sulfurous acid, carbon monoxide, and the hydrocarbons from the gasoline that did not burn.

CAUTION: The symptoms of carbon monoxide poisoning are: headache, or a pounding in the head; drowsiness; optical illusions; nausea; uneven heartbeat; confusion. Never run your motor with the garage doors closed. Always keep your window opened at least a crack if you are backed up in heavy traffic with the other guy's exhaust spewing into your car.

The exhaust system starts with the *exhaust valve* in the piston. This opens up to let the burned-up gases out into the *exhaust manifold,* a piece of metal ductwork that leads from each cylinder, channeling the explosive noises and the gases to the *exhaust pipe*, which takes them to the *muffler,* which cools the gases, and to a *resonator*, which muffles the explosions and then sends the quieted, cooled gas out the *tail pipe* into the outer atmosphere and into our neighbor's lungs. If you have ever driven in Los Angeles or Mexico City on a smoggy day you will know what this means, as the tears run down your face from the fouled-up air that irritates your eyes until they are permanently red for as long as you stay there.

The big enemies of the exhaust system are rust and corrosion. If you live in places where they spread salt on the roads, or if you live by the sea, you will have this problem a lot.

In the average car most exhaust repairs (except on the emission-control systems) are not so much complicated as they are difficult due to the parts being rusted together. It takes more strength and perseverance than brains to repair an exhaust system.

Just as your breath can tell you many things about your body's health, your car's exhaust fumes can tell you a lot about your engine's health — from the way it sounds to the color of the smoke and the smell of the fumes. See Troubleshooting, page 178.

EMISSION-CONTROL SYSTEMS

Today's exhaust systems have *emission controls* of various types, namely: the *air-injection system*, which injects air into the exhaust manifold to complete combustion; the *vapor separator*, to prevent gasoline vapors from evaporating into the atmosphere; the *positive crankcase ventilation* (PCV) *system*, to allow the engine to "breathe"; the *exhaust gas recirculation system*, which recirculates the exhaust gas into the carburetor; and the *catalytic converter*, to convert noxious gases into harmless water vapor. These systems cause us to get less power from our engines and therefore we use more gas to go fewer miles and thus further deplete our resources. Good old American know-how at work again. Since these systems are

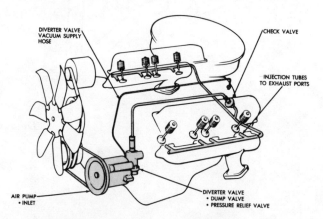

Emission Controls: Air-Injection System. Courtesy of the Chrysler Corporation

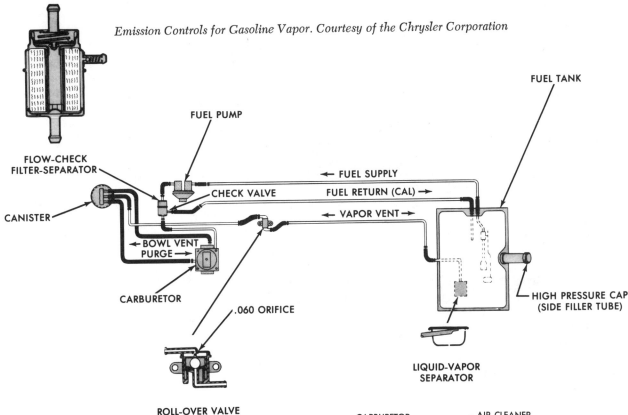

Emission Controls for Gasoline Vapor. Courtesy of the Chrysler Corporation

mandatory for the time being, the only way to beat the system is to get a three-quarter-ton van or truck — for some strange reason they are not required to have these emission devices.

To quote the Chrysler people, "Hydrocarbons (HC) are the unburned gasoline vapors leaving the engine combustion chamber. A certain amount of HC can be expected due to cold spots in the combustion chamber. Excessive HC is normally caused by (1) engine misfire or (2) overly rich or lean mixtures. Carbon

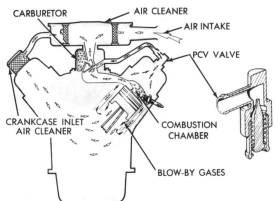

Emission Controls: Positive Crankcase Ventilation. Courtesy of the Chrysler Corporation

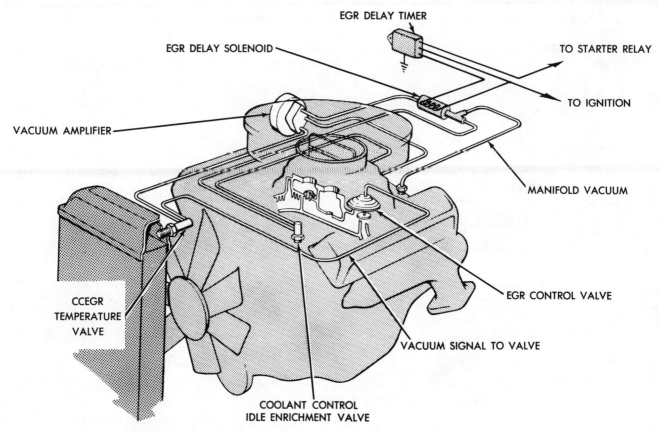

EGR DELAY TIMER

EGR DELAY SOLENOID

TO STARTER RELAY

TO IGNITION

VACUUM AMPLIFIER

MANIFOLD VACUUM

CCEGR TEMPERATURE VALVE

EGR CONTROL VALVE

VACUUM SIGNAL TO VALVE

COOLANT CONTROL IDLE ENRICHMENT VALVE

Emission Controls: Exhaust Gas Recirculation. Courtesy of the Chrysler Corporation

Monoxide (CO) is the result of partial burning of the fuel mixture due to insufficient oxygen. The air/fuel mixture is either providing too much fuel or not enough air."

On page 47 is a view of an emission-control system and the accompanying maintenance chart to keep your vehicle properly (and legally) adjusted. These systems have gotten so complicated that, unless you have special testing equipment and knowledge, you must take the car to a qualified person for testing and adjustments.

THE COOLING SYSTEM

Unless you have an air-cooled engine like the VW, Porsche, or Corvair, your water cooling system will consist of the following components:

Radiator, radiator cap, hoses, water pump, thermo-

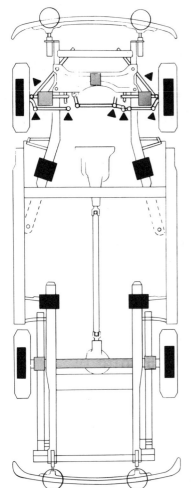

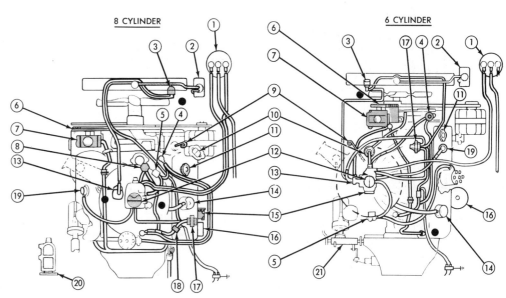

LUBRICATION
▲ SUSPENSION AND STEERING LINKAGE BALL JOINTS
LIFTING
■ FRAME CONTACT OR DRIVE ON HOIST
□ FLOOR JACK OR HOIST
O BUMPER JACK (AT BUMPER SLOT ONLY)

LUBRICATION AND MAINTENANCE GUIDE
ALL MODELS

8 CYLINDER

6 CYLINDER

(1) FUEL VAPOR STORAGE CANISTER
(2) COOLANT RESERVE TANK
(3) TEMPERATURE VALVE (CCEGR)
(4) THERMAL IGNITION CONTROL VALVE (TIC)
(5) ORIFICE SPARK ADVANCE CONTROL VALVE (OSAC)
(6) AIR PUMP
(7) POWER STEERING PUMP
(8) COOLANT CONTROL IDLE ENRICHMENT VALVE (CCIE)
(9) CRANKCASE DIPSTICK (OTHER V8, LEFT SIDE)
(10) FUEL FILTER
(11) OIL FILL CAP

(12) CARBURETOR CHOKE SHAFT
(13) EGR CONTROL VALVE
(14) CRANKCASE INLET AIR CLEANER
(15) MANIFOLD HEAT VALVE
(16) OIL FILTER (OTHER V8, LEFT FRONT)
(17) VACUUM AMPLIFIER
(18) EGR TIME DELAY CONTROL
(19) PCV VALVE
(20) MASTER CYLINDER
(21) CLUTCH TORQUE SHAFT
● COOLING SYSTEM DRAINS

Lubrication and Maintenance Guide. Courtesy of the Chrysler Corporation

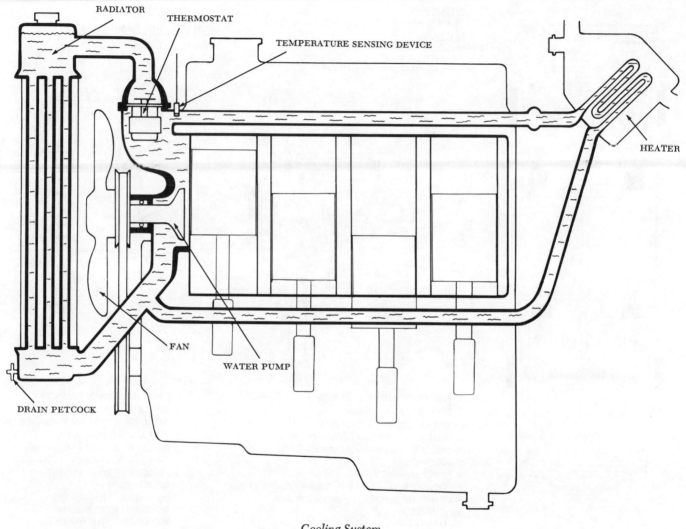

RADIATOR

THERMOSTAT

TEMPERATURE SENSING DEVICE

HEATER

FAN

WATER PUMP

DRAIN PETCOCK

Cooling System

stat, transmission oil cooler, fan and *fan-belt-pulley assembly, heater* and *air conditioner* units. All of these dissipate the heat generated by the engine's moving parts caused by friction and the combustion process.

If your engine could talk it would probably tell you that it prefers to run at a temperature of 180° F; at that temperature, the oil flows nicely but is not hot enough to break down its lubricating qualities.

The *radiator* is that big flattish item with the honeycomb face in the very front of the engine compartment of the car. Its thousands of cells provide area to cool the water that has run through the hot engine and run off again, taking the engine heat with it. Radiators get corroded, radiators get dirty — that is, filled up with the bodies of bugs and flying insects that collect in the normal course of driving. Radiators get banged in a lot since they are located at the very front of the car. Radiators even get stolen, because they contain a lot of valuable copper. They also get drained by means of a little petcock at the bottom, which is merely a valve you open to drain off the old coolant when you want to replace your cooling-system fluid. The *radiator cap* is a screw-type cap that removes to allow you to add water and coolant from time to time. With luck, your radiator should last the life of the car, ditto your radiator cap.

The *water pump* is the next important item in the system. As its name implies, it pumps the water through the system. As all pumps can break down, so can your water pump. It shouldn't, but sometimes it does. Replacing it is usually a fairly simple job, unless you have air conditioning, and then it can be complicated. You can buy rebuilt ones.

The *fan's* function is to draw the air through the radiator; so it can do this it is placed *behind* the radiator, closest to the engine. It is activated by the fan-belt pulley that is attached to the crankshaft of the engine.

The *thermostat* is the next important item. This is a little device located at the top of the engine block where the hose from the radiator fits in. It opens and closes a valve. When the engine is cold, it closes off the flow of water to the engine from the radiator. The water already in the engine heats up quickly. When it gets to a certain predetermined temperature, the thermostat opens the valve and lets the hot water out to circulate through the radiator, thus dissipating its heat, and then recirculates it back into the engine to start the cooling process all over again. These little mechanisms are the brains of the cooling system. They wear out and need to be replaced. See Maintenance, page 161, for replacing a thermostat.

Thermostats come in different heat ranges; for example, a 180° F thermostat begins opening at that temperature and opens completely at around 200° F, whereas a 190° F thermostat begins opening at that temperature and is fully opened at around 218° F. Varying factors decide which one you should use. Check your owner's manual before replacing your thermostat to ascertain proper specifications.

Cooling systems have improved considerably since the advent of the water pump and modern antifreeze.

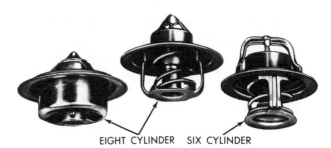

EIGHT CYLINDER   SIX CYLINDER

Thermostats. Courtesy of the Chrysler Corporation

I can still remember a harrowing ride in a raging blizzard when I was about five years old with my Mums in her 1930 Essex coupe with the rumble seat and the thin yellow stripe around the cab. We were driving from Wilkes-Barre, Pennsylvania, back to Bloomsburg, Pennsylvania, about forty miles distance. It was one of those old-fashioned snowstorms and you couldn't see ten feet in front of you. My mother is a tiny woman but she was one hundred pounds of pure courage. The radiator started boiling over about ten miles out of Wilkes-Barre. It was hell even trying to see far enough to pull off the road without pulling into a deep ditch. In those days it was a two-lane highway. We would stop and let the radiator cool off for about fifteen minutes, then we would start off again. We would get about five miles and it would boil over again. The snow kept pounding and swirling down, getting deeper and deeper. The light was failing fast although it was only about 3:00 P.M. The road conditions grew worse. That we finally made it was a miracle. It took us four hours for an hour-and-a-half drive. Had old Essex been equipped with a water pump and up-to-date ethylene-glycol antifreeze instead of plain alcohol we wouldn't have had any trouble. We were just ten years too early for the water pump, which came into being around 1940.

The *transmission oil cooler* is a separate unit that sits under the radiator and does just what its name implies, cools the transmission oil.

The hoses in the cooling system are of primary importance. They should be in good repair at all times and properly connected and clamped. See Maintenance, pages 141 and 161, for more on hoses.

TIP ABOUT ENGINE OVERHEATING. If you are:

pulling a trailer
stuck in heavy, slow-moving traffic

pulling your load up a steep hill or long, steep mountain road

your engine's cooling system may not be up to the strain. Therefore it needs an extra assist from you, the driver. You can help the situation and provide additional cooling by shifting into a lower gear. The lower the gear, the more your engine will cool.

In heavy traffic, when you are at a standstill, put the car into neutral and gently race the engine; that will provide extra cooling also (the fan will cool the radiator).

THE OIL SYSTEM

As we all know from the Tin Woodman in *The Wizard of Oz,* without a little oil in our joints, we wouldn't get very far on the "yellow brick road."

Oil has many functions other than lubrication to reduce friction caused by one metal part rubbing against another: it reduces heat; it reduces corrosion; it creates a seal; and it absorbs waste.

Without oil, engines would seize up and never work again. Oil is the lifeblood of the engine, and you should change the oil and the filters at least as often as the manufacturer recommends and buy only premium oil. Skimping on oil is stupid. Think of buying oil as you would of buying a present for your love — nothing but the best and the best is none too good. If you want to save money, buy your good oil in five-gallon (or larger) containers.

When you pour oil into your car from the can it goes to the *sump*, or *oil pan*, located at the bottom of your engine. The sump has a plug that you unscrew when you wish to change and drain your oil, and it also has a *filter* to collect impurities from the oil. It has an *oil pump* that pumps the oil up through the engine's *oil galleries*. There is an additional *oil filter*

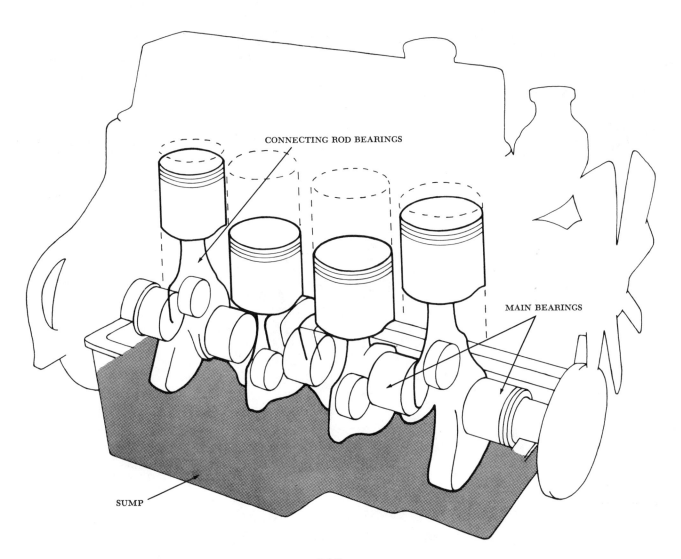

CONNECTING ROD BEARINGS

MAIN BEARINGS

SUMP

Oil System

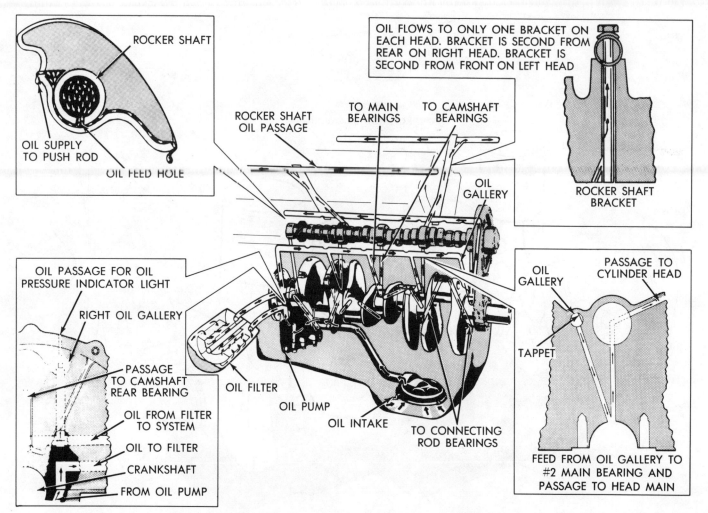

ROCKER SHAFT

OIL SUPPLY
TO PUSH ROD

OIL FEED HOLE

OIL FLOWS TO ONLY ONE BRACKET ON
EACH HEAD. BRACKET IS SECOND FROM
REAR ON RIGHT HEAD. BRACKET IS
SECOND FROM FRONT ON LEFT HEAD

ROCKER SHAFT
OIL PASSAGE

TO MAIN
BEARINGS

TO CAMSHAFT
BEARINGS

OIL
GALLERY

ROCKER SHAFT
BRACKET

OIL PASSAGE FOR OIL
PRESSURE INDICATOR LIGHT

RIGHT OIL GALLERY

PASSAGE
TO CAMSHAFT
REAR BEARING

OIL FROM FILTER
TO SYSTEM

OIL TO FILTER

CRANKSHAFT

FROM OIL PUMP

OIL FILTER

OIL PUMP

OIL INTAKE

TO CONNECTING
ROD BEARINGS

OIL
GALLERY

PASSAGE TO
CYLINDER HEAD

TAPPET

FEED FROM OIL GALLERY TO
#2 MAIN BEARING AND
PASSAGE TO HEAD MAIN

Oil System. Courtesy of the Chrysler Corporation

that usually screws on and off and should be replaced every other oil change (or, in dirty driving conditions, every oil change). Note your car's recommended procedures for oil changes and adhere faithfully to them; the life of your engine depends on it.

When my father was teaching me to drive he always told me to make it a habit to have my oil checked every other time I bought gasoline and particularly before starting out on a long trip or arduous mountain journey.

You check your oil by means of the dipstick. That usually is a long, thin, wire rod with a ring on the end of it for you to pull it out by. The dipstick tells you how much oil you have. It usually says "add" when you need oil. That means add one quart. Or, if it is lower than that, add two or even three quarts, depending on what the dipstick tells you. Don't add more oil than the stick indicates.

If your car is equipped with a warning light that flashes on when your oil pressure is low, heed it, by all means. If you have an oil gauge, get into the habit of looking at it while you are driving, much as a pilot checks his instrument panel constantly to be sure all systems are functioning properly. If the pressure is below the usual reading, check your oil.

All the while the car is in motion, oil is circulating throughout the engine, lubricating the different rods, pistons, bearings, valve lifters, rocker arms, and so on, just as your blood is constantly circulating through your veins.

Although it is important to keep your oil level topped up, I once had a 1952 Ford that immediately, as soon as I filled up the oil, threw the last quart. Otherwise I didn't use any oil. As soon as I discovered that, I just kept it a quart low with no harm done. Each car has its own foibles, like each person.

It is important that you make sure when you take the car in for an oil change that they actually change it and put in new oil of the proper viscosity. Viscosity means thickness. Since oil has many functions it shouldn't be too thick, or the parts of the engine won't move freely enough; it can't be too thin, or it will "break down," that is, be too thin to lubricate properly. Oil thins as it is heated and thickens as it cools.

The Society of Automotive Engineers, SAE, has set certain standards or grades for oil viscosity at given temperatures, for instance, SAE 5W, 10W, 20W, 30W, 40W, and 50W — those are the single-grade oil viscosity measurements. The lower the number, the thinner the oil. If you lived in Alaska you would probably use 5W because it wouldn't thicken up in the extremely cold temperatures. In the tropics you might use 40W. In recent years the oil companies have introduced multigrade-viscosity oils that have several different ranges or combinations of oil in them. Living in Connecticut, where the temperature can go as high as 100 degrees Fahrenheit in summer and drop to —25 degrees Fahrenheit in the winter, I use a multigrade SAE 10W–40, the "10" allowing me to start in cold weather while the "40" protects the moving parts by being heavy enough not to break down.

The hotter an engine runs the more important it is that you have a high-quality oil that will not break down at the fantastic temperatures an engine builds up at continued high speeds (often higher than 1,200° F). Bear in mind that the SAE rating has nothing to do with the quality of the oil, just the viscosity. Always buy premium oil. Clean oil is clear and amber colored. If your oil looks dirty, change it; don't wait for the recommended lubrication and oil-change period (see Maintenance, page 157).

LUBRICATION AND MAINTENANCE CHART
NORMAL SERVICE

ENGINE COMPARTMENT

ENGINE COOLANT - BATTERY

① Reserve Tank - Keep coolant level between 1 and 2 qt. mark with 50/50 Ethylene Glycol and Water.

● Drain Locations - Drain and flush first 24 months or 30,000 miles then every 12 months or 15,000 miles.

Battery - Every 2 months (standard battery) check electrolyte level, maintain level with mineral free water to bottom of filler well hole.

ENGINE OIL - STEERING FLUID

② Crankcase Dipstick - Check oil when refueling, keep between "Add one Quart" and "Full".

③ Fill Cap - Oil - Use ONLY oils with "SAE" Grade and "SE" Classification.

④ Oil Filter (Other V8 Left Side) - Change with first (THEN EVERY SECOND) oil change.

⑤ Power Steering - Check fluid level each oil change. Add/use P/N 2084329 or equivalent.

FUEL - CHOKE - EXHAUST - BRAKE MASTER CYLINDER - TRANSMISSION (AUTOMATIC)

⑥ Fuel Filter - Replace every 30,000 miles.

⑦ Fuel Vapor Storage Canister - Replace filter every 30,000 miles.

⑧ Choke Shaft - Every 6 months or second oil change clean with solvent.

⑨ Manifold Heat Valve - Every 30,000 miles (COLD) while rotating valve spray Solvent P/N 3419129 or equivalent to shaft ends.

⑩ Brake Master Cylinder - Every 6 months Check fluid level, maintain level ¼ " to top of reservoir, use brake fluid conforming to DOT 3.

⑪ Transmission (Automatic) - Every 6 months Check fluid level (Engine hot, in neutral)

VENTILATION SYSTEM - RUBBER/PLASTIC HOSES - DRIVE BELTS

⑫ PCV Valve - Every 5,000 miles check function. Every 30,000 miles replace valve.

⑬ Crankcase Inlet Air Cleaner - Every 30,000 miles Clean and re-oil.

⑭ Carburetor Air Cleaner - Every 30,000 miles replace filter element.

Hoses - Every second oil change Inspect for leaks and/or deterioration, replace if necessary.

Belts - Every Oil change check, Adjust or replace if necessary.

ENGINE AND EMISSION COMPONENTS, SEE GROUPS 9 AND 25 FOR SERVICING

Tappets (6 Cylinder Engine) - Every 15,000 miles check and adjust.

Spark Plugs (All Engines) - Replace every 30,000 (With Catalyst) or 15,000 miles without

⑮ Temperature Valve (CCEGR)

⑯ Thermal Ignition Control Valve (TIC)

⑰ Orifice Spark Advance Control Valve (OSAC)

⑱ Air Pump

⑲ Coolant Control Engine Vacuum Switch (CCEVS)

⑳ EGR Control Valve

㉑ Vacuum Amplifier

㉒ EGR Time Delay Control Valve

CHASSIS

① Suspension Ball Joints - Every 6 months, Inspect seals-Replace if damaged or leaking.

② Steering Linkage Joints - Every 3 years or 30,000 miles relubricate with P/N 2525035 or equivalent.

③ Upper and Lower Control Arm Bushings - Inspect for deterioration every oil change.

④ Front Wheel Bearings - Inspect, Clean, Relubricate with P/N 3837794 or equivalent AT LEAST every 22,500 miles or whenever brakes are serviced.

⑤ Brake Linings - Inspect every 15,000 miles and/or during wheel bearing service.

⑥ Brake and Power Steering Hoses - Every 6 months inspect for deterioration and leaks.

⑦ Transmission - Manual - Every 6 months check fluid level. Maintain fluid level at bottom of filler plug hole with DEXRON Automatic Transmission Fluid.

Shift Mechanisms - Lubricate with P/N 2932524 or equivalent. Column (3 Speed) as required. Floor, 3 speed (Through titting) every 7,500 miles, 4 speed (Pack) every 10,000 miles or 6 months.

⑧ Universal Joint Seals - Every 6 months inspect for leakage, replace joint if leakage is evident.

⑨ Rear Axle - Lubricant, No periodic level check required. Examine for leakage during engine oil change, use P/N 3744994 or equivalent, if required.

Lubrication and Maintenance Chart. Courtesy of the Chrysler Corporation

OTHER LUBRICATION Besides your engine, which needs oil to keep those parts moving smoothly against each other, the rest of the car also has moving parts that need periodic shots of various grades of oils and grease.

I have included here (see opposite) a page from the Dodge shop manual showing the various lubrication joints and different lubricants that they specify for their products.

3. The Electrical System

Since approximately 90 percent of the trouble you will ever have with your automobile will stem from some part of the vast electrical system, I want to briefly touch on some of the terminology and concepts, if for no other reason than that it may save you from a "shocking" experience, unpleasant but not fatal.

Electricity, like the ocean, can be a powerfully destructive force if unleashed in the wrong place at the wrong time under the wrong circumstances. Conversely, that vast power, when properly harnessed and channeled, can be made to accomplish fantastic feats for us such as pushing our auto down the highway at alarmingly high speeds to get us from one place to another.

A diagram of the electrical system of our modern motorcar, as seen from the top, appears on page 57.

Mini Electrical Lesson

Volt — a measure of electrical "pressure." It requires 1 volt to overcome a resistance of 1 ohm.

Ohm — the measure of the "resistance" of a material to the flow of electricity. That is to say, a material such as copper that has a _low_ ohm reading easily allows the flow of electrical current through it. Hence it is called a _conductor_. On the other hand, a material such as rubber has a _high_ ohm reading and does _not_ readily allow the flow of electricity through it. Hence it is called an _insulator_.

Ampere — a measure of the quantity of electricity that can flow through a wire (conductor), governed by the size of the wire. _Thin wires allow small amounts of current through; thick wires allow large amounts._

Watt — a measure of electrical _work_ and the end product of volts multiplied by amps: volts × amps = watts. For instance, in a 12-volt battery system your headlights require about 8 amps to light up; 12 volts × 8 amps = 96 watts (which is the amount of electricity used up by burning your headlights).

Your electric bill at home is based on _watt hours_. That is simply the measure of watts consumed over time:

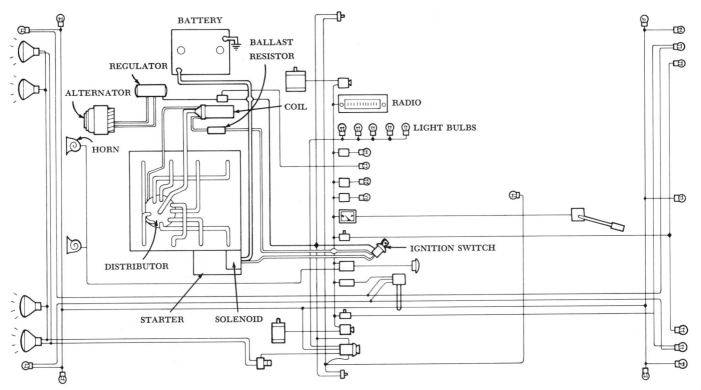

Electrical System—Aerial View

1 watt for 1 hour = 1 watt hour
96 watts for 1 hour = 96 watt hours
96 watts for ½ hour = 48 watt hours

Since you use so many watt hours in your home the bills are computed in *kilowatt*, or thousand-watt, hours.

Electrical units that are in *motion*, such as motors, are measured in amps. Units that *heat* up, like cigarette lighters, electric stoves, light bulbs, and so on, are measured in watts.

How many times in my automotive life have I heard countless mechanics say to me, "Well, lady, you got a short circuit somewhere!"

I would always nod knowingly and reply, "Yes, well fix it" — not knowing what the hell they were talking about until I took the Know-How Course, which explained to me that a "short circuit," or "short," is always somewhere on the "hot line," or positive wire, leading to an electrical connection from the battery. The wire has somehow become exposed, that is, the insulation has worn off so that the wire is either rubbing or "grounding" to the body of the car or to a piece of metal (like a bolt) that is attached to the body of the car. It is "shorting out" because it is actually completing a circuit before it is supposed to — hence the term "short circuit." Or, it can be rubbing against another exposed wire. This can cause a fire, so it is important to find the short if possible.

My agent told me she had an old Chevy convertible that had an elusive short somewhere in the ignition system that innumerable garages and electrical experts could not locate. It left her stranded in a snowstorm on two separate occasions. She finally traded the car in on a new model without ever tracing the short.

FUSES, WIRES, AND CABLES

Because the electrical system is so extensive, it is divided into subsystems or circuits, each performing different functions. Some are interdependent; all are interrelated.

In these interrelated circuits more than two hundred feet of wires and cables (two or more enclosed wires) may be used in one automobile. For expediency in troubleshooting so that the manufacturers themselves would know what they were doing they have color coded these wires for the different systems. For instance (with three exceptions — the battery ground strap, battery leads, and ignition high-tension wires, which are black), my Dodge van has eighteen different colors.

Your car like your home also is equipped with *fuses*, and sometimes *circuit breakers* to protect it from an electrical fire when something goes wrong in a circuit. The fuse or circuit breaker is, you might say, a weak link in the electrical chain and is so designed to give out at the first sign of trouble, thus breaking the circuit in a particular system and thereby saving the system from burning up (and sometimes saving the entire car and its occupants) until the cause of trouble can be traced to a faulty switch, a loose connection, a short-circuited wire, a worn-out or defective accessory, or a broken wire somewhere along the way. Some circuit breakers are actually integrated into the unit switch or wire itself.

The fuses you find in your fuse box at home are probably round with isinglass windows and screw into the fuse box, as opposed to the fuses in your car, which are cylindrical cartridges and just push or snap into the clips in the fuse box. However, they share the one thing in common that makes them a "fuse" — a fine, thin wire that is designed to melt at the least sign

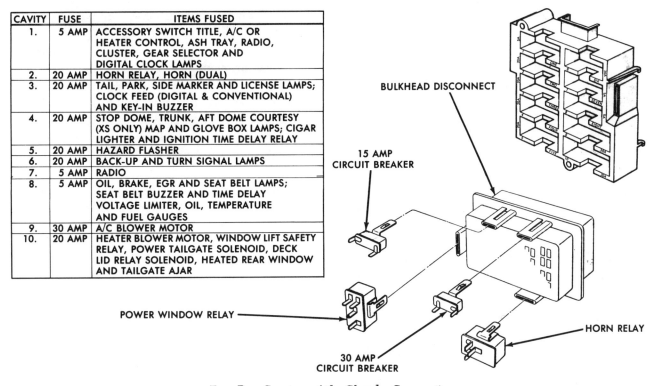

CAVITY	FUSE	ITEMS FUSED
1.	5 AMP	ACCESSORY SWITCH TITLE, A/C OR HEATER CONTROL, ASH TRAY, RADIO, CLUSTER, GEAR SELECTOR AND DIGITAL CLOCK LAMPS
2.	20 AMP	HORN RELAY, HORN (DUAL)
3.	20 AMP	TAIL, PARK, SIDE MARKER AND LICENSE LAMPS; CLOCK FEED (DIGITAL & CONVENTIONAL) AND KEY-IN BUZZER
4.	20 AMP	STOP DOME, TRUNK, AFT DOME COURTESY (XS ONLY) MAP AND GLOVE BOX LAMPS; CIGAR LIGHTER AND IGNITION TIME DELAY RELAY
5.	20 AMP	HAZARD FLASHER
6.	20 AMP	BACK-UP AND TURN SIGNAL LAMPS
7.	5 AMP	RADIO
8.	5 AMP	OIL, BRAKE, EGR AND SEAT BELT LAMPS; SEAT BELT BUZZER AND TIME DELAY VOLTAGE LIMITER, OIL, TEMPERATURE AND FUEL GAUGES
9.	30 AMP	A/C BLOWER MOTOR
10.	20 AMP	HEATER BLOWER MOTOR, WINDOW LIFT SAFETY RELAY, POWER TAILGATE SOLENOID, DECK LID RELAY SOLENOID, HEATED REAR WINDOW AND TAILGATE AJAR

BULKHEAD DISCONNECT

15 AMP CIRCUIT BREAKER

POWER WINDOW RELAY

30 AMP CIRCUIT BREAKER

HORN RELAY

Fuse Box. Courtesy of the Chrysler Corporation

of trouble, that is, too much heat shooting through it. Each circuit has its own fuse so you know where to start looking for the trouble. Your owner's manual or shop manual should designate the location of the fuse box and, if it is not written right on the box or its cover, it should tell you the system to which each fuse belongs. Remember, you should not only change the fuse but be sure to have the cause of the burned fuse traced and repaired. It could be: a faulty switch, a burned-out bulb, a short in the wiring, a loose bulb, a defective unit such as your heater or clock or many times the cigarette lighter, or even a faulty fuse itself or faulty circuit breaker.

TIP: Locate your fuse box *before* trouble strikes. Some cars conceal it like buried treasure. Carry some extra fuses with you in the glove compartment. They are sold at most service stations and all auto supply stores.

CAUTION: DO NOT USE A LARGER FUSE THAN THE ONE SPECIFIED FOR YOUR AUTO. Replace with *identical* size that is imprinted on the fuse. *Be sure* to turn off your engine before replacing the fuse or you might get a shock!

If you have difficulty removing the burned-out or defective fuse, DO NOT use anything metal like a screwdriver or hairpin to help you, use a wooden pencil or stick or plastic pen. With something metallic you might inadvertently complete the circuit and not only get shocked but possibly burn out all the wires of the instrument panel on a twelve-volt system.

Most fuse boxes are located somewhere under the dashboard, most times on the *fire wall* (that is the wall that separates you from the engine compartment; if your engine is in the front the fire wall is in front of you, if your engine is rear mounted it is in back of you).

Fusible link — merely a smaller wire than the rest of the wires in the circuit, making it "the weak link" that will be the first to melt (the same principle as a regular fuse). They are always found in the hot wire. You can find them at the battery, at the starter solenoid, but not on the starter-motor circuit, which is a heavy-duty circuit. Sometimes they are red in color, never extremely long.

Circuit breakers — in autos are usually found protecting electric motors from momentary overloading. At home, when your circuit breaker is overloaded it shuts off and you have to head for the circuit box to snap the switch back on to reactivate it. In autos, they automatically come back on or *reset* themselves. The headlight system usually has a circuit breaker.

NOTE: It is located on the hot wire or hot terminal (+).

In-line fuse — just what the name implies. It is a regular cartridge fuse that is located in a socket in the hot wire itself. You pull the socket apart by twisting it and voilà, there is the fuse. Some of the places these can be found on Chrysler, Ford, and GM cars (not AMC) are: automatic headlight dimmers and speed controls, air conditioners, spotlights, headlight relays, blower motors, tailgate-lock solenoids, and deck-lid solenoids.

A word about electrical wires and cables — like fuses, they are designed to do different jobs and carry different loads just like the wiring in your home — your home air conditioner requires a thicker, heavier load bearing electric cord than a table lamp because it uses more electricity than a table lamp. Think of electrical wiring as you do a garden hose — the thicker the hose, the more water can flow through it. Therefore, BE SURE when you are replacing faulty or broken wiring to replace it with wiring of the same type and size. The same rule applies to bulbs and switches.

ELECTRICAL AXIOM: The farther a current travels from the source, the lower its voltage becomes.

SIZE OF WIRE AND CURRENT IT CAN CARRY

	light load (to 7 amps)	medium load (7 to 10 amps)	heavy load (10 to 15 amps)
to 25 ft. — use	#18	#16	#14
to 50 ft. "	#16	#14	#12
to 100 ft. "	#14	#12	#10

Credit: *Know-How*

NOTE: To work on your electrical system you should have on hand: a roll of electrical tape; a pair of pliers with insulated handles; a screwdriver or two with insulated handles; a set of lightweight "jumper" cables; a test light. And if you are going to be replacing wires you may need a soldering iron or a crimp connector and some crimpers.

CAUTION: In my dealings with Christmas lights and extension cords I have learned the hard way — by bad experiences — to stay away from wiring made in the Orient unless it is Underwriters' Laboratory approved.

The Starting, or Cranking, System

Using the analogy of the human body, surely the *battery* can be called the heart of the system because without it nothing works. Most car batteries are either *six volt* or *twelve volt*, mostly the latter. "Volt" is an electrical term indicating how much force, or pressure, the battery is capable of producing to push along the "blood" — the electrical current — to the various parts of the car that run by electricity.

NOTE: The capacity of a battery is measured by *ampere (amp) hours*. The higher the amp rating, the better the battery and, concomitantly, usually the more expensive. Look in your owner's manual (or on the battery) to see what strength your battery is. DO NOT replace a six-volt battery with a twelve-volt battery or vice versa. DO NOT replace your original battery with a battery of lesser amp rating. However, if, for instance, after your purchased your car you had additional electric equipment installed (such as an air conditioner or anything that draws heavy current) you may well find you require additional current and may want to replace your battery with one of higher amp rating. That merely means you are increasing your electrical storage capacity to supply your added equipment. Applying the same principle to your flashlight, the more batteries the flashlight holds, the more powerful a beam is emitted and the longer it lasts. The difference is that your car battery is a "wet cell," meaning it is rechargeable, and your flashlight batteries are usually "dry cell," meaning you can't recharge them (with a few exceptions).

The battery acts as a storehouse to supply the current to your car when the engine is *off*, for instance, if you want to listen to the radio or blow your horn.

However, the two main functions of the battery are to start the *starter motor*, which initially turns over your engine, and to supply the spark to the spark plugs, which keep the engine running.

The battery belongs to the *starting*, or *cranking*, *system*, one subdivision of the electrical system.

The components of the starting system, or cranking system, are: the *starter* (or *ignition*) *switch*; the *battery*; the *solenoid switch*; the *starter motor*; and, if you have an automatic transmission, the *neutral switch*.

To get our bodies moving in the morning usually requires some outside stimuli such as a few cups of hot tea or coffee, a couple of eggs, and perhaps a rasher of bacon and a shower. On bitter cold mornings it is even more difficult to "get the heart started" and the body warmed up enough to function; it's the same with a car.

The starting system is sometimes referred to as the cranking system because in the old days that's what they used, a crank. In fact, my first car was a twenty-year-old 1929 model, a Ford coupe with a rumble seat. It came equipped with a crank to get the car started in cold weather. The crank performed the same function as the starter motor. It turned the engine's crankshaft over and over and over pushing the pistons up and down in the engine, which created a partial vacuum that sucked air/fuel into the combustion chamber, where it was then ignited by the spark from the spark plugs and whoopee, your engine started to sputter and sputter and finally caught and in a few seconds was putt-putting you down the highway. That was when all went well. When all didn't go well, sometimes the engine would backfire, whipping the crank around and sending you spinning off into the snowbank on your backside and maybe

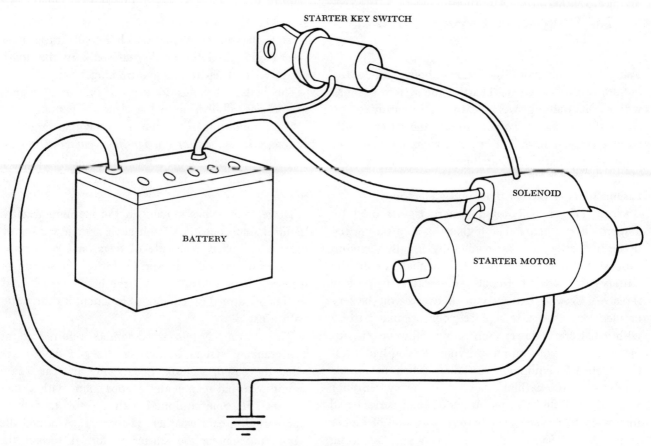

STARTER KEY SWITCH

SOLENOID

STARTER MOTOR

BATTERY

Starting System

breaking your arm in the process. Owning an automobile in those days was truly living dangerously.

Today we are more sophisticated. We simply place our key into the *ignition switch* and turn it to the right. By so doing we complete the electrical circuit that activates the starter motor.

Completing a circuit: a circular journey, or one beginning and ending in the same place, a round. Every time you want anything to work by electricity,

whether it be a simple light bulb or a huge motor, you must have a complete circuit. *Electrons* (electrical current) happen to flow from the negative (—) to the positive (+). Don't ask why. That's the nature of the beast. Therefore all the electrical units in your auto will have both a negative and a positive connection, or *terminal*. (A terminal simply means an end.)

To save money on copper wire, which is expensive, the early auto manufacturers realized that since the body of the car was made of steel (metal) and metal, like wire, is a conductor of electricity, all they had to do to complete a circuit back from any electrical unit on the car, whether a headlight, a starter motor, an air conditioner or radio or whatever, was to *ground* (attach) one terminal (usually the negative terminal) to the body of the car instead of running a wire all the way back from the unit to the battery — which, in modern cars, saves about a hundred feet of copper wire.

Almost all cars since 1954 have negative ground connections because they start more easily and run better. Consider the battery as the source, the well-spring, the font-of-life of all the electrical life in your car. Every electrical unit is connected to the battery by wires. The battery is connected, or grounded, to the car by a metal strap (from its negative terminal). Therefore, all that has to be done to complete a circuit from any electrical unit is to run one wire from the positive terminal (+) of the battery (the hot wire) to the unit and ground the unit to the car body. You have a complete circuit because the steel car body acts as the returning wire.

In electrical schematics a ground, or earth, is designated by this symbol:

If you will notice on the diagram of the starting system, a thin wire leads from the ignition switch to the heavier-gauge wire that leads from the battery to the solenoid to the starting motor. The wire from the battery to the solenoid of the starter motor is heavier gauge because the starter motor uses a larger jolt of electricity than any other electrical unit of the car, anywhere between 150 and 500 amps, depending upon the size of the engine, the thickness (viscosity) of the oil, and how cold it is.

ELECTRICAL AXIOM: It takes more energy to get a box started to move than it does to move it after it is moving.

For safety's sake as well as economy, the auto designers installed a *solenoid switch* in the system. It is merely a relay switch that permits the high current from the battery through to the starter motor without exposing the driver to it. It also saves using heavy expensive cable. This initial electrical demand imposes a heavier drain on your battery's power than any other single motor or electrical device on your car, because not only must it impel the starter motor but simultaneously it also must send some juice (electricity) to the ignition system as well. Therefore, if your battery is weak or kaput, this is the time you will probably get your first clue. Either it will completely fail to turn the starter motor and/or engine over at all or it will revolve (rev) so slowly you will almost feel the pain yourself. It will sound like a slow *uhhh — uhhh,* a dying gasp.

IMPORTANT NOTE: Get into the habit of making sure *all* the extra appliances or accessories, such as lights, heaters, fans, blowers, air conditioners, windshield wipers, radios, tape decks, and so forth, are turned off *before* you turn the ignition key to the start position — *every little drain hurts* and in dire situations can make the difference between getting your car started or not, particularly in cold weather. If a battery is discharged the electrolyte fluid in the battery can freeze. In cold weather your engine is much harder to turn over because the oil in the crankcase thickens and the battery is less efficient because of the cold. In fact, in cold climates it takes more than twice as much juice (amps) to start your car at the average winter temperature than it does at the average summer temperature.

In Connecticut I had a 1973 VW van that wouldn't start at all without a "jump" from a neighbor's battery every single day for one entire winter. I had my battery tested and it tested out okay. Being a sweetheart, I didn't trade it in until I got to Florida. Hopefully the person who bought it there will keep it in a warm place!

Let's take a quick wraparound look at batteries and their properties. The most commonly used *battery capacity* rating is called the Twenty Hour Rating in AMP Hours (if it can be discharged at 1/20 of its rated capacity for 20 hours and still produce 10.5 volts at the end of the test). For instance, on my Dodge van, written on the top of the battery it says: "Cold Cranking 305 Amps at 0 degrees F. Reserve Capacity 68 minutes. (Group 24.)"

Battery capacity is determined by (1) the number of plates, (2) the size of the plates, and (3) the amount of sulfuric acid in the electrolyte. The voltage is determined by the number of compartments, or *cells*. All cells have voltage of 2.1 volts — that is, 3 cells = 6 volts, 6 cells = 12 volts.

What a battery actually does is to convert chemical energy into electrical energy. To prove my point about how cold weather affects your battery, here are some statistics put out by Ford Motor Company.

PERCENTAGE OF BATTERY EFFICIENCY AT VARIOUS TEMPERATURES

80° F	100%	20° F	58%	0° F	40%
50° F	82%	10° F	50%	−10° F	33%
30° F	64%				

So, if you live in a part of the country where it gets really cold, it will pay you to invest in a powerful battery that will get you started in bitter weather.

To give you some idea of how much electricity the different accessories on your car use:

	6 Volt System	12 Volt System
Headlights	13.5 amps	8.0 amps

Let us say that the average car battery is rated at 60 amp hours (storage capacity). What that means to you, the user, assuming your headlights require 10 amps of power, is that you can leave your headlights on for 6 hours before your battery will be dead or have no more potential. But, if you crank your starter motor over (which could easily require 300 amps), you only have 2/10 of an hour, or 12 minutes, cranking time before your battery has no more potential.

CURRENT REQUIREMENTS FOR LIGHTS, IGNITION, AND ACCESSORIES

Accessory	Battery System	
	6 Volt	12 Volt
License-plate light	0.6 amps	0.4 amps
Taillights	1.5 "	1.0 "
Instrument lights	1.2 "	1.5 "
Ignition	3.3 "	3.0 "
Heater	8.7 "	5.0 "
Radio	5.5 "	1.8 "

Most automobiles come equipped with a 60-amp battery that is sufficient for normal usage. For more on battery testing and maintenance, see Maintenance, pages 137–138 and 159.

The next part of the cranking system we look at is the solenoid switch, mentioned before, which is merely a small device that contains a coil of many, many copper wires and an iron plunger. One of its terminals is attached by a heavy copper-wire cable to the battery, the other terminal to the starter motor. When you turn your starter switch you send a small amount of electricity through the coil in the solenoid, which activates (by magnetism) the iron plunger, which closes the *contact points*, sending heavy current through the cables to the starter motor. The solenoid is usually located either on top of the starter motor or fender wall or on the fire wall. Occasionally solenoids go bad and must be replaced. See Trouble-shooting, page 166.

The *neutral switch* (on automatic transmissions only) is merely a safety device located on the

gearshift. You must have the car gearshift in either "neutral" or "park" to complete the electrical circuit that permits the flow of current to the solenoid and enables the car to start. It is designed that way to keep you from starting the car in gear and going careening off the hillside or wherever your wheels were headed.

NOTE: If you turn on your ignition key and nothing happens, make sure your gearshift is seated in the proper place, either "neutral" or "park."

The starter motor is usually located beneath the engine. As shown on page 68, the starter motor has a toothed *pinion gear*, which engages with the *ring gear* (another toothed device) on the engine's fly-wheel. As the starter motor turns its pinion gear, that turns the flywheel of the engine, which turns the crankshaft, which moves the pistons, which suck in the fuel, which the spark plugs ignite, which pushes down the pistons, which turn the drive shaft, which turns the wheels around and off you go. That's it in a nutshell.

Usually you do not have trouble with starter motors for the first 50,000 miles.* If you do, you can buy either a rebuilt one from a reputable auto-supply house or a new one. Rebuilt ones are perfectly all right. Repairing a starter motor is not a job for amateurs, but replacing one is simple.

In both theory and practice, the starter motor merely overcomes the inertia of the engine and gets it moving. Once the engine has started and is running under its own power, the starter motor retracts its gear and goes back to sleep until the next time you need it.

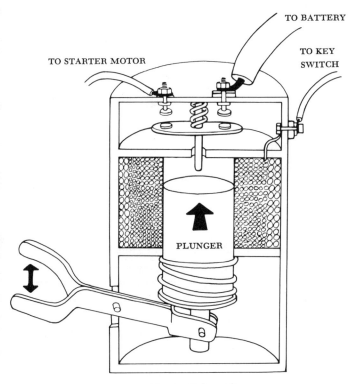

TO BATTERY

TO KEY SWITCH

TO STARTER MOTOR

PLUNGER

Starter Solenoid

* However, you can burn up your starter motor by cranking it too long. If you have trouble starting, turn it over a few times and rest. A few more turns and rest. Don't lean on it too long.

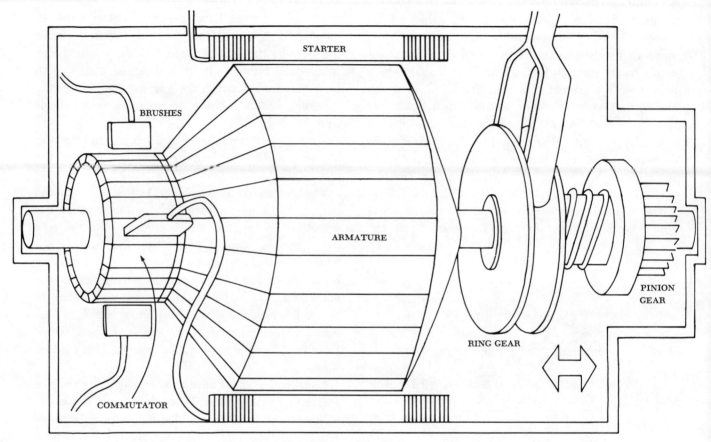

Starter Motor

THE IGNITION SYSTEM

If the engine had a song to sing, it would be to the ignition system — "Baby Won't You Light My Fire?" That is where the spark to ignite the fuel in the cylinders comes from, the ignition system.

The ignition system is divided into two separate subsystems, the *primary circuit* and the *secondary circuit*.

The primary circuit consists of: Usually a hand-operated *ignition switch* activated by a key, located on the dash or steering column, and a *coil*.

When you turn on your ignition switch you complete an electrical circuit between the battery and the coil. The battery sends along its low voltage (12 volts, to be precise, if you have a 12-volt battery) to the coil.

The purpose of having a coil is to turn that low voltage into high voltage because you need high voltage (by high I mean 20,000 to 30,000 volts) to create enough of a spark to jump a gap and ignite the fuel in the cylinder chamber for the power stroke. This

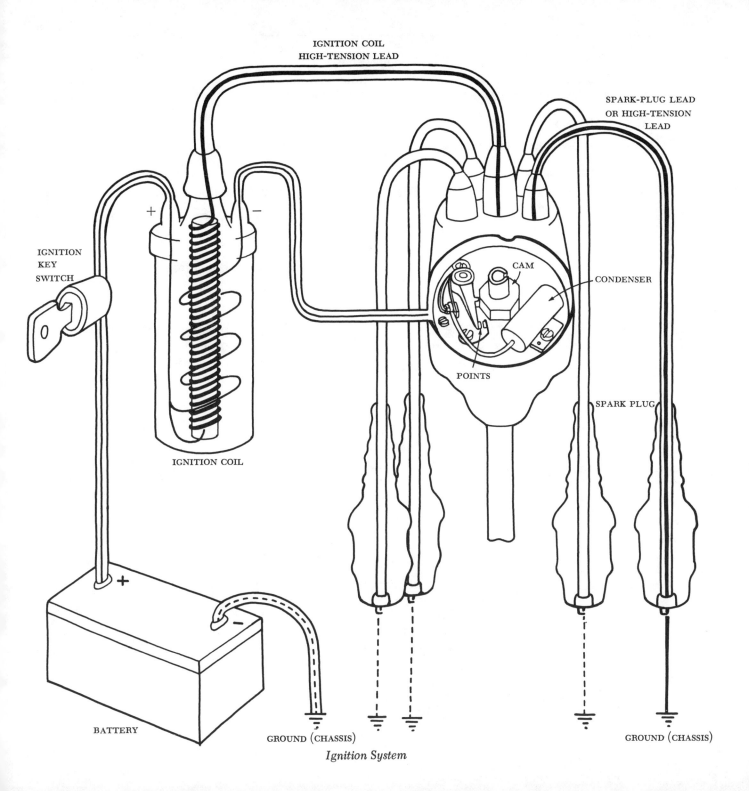

IGNITION COIL
HIGH-TENSION LEAD

SPARK-PLUG LEAD
OR HIGH-TENSION
LEAD

IGNITION
KEY
SWITCH

CAM

CONDENSER

POINTS

SPARK PLUG

IGNITION COIL

BATTERY

GROUND (CHASSIS)

GROUND (CHASSIS)

Ignition System

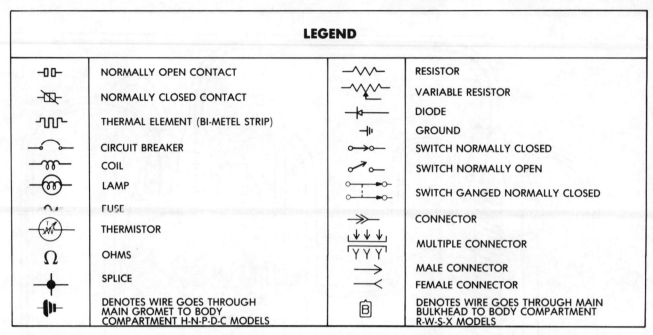

LEGEND		
NORMALLY OPEN CONTACT		RESISTOR
NORMALLY CLOSED CONTACT		VARIABLE RESISTOR
THERMAL ELEMENT (BI-METEL STRIP)		DIODE
CIRCUIT BREAKER		GROUND
COIL		SWITCH NORMALLY CLOSED
LAMP		SWITCH NORMALLY OPEN
FUSE		SWITCH GANGED NORMALLY CLOSED
THERMISTOR		CONNECTOR
OHMS		MULTIPLE CONNECTOR
SPLICE		MALE CONNECTOR
		FEMALE CONNECTOR
DENOTES WIRE GOES THROUGH MAIN GROMET TO BODY COMPARTMENT H-N-P-D-C MODELS		DENOTES WIRE GOES THROUGH MAIN BULKHEAD TO BODY COMPARTMENT R-W-S-X MODELS

Electrical Symbols. Courtesy of the Chrysler Corporation

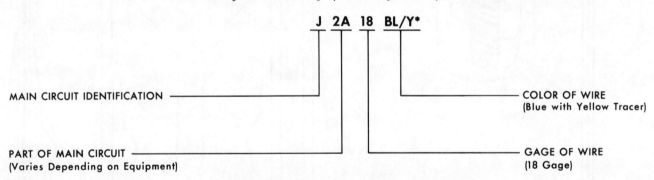

J 2A 18 BL/Y*

MAIN CIRCUIT IDENTIFICATION

PART OF MAIN CIRCUIT
(Varies Depending on Equipment)

COLOR OF WIRE
(Blue with Yellow Tracer)

GAGE OF WIRE
(18 Gage)

Code for Wire. Courtesy of the Chrysler Corporation

COLOR CODE			
BK	BLACK	P	PINK
BR	BROWN	R	RED
DBL	DARK BLUE	T	TAN
DGN	DARK GREEN	V	VIOLET
GY	GRAY	W	WHITE
LBL	LIGHT BLUE	Y	YELLOW
LGN	LIGHT GREEN	*	WITH TRACER
O	ORANGE		

Courtesy of the Chrysler Corporation

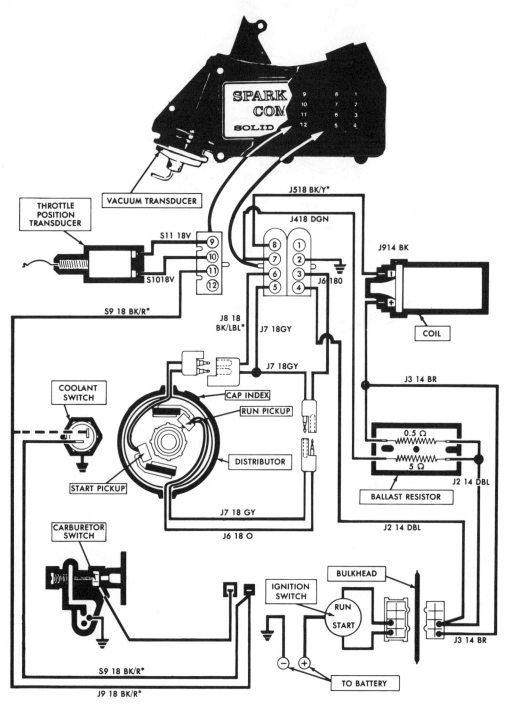

Wiring Diagram for Electronic Ignition. Courtesy of the Chrysler Corporation

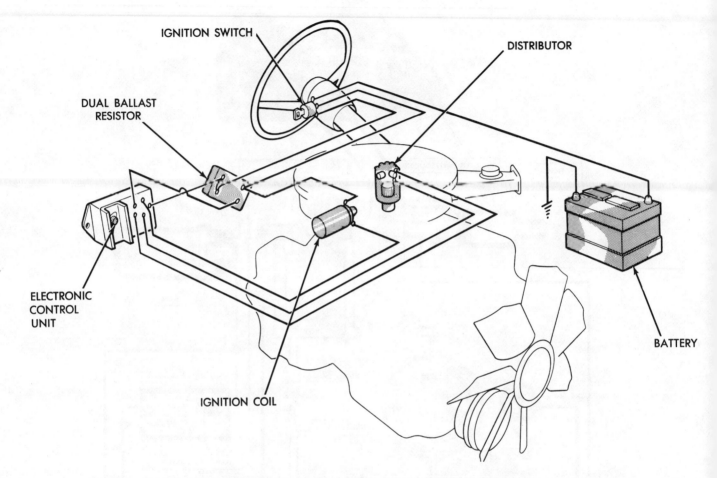

IGNITION SWITCH

DISTRIBUTOR

DUAL BALLAST
RESISTOR

ELECTRONIC
CONTROL
UNIT

BATTERY

IGNITION COIL

Electronic Ignition System. Courtesy of the Chrysler Corporation

magic is performed inside the coil by two sets of windings around an iron core: the primary winding of a couple hundred turns of fine wire (called the primary, or low-voltage, circuit) and the secondary winding (called the secondary, or high-tension, circuit), which has several thousand windings — perhaps an entire mile of wire in toto. The high voltage created is sent up

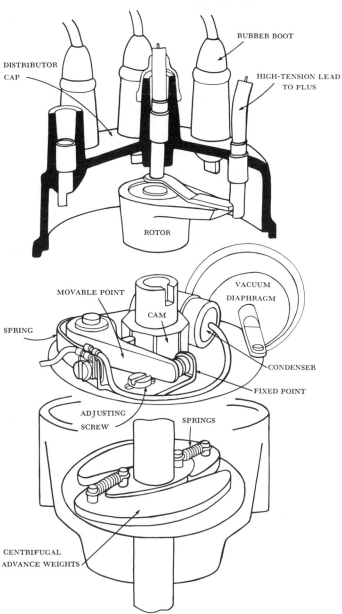

Distributor Sections

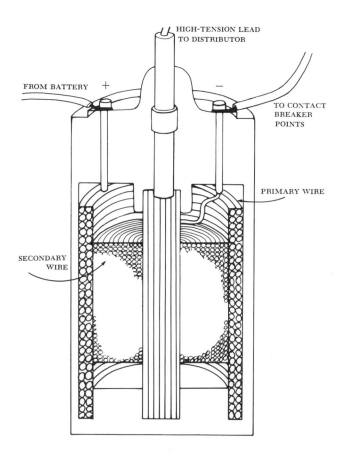

Ignition Coil

through the coil to a high-tension lead (a heavy black wire) that takes it to the distributor, where that high voltage is broadcast to each spark plug in the proper firing order.

Now there is still the low-voltage circuit at work in the coil that sends yet another (low-tension) lead out of the primary winding of the coil to the inside of the distributor, wherein lies the *condenser*. This is a small cylindrical piece that looks like a small tin can. Its function is to see that the *breaker points* (which are very delicate little metal arms with small round knobs on the ends) don't get too much current through them at once, or they will fuse together or get pitted. Then they have to be filed off or replaced.

The breaker points (or in the case of electronic ignition systems such as Chrysler's, a *reluctor,* which has replaced these points and performs the same function) open and close the electrical circuit intermittently,

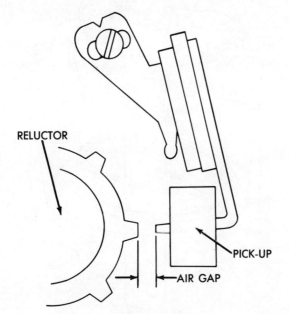

RELUCTOR

PICK-UP

AIR GAP

Electronic Ignition. Courtesy of the Chrysler Corporation

which allows the coil to perform its function — building up and collapsing a magnetic field whereby it makes high-voltage current from the low-voltage current.

The breaker points (or the reluctor) are activated (opened and closed) by the distributor shaft that is attached to and turned by the camshaft. These points must be set only so far apart and no farther. For further information see tune-up procedures, pages 143–156.

The secondary circuit of the ignition system begins with that heavy-duty wire coming out of the coil, leading into the high-tension terminal of the *distributor cap*. From there the current is transferred to the *rotor*, located underneath the car, which sends it along to each spark plug in turn, according to the firing order of the engine.

The spark plugs are the last stop for the ignition circuit. Your engine works only as well as your spark plugs.

There are different spark plugs for different engines, different speeds, different load factors, different combustion chambers, different mixtures of fuel, different compression ratios, and different operating temperatures.

Cold plugs are used in high-performance engines. They have short insulators, the heat having a shorter distance to travel.

Hot plugs have long insulators, the heat having a longer way to travel. These are used in low-performance engines.

Most plugs have a longer way to go to seat in the engine. These engines require *long-reach plugs*.

Short-reach plugs have short threads that fit into an engine so designed.

Some plugs have *gaskets* to ensure a tight seal. Others have a *tapered shoulder* that accomplishes the same thing without a gasket. It is important that you use the correct spark plug. The specific one for your car will be listed in your owner's manual.

Friends of mine bought a new Ford van this year. They complained bitterly that they were getting only six miles to a gallon, after one month's use. They took it back where they bought it and discovered that someone either at the factory or at the dealer had put in the wrong spark plugs. As soon as they were replaced by the correct plugs the mileage doubled to twelve miles per gallon. They're still complaining!

The average life of a spark plug under normal driving conditions is around 10,000 miles (unless you have an electronic ignition system, then they are supposed to last until 15,000). If you are getting less, something is not right. See Maintenance, pages 138–140, for replacing spark plugs.

The Charging, or Generating, System

This system is composed of either a *generator* or an *alternator*, one or the other of them being used as the dynamo of the electrical system. Since the battery is considered the heart of the electrical system, consider the dynamo as the supplier that keeps the heart beating, or *charged*. Without food being turned into blood to keep the cells nourished, we wouldn't last long. Without the battery having its electrical supply replenished, it wouldn't last long either, perhaps an hour instead of three years. Hence the generator or alternator.

As soon as the engine is started and running on its own power, the dynamo (generator/alternator) is drawn into action through a series of pulleys and belts that are driven by the crankshaft. The mechanical energy of the engine's rotating crankshaft is being turned into electrical energy. Through this action, electrical current is produced to (1) recharge the battery, or replace the electricity needed to start the starter motor and get the engine started, (2) run all the accessory equipment of the auto (such as the radio, lights, horn, heater, and air conditioner) once the engine is running under its own power, and (3) supply the engine with sparks.

In the early days, and all the way through the fifties, cars were equipped with generators, which produce *direct current* (DC). A generator is composed of hundreds of copper wires wound around coils; magnets; armatures; brushes; cooling fins; bearings; pulley wheel; commutator; and a few other things. It is the nature of the beast that the output from a generator is limited to about 30 amps and that it runs at a maximum speed of about 6,000 rpm. The difficulty with early generators was their inability to produce sufficient electricity to charge the battery if the engine was running at less than 1,200 rpm. Therefore, since most cars idle (sit still with the motor running) at anywhere from 600 to 900 rpm, all the time the car was not in motion the battery was discharging. No good. If you idled your car too long your battery went dead.

Therefore the alternator was developed. This is also a dynamo but it produces *alternating current* (AC). It charges the battery at a speed of a mere 600 engine rpm and produces around 45 amps, and has a maximum speed of double the generator, or 12,000 rpm. (The AC current is changed back to DC by means of a *diode*, or *rectifier*, so the battery can use it.)

As you may have guessed, this system is called the charging, or generating, circuit because it actually manufactures electricity to run the car and, with the remainder, recharges the battery. A nice give-and-take arrangement since the battery starts up the whole thing to begin with.

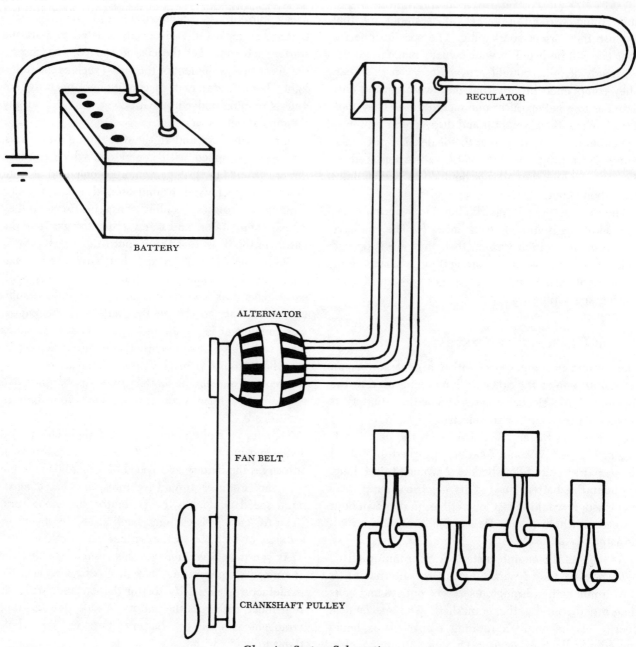

Charging System Schematic

You can locate the alternator (or generator on the older models), which is attached to the front of the engine, by tracing the belt that runs from the crankshaft pulley to its other pulley, which will be at the alternator. If there is more than one set of belts running from the crankshaft pulley (such as those for an air injection pump or power steering pump) the alternator will be the unit that also has wire cables leading to the battery.

When all systems are A-okay, that is, when you have a good, fully charged battery, your alternator should, under normal conditions, keep your battery in full charge. What it won't do is revitalize a bad battery (a battery that is low in charge because it is wearing out).

In 1950, on a Jack Kerouac–like trip across the country to Sun Valley, I was driving a 1946 Ford convertible through Kansas in the middle of the night and bam, my generator burned out. To be towed about twenty miles into Kansas City and have a rebuilt generator installed cost me about twenty-eight dollars. Those were the days! It burned out because I had been "pushing it" nonstop, except for pit stops, for twenty-four hours at too high a speed and it just couldn't stand the heat.

Anything that goes awry with your charging system is supposed to show up on your *ammeter*. An ammeter is the gauge that *used* to be on your dashboard and whose function was to measure the flow of electricity to and from the battery. Manufacturers replaced the ammeter with warning lights. I happen to have an honest-to-God ammeter on my Dodge van but it, like the oil-pressure gauge, cost extra. The difference to the car owner is that an ammeter shows *instantly* when something is wrong, that the system is discharging when it should be charging, or vice versa. The warning light (which says either "gen" or "alt" when the red light comes on) tells you only that there is trouble when most of the damage may have already been done; it's like locking your barn door after the horse has been stolen.

There are, however, other symptoms that might alert you before the red light comes on that something is wrong: (1) if your battery needs water more than once every couple of months (except in hot weather); (2) if your battery needs recharging often; (3) if your bulbs seem to be burning out a lot. These can all happen before the warning light signals.

In the event your generator or alternator goes bad, it can be replaced with either a new or a rebuilt unit. If you get a rebuilt unit, make sure you get some sort of guarantee along with it.

The other unit required in the generating system is a control called a *voltage regulator*. This is needed to make sure the alternator doesn't send more juice than the battery or other electrical units can use at one time. In other words, it regulates the voltage output of the alternator. The voltage regulator is usually located on the fire wall or the fender wall.

Occasionally voltage regulators go bad and must be replaced. They should not be repaired. If either the voltage regulator or the alternator goes bad, the other should be checked as well, because trouble in one causes trouble in the other. (See Troubleshooting, page 169.)

THE INSTRUMENT PANEL

Most of the gauge lights in your auto will be found on the dashboard, or instrument panel. Many of them are there to warn you of impending doom while some others are there to remind you of certain things you might forget to do, such as to release your emergency brake before driving off.

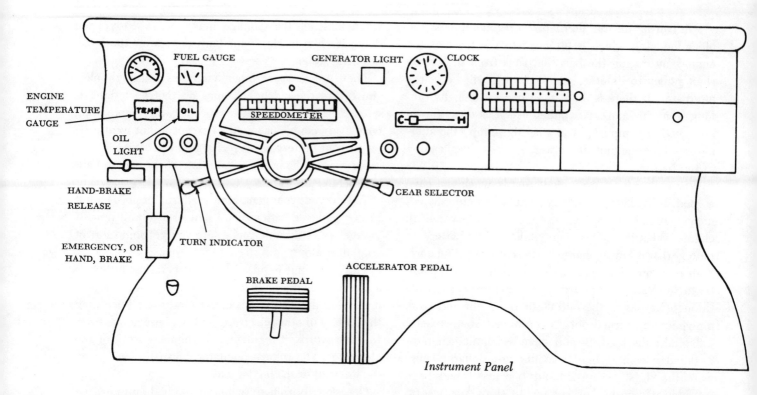

Instrument Panel

On a typical instrument panel there are gauge lights that light up if:

> your oil pressure is low
> your engine is running too hot
> your battery is discharging
> you are low on gas
> your transmission needs fluid
> one or more of your doors isn't closed securely
> your seat belts aren't fastened
> your bright lights are on
> your brake-fluid pressure is low

If some of these gauge bulbs burn out it is very important to replace them. If your brake fluid is low, you could be in grave danger. If your transmission fluid is low or your oil pressure is low, your engine could be in grave danger.

I once had my dream car, a 1959 220 SE yellow convertible Mercedes-Benz that I picked up at the factory in Stuttgart and drove all over Europe before bringing it back home with me by ship. I was driving along one late summer afternoon in a hurry to get to a friend's house when a red light flashed on my dash. All it said was "oil." I was only a few miles from her house so I continued until I was almost there and smelled an odor from the engine that told me I had better stop. I walked the rest of the way and called my mechanic.

After I told him what happened he said, "How far did you drive after the light went on?" I replied, "Oh, only a couple of miles." He groaned and said, "I'll be right over to tow it in. Don't drive it another inch."

It seemed that the night before I had hit a rock that had punctured a small hole in my oil pan and all the oil had drained out. It cost me nine hundred dollars to have it fixed and would have cost a lot more had I driven another mile . . . I would have had to replace the entire engine. I swore then, in more ways than one, that I would never disregard those little dashboard lights again. I didn't until one Saturday afternoon last summer when I was driving a friend's little VW bug on Nantucket and a red light that said "gen" flashed on. I mentioned it to my friend who owned the car. She said, "Well, the garage is closed until Monday."

We drove all weekend with the red "gen" light still burning. Monday morning the little car just up and died on us. We had burned out the alternator system and it cost almost two hundred dollars to repair. Had we taken care of it when the light first appeared it would have cost about five bucks!

Those lights are signals that something important is happening. Ignoring them can be as fatal as ignoring your first heart attack. However, I don't recommend opening up the dashboard unless you are a competent mechanic. Talk about Pandora's box — there is a maze of wiring and connections under there. The slightest wrong move or catching something on a button or cuff link could upset the entire apple cart. Best take the car to a certified dealer who is familiar with that particular model.

In the midst of writing this chapter I was experiencing a clicking noise in my radio/tape deck — as though the current were intermittently cutting out. My radio/tape deck was installed by a van customizing establishment in Florida. They removed the original AM radio and replaced it with a fancy quadraphonic sound system. My first clue that it hadn't been properly installed should have been when I saw a Rube Goldberg bunch of wires wrapped around my steering column and halfheartedly taped against the fire wall. I inquired of my Know-How Course instructor, Guy Alland, what the trouble could be. He said, "It's probably a speaker wire shorting out somewhere. Check them out."

I did, over the weekend. Sunday morning I traced the speaker wires from the speakers back to the radio. They all seemed fine. Then I saw another wire and began to follow it, when all of a sudden smoke started to pour out from under the dash. I had visions of the whole van and all my personal belongings, including my Honda trail bike that was strapped on the back, going up in one big blaze. I ran around the side of the car and whipped out a spray can of fire extinguisher that is supposed to have a wide, all-encompassing spray, like a bug bomb. A sad little squirt came out. I shook it vigorously. Another sad little squirt! I started to yank all the wires I could see out of the radio. It worked. The hissing smoke stopped instantly. My heart started to beat again and my legs began the nine-day tremble. I had spoken to Guy earlier in the week about removing the dashboard panel to replace a gauge light. He said, "Never do that. There is such a maze of wires and connections under there you'll regret it for the rest of your life!" So I resisted the temptation to take off the panel and examine the damage myself. Naturally, since it was Labor Day weekend, the garage was closed until Tuesday. Tuesday I called the Dodge garage and told them what had happened. The service manager groaned. "Oh God! Can you start the car?"

After the fire I had very tentatively tried the starter, thinking it might set off another fire or not start at all. But all was well. "Yes, I can start it."

"Well, bring it right down, we'll take a look," he said, not sounding too hopeful.

Discretion being the better part of valor, I borrowed a proper fire extinguisher from my hostess and tucked it under the driver's seat, just in case. I felt as if I was riding on a crate of eggs all the way to the garage but I arrived without any problem.

The mechanic assigned to my case attacked the dashboard panel with no trepidation whatsoever. He had some difficulty with the speedometer cable but finally wrenched the panel free from its housing, disclosing the huge gaggle of wires that connect all the various gauges on the panel. Sure enough, the wires to the oil gauge, the ammeter, and the gas gauge had burned through. But the culprit was the wire that had connected the original AM radio in the van. When the customizing place replaced it with their fancy system they cut the old radio wire (a live wire) and just left it dangling in the breeze without taping it up. Eventually it worked its way against the body of the car and caused the short circuit and damn near burned up my whole life.

MORAL OF THE STORY: Be sure to tape up all leftover ends of wires. BE SURE TO CARRY A PROPER FIRE EXTINGUISHER. And if you live in country where the weather goes below freezing, make sure your fire extinguisher is *that* kind. Some of them only work if the temperature is above 32 degrees Fahrenheit.

ACCESSORIES

LIGHT BULBS Light bulbs in your car are no different from light bulbs in your house, in that some are easier to get to than others. At least you don't need a stepladder to replace the bulbs in your car. Usually a few screwdrivers will be all that you need — and the new light bulb, of course. (In an expensive car there can be as many as fifty different light bulbs.)

Before you start unscrewing your dashboard or taillight or sidelight or dome-light assembly, check the fuse box to make sure that the fuses are not burned out. If they are okay then it is most probably the bulb that has burned out, or vibrated loose, or accumulated some residue on the metal tip or in the light socket.

If it is a light in your taillight assembly (turn signal, stoplight, or emergency flasher) that is not working, you should get your Phillips screwdriver and head for the rear end. You will find a couple of screws in the lens cover. Failing that, open the trunk, for the lens cover or unit is probably secured with screws from the inside out.

Many taillights have to be replaced from the inside, that is, through the trunk compartment. Sometimes the entire light unit lifts out from its friction-held retainer or mooring. If the light socket is corroded or rusted it can sometimes be cleaned off by scraping it with a penknife, sandpaper, or wire brush. If the wires are corroded or rusted out and have to be replaced, cut the wire back as far as necessary until you reach good wire and then add your new wire with your crimper set. Then wrap securely with electrical tape at least one inch on each side farther than the splice itself.

NOTE: Keep in mind that only about 20 percent of the electrical trouble encountered is due to wiring.

The bulbs have two little metal prongs, one on each side. Most tail- and sidelights have these fittings as do interior dash and dome lights. *Push* the bulb in and *twist* counterclockwise, which will release it from the socket. Examine it. If the little filament is burned out, replace the bulb. If it isn't, then either the bulb had vibrated loose and merely needs to be firmly screwed back into the socket, or it may have accumulated some corrosion or rust on the metal tip that connects in the socket and needs cleaning or scraping off. If such is the case, there is probably residue in the socket also that needs cleaning. If there is, *don't* stick your knife or screwdriver into the socket without disconnecting the negative terminal cable from the battery because that is a live connection in there and you may get a shock or blow your fuses. After you have cleaned the bulb and the socket and replaced the battery terminal, check your fuse, and if it still doesn't work, then you have either a loose connection or a broken wire.

To use the test light: Make sure your light switch is "on" — then ground your test light by attaching the alligator clip to a clean piece of metal — the rim of the socket will do nicely — and stick the probe into the brass buttons in the socket. If it lights up, your bulb is bad. If it doesn't light up, there is a broken wire somewhere in the circuit or a bum connection in the lamp unit itself. Depending upon which section of the car you are dealing with, you can get to all these units through the trunk, or under the hood or in the tire wells, to remove them and check them out. Be sure all the screws are tight and that there are no broken or frayed wires. Tape all suspect wiring with electrical tape. If you find a broken wire, you can either solder it or twist it together, making sure that all exposed wire has been thoroughly wrapped with electrical tape.

TIP: Unless you are experienced with the use of solder and soldering iron, have a professional do it.

Along with extra fuses in the glove compartment, it pays to carry a few extra bulbs; altogether they take up less room than a pack of cigarettes.

HEADLIGHTS Next to your brakes, your headlights are probably the most important part of your car if you do any night driving. They should be properly adjusted for high and low beam and for correct distance and candlepower. They are really life-and-death items.

If oncoming cars blink their lights at you at night for no apparent reason, you undoubtedly have something wrong with your headlights (unless you are driving in the wrong lane). Either your high beam is blinding them (set too high or crooked) or perhaps one of your lights has blown out (a dead eye). In any event, your headlights should be checked once a year according to most state laws.

Headlights are "sealed beam," which means that the entire light is the bulb and lens and reflectors — all sealed into one airtight unit. You cannot break it down. The entire unit, however, is very easy to replace. The normal headlight life is about 460 hours, if they are wired properly. Improper wiring — if too heavy a wire is used — increases the brilliance but burns out the bulb faster.

Sealed-beam headlights have two beams, a high beam (usually 60 watt) that throws the light farther ahead of you, and a low beam (usually 40 watt) that drops the light beam closer to the ground. These lights can be dimmed, or dropped closer to the ground, by means of a *dimmer switch*, which is usually located somewhere on the floorboards on the driver's side, usually on his left. However, many foreign and some American autos have the dimmer switch located on the steering column. When you "dim" the lights it switches off one filament and switches on the other.

Most master light switches are located on the dashboard to the driver's left. They usually have three positions, which affect three different sets of lights: (1)

the parking lights, taillights, and license-plate light; (2) instrument dashlights; (3) headlights (usually the all-the-way-out position).

BEAR IN MIND THAT NOT ALL HEADLIGHTS ARE THE SAME STRENGTH. BE SURE THE REPLACEMENT IS IDENTICAL TO THE ONE YOU REMOVE. The number is stamped somewhere on the old headlight.

NOTE: Some cars have two headlamps (stacked headlamps) on each side of the car. Type I are single beam (one filament) or high beam. Type II are high/low beam (dual filaments). Replacing a headlight takes only a few minutes and requires a Phillips screwdriver (medium) and a regular screwdriver (medium).

PROCEDURE:

Unscrew and remove *trim-ring* (2 Phillips screws).

Unscrew *retaining ring* (3 regular screws).

Pull the bulb slightly forward until you see the electrical connection to which it is attached. Detach it and remove from the socket.

DO NOT FOOL with the screws in the socket at the top and 90 degrees down on the right — they are vertical- and horizontal-adjustment screws for the lights. Touch these only if the lights need adjusting. Plug in the replacement bulb properly and replace all the screws. *Properly* means top to top — some are marked "top." If not, make sure the printing is readable — *not upside down.*

More than once in my life have I been stopped by state police who were spot-checking headlight alignment, even in Spain. Why do they bother? Because headlights that are out of alignment or too bright are one of the major causes of accidents in night driving (after drunken driving and falling asleep at the wheel). Although really bright headlights are all the better to see with on a dark night, they are also all

the better to blind the drivers of oncoming cars, which then plow head-on into you. A headlight alignment takes a few minutes at a properly equipped garage.

Your low-beam lights should point down lower to the ground and a bit off to the right; your high beams should shoot out straight much farther and cover a wider area. *Low beams are recommended for heavy fog.* If you drive on rough roads or have been involved in a collision, chances are your headlights may have been knocked out of adjustment. Sometimes just normal vibrations can cause the screws to loosen and the retaining ring to shift.

In your house, when all the lights go out at the same time you don't run around replacing all the bulbs, since it is highly unlikely that all the bulbs would burn out at the same time. It is much more likely to be a fuse or a main-switch problem. Same with your car. If *both* your headlights are out, the cause is probably *not* the sealed-beam lamps themselves but a loose connection, frayed wire, or master-switch or circuit-breaker problem. Prepare for a long search, starting at the wires leading from the headlights and tracing them back through the engine compartment. The lighting system is connected to the alternator, the charge indicator, the battery, and the ground connection. Each lighting circuit shares a part of its circuit with the other lighting circuits, usually branching off the main circuit at the most reasonable junction. In other words, it is a veritable maze of wires and can confuse even a professional.

If faulty wiring is the trouble, you can begin the search by getting a schematic of your car's wiring — which is in the repair manual — or, more likely, take it to a mechanic who is good with electrical systems.

NOTE: A headlight lens is a prism especially designed to yield the optimum amount of light and to direct it

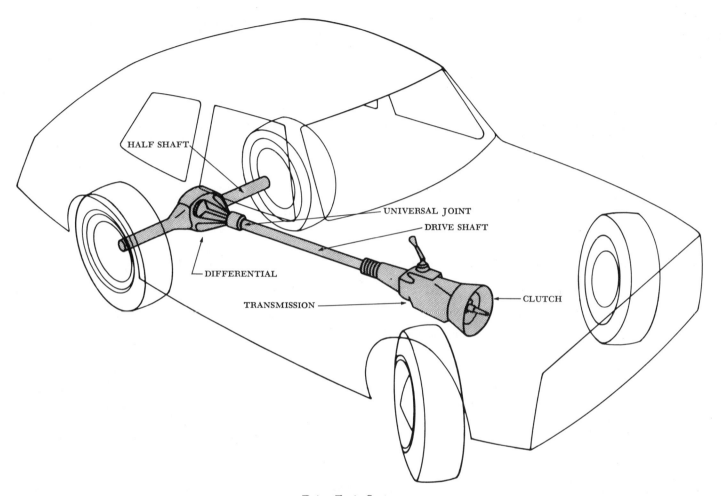

HALF SHAFT

UNIVERSAL JOINT

DRIVE SHAFT

DIFFERENTIAL

CLUTCH

TRANSMISSION

Drive-Train System

gears. All you had to do was step on the gas. This fantastic innovation made it possible for thousands of inept people to get their driver's licenses and make the highways even more treacherous than they had previously been, as is the case today.

That "point of departure" I mentioned is also the very tricky place at which to linger is to "ride the clutch." This is to be avoided at all costs since it wears your clutch down to a nubbin in no time flat. Like your brake pedal, your clutch should not be used to rest your weary legs. The average clutch on the average car with the average driver should last about 40,000 to 60,000 miles.

Clutches can be adjusted sometimes if they are slipping or dragging. A slipping clutch means that the friction material that is bonded or riveted to the *clutch plate* becomes glazed or smooth, unable to perform its function of applying friction properly; it slips against the clutch plate, usually as a result of being contaminated by oil or wear and tear. A dragging clutch means the opposite, that it is sticking or holding on to the clutch plate after you have released the pedal. This may also be caused by wear and weak clutch springs, which are replaceable and sometimes adjustable.

The gears are:

Low, or *first,* gear — used when you want to start from a dead stop.

Second gear — used to gain speed after you have the car moving; used as a braking gear going downhill; used as a power gear to ascend a steep incline.

Third, or *high,* gear — your normal driving gear at highway speeds.

Reverse — used when you want to go backwards.

Overdrive — merely another gear that is a higher gear than your top-speed gear and that enables you to move along at a reduced engine speed without sacri-

ficing road speed. It uses less gas because it employs a higher gear ratio.

Some cars are equipped with four or even five forward gears. Some trucks are equipped with more than thirty forward gears.

If you are interested in saving gas — buy a manual transmission. You save about 3 miles per gallon.

Universal joint. I was thirty-five years old before I found out that it didn't mean an international bar. I found out because the one in my almost new (12,000 miles) Mercedes was causing a terrible grinding sound almost under my seat. It happens to be a part of the drive-shaft assembly that is there to absorb stress. The drive shaft is made of steel and is long and thin. As the car goes over bumps and uneven places it would break in two if there wasn't a universal joint to allow it to "bend." The universal joint allows the drive shaft greater flexibility, both sideways and back and forth.

Differential. A good name for this part of the system. It is merely a set of compensating gears. Its function is to compensate for the difference that your wheels have to travel around a corner; for instance, if you are making a sharp right turn, your right wheel travels almost nowhere while your left wheel has some distance to go to catch up. Just as when *you* are running around a sharp corner on foot. Differential gears send the power to the wheel that has the farthest to travel. For the most part, you should not anticipate trouble with the differential.

AUTOMATIC TRANSMISSIONS

As the nomenclature implies, the automatic transmission does your work for you; it selects and changes the gears as the speed and conditions require.

This is a very complicated system, similar to our

nervous system. When you want to move a part of your body, the brain sends messages through the nerve system to the muscle system, until finally the message gets through and your arm flies up. In your car, when you take your foot off the brake and step on the gas, it sets up a chain reaction that eventually, through a maze of epicyclic gears of varying sizes and ratios, and fluids and valves and brake bands, planet carriers and clutches, input and output shafts and sprag wheels, transmits the power to the wheels, setting them in either a forward or reverse motion, propelling you and your's down the road to Morocco.

I do not, repeat, do not advise anyone but a professional to try to do anything with the automatic transmission system beyond checking the fluid periodically to see if there is enough. It takes expert mechanics and expert's tools and testing devices to work on the automatic transmission of your car.

TIRES

When automobiles were first made, they had solid rubber tires mounted on the wheels. Granted, they weren't troubled with flats, but it was a bumpy ride.

Then came inflatable (pneumatic) tires. When they first came out you had to carry several spares for a short trip and could count on at least one or two flats every hundred miles. Today we are more sophisticated and can, many times, drive thousands and thousands of miles without having one flat tire (with luck and some good management). For instance, statistics tell us that between 85 percent and 90 percent of blowouts occur when your tire's tread is 90 percent used up.* Therefore, don't jeopardize your life and the lives of others by waiting too long to replace your

* And it's 44 times as liable to go flat.

tires. One-sixteenth inch of tread left is the general guideline to tell you you need new tires. Some tires have built-in tread-wear indicators, that is, they have "bars" that surface around the tire when the tread is down to 1/16″. Another good way to tell is to insert a penny in the grooves of the tread in several places. Push Lincoln's head into the tread groove; if there is any space showing between the top of his head and the tip of the coin — in fact if you can see *all* of his head — you are pushing your luck. You need new tires, pronto.

There are many different types of tires to choose from and a multitude of factors enter into the choice. Let us start with the anatomy of a tire:

The *casing,* or *carcass* — its components and the way they are constructed determine the characteristics of the tire: the type of ride — soft or hard, smooth or bumpy, quiet or noisy; whether the tire will stand up in the cold, in the wet, and under varying speeds; whether it will corner well; and so on. The components may be layers of corded fabric of cotton, nylon, rayon, glass, fiberglass, polyester, and even steel, which are bonded into a rubber or synthetic rubber base.

These layers, or *plies,* are always applied at bias angles to each other and come in pairs, that is, most passenger-car tires are either two-ply, four-ply, or six-ply. Because the layers are alternately applied on the bias, these tires are called *bias-ply.*

A ply-rating can be misleading, however, since a tire that is "four-ply rated" may only have two plies. This is because the old ply rating indicated a strength and load-carrying ability, but with the advent of stronger synthetic materials than the original cotton the same or an even greater load-carrying ability and strength has been achieved with fewer plies. Of the three types of tires, bias-ply are the least expensive,

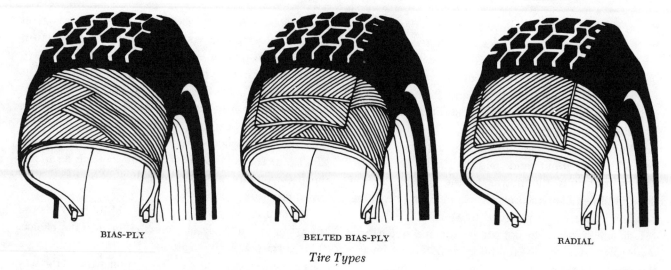

BIAS-PLY   BELTED BIAS-PLY   RADIAL

Tire Types

and they give a good soft ride. At high speeds they tend to heat up and consequently wear badly.

To improve upon the bias-plies, *belts,* or *breakers,* have been added, which are usually fiberglass or polyester and glass (polyglass). These tires are called *bias-belted.* They are more expensive than bias-ply tires. They are also stronger and tend to "squirm" less, which reduces the heat factor.

The best, the most expensive are *radial-ply.* These tires come belted with either nylon, glass, or steel. They should last the average driver for 40,000 to 50,000 miles, and in addition they get much better gas mileage. These are the preferred tire if you can afford them. They are excellent for high-speed driving but can be noisy and unsmooth at low speeds.

The *beads* — the steel wires encased in rubber that hold the two rims (inside and outside) of the tire together and keep it encircling the wheel.

The *sidewall* — the side of the tire, as the name implies. If you have white sidewalls they are more expensive and naturally, like white shoes, harder to keep clean. On the sidewalls of some tires is an extra strip of rubber called a *rubbing (curb) strip.* In defective tires sidewalls can break and you should get a refund or at least an adjustment from the dealer.

The *tread* — might be considered the shoe of the automobile. As do footprints, treads come in varying sizes, designs, and surfaces. They are also of rubber or synthetically blended rubbers, and are bonded to the casing of the tire.

Treads are patterned differently for different uses. Snow treads and mud treads have deep grooves to grip down into the snow or mud. Another addition to this type is the *steel-studded* tire for use in places that have extreme icy road conditions. (Some states do not allow these steel studs due to the excessive wear and tear on the surface of the roads.) Snow and mud tires are not recommended for long trips or high speeds as they tend to heat up. Heat destroys tires quicker than anything except maybe a hatchet.

Some treads are specially designed for high speeds; some for normal speeds; some for cornering at high speeds; some for wet driving at high speeds; and so forth.

CAUTION: When you change the tires on your car make sure you don't mix the treads. It is not only dangerous but in some cases illegal.

Tires are coded for recommended maximum speeds. Be certain you get the right tire for your car's suspension system and the speed at which the car will be driven. DO NOT buy retreaded tires for open road or turnpike use. They will be not only a waste of your money but a safety hazard as well. Retreaded tires do not hold the retreading at high speeds and you will soon find yourself sitting on the roadside with a flat tire on the car and a useless piece of rubber a few feet away.

Good tread also keeps your car from *hydroplaning* on wet roads, which is a term for literally riding on top of the water, thereby losing traction and control of your car.

Tire profiles are like people profiles in that you can see how the tire looks from a different angle. Its "profile" size and series number is determined by the width (sidewall to sidewall) in relation to its tread-to-wheel rim height (see illustration below). The series numbers start at 83 (for narrow width) and descend to 78, 70, 60, 50. The lower the series number, the wider the tread, the better the traction.

The *valve* — the place where you put air in your tire. In a tubeless tire it is sealed into the rim of the tire. In a tire with a tube it is in the tube. It has a one-way valve core that allows air in but not out (when it is functioning properly). This core has a tiny spring that sometimes wears out, and then you need a new valve. There is also a center pin and a cap on the valve that keeps the dirt out.

Air — the last but not least part of your tire, whether it be tubeless or tube-type.

It is of the *utmost importance* to keep your tires inflated to the manufacturer's specifications, which are usually written on the sides of the tires as well as in your owner's manual and sometimes other places such as the inside of the glove box or even on the gas-tank cover. A tire gauge is called for, your very own, because the majority of gas-station air pumps are notoriously inaccurate. Where I live I have yet to find one accurate within two pounds.* Some are off as much as seven and eight pounds. Most vary from three to five pounds off.

When you hear the expression "first line" tires, don't be misled. It does not mean the finest tires money can buy, it merely means the tires the manufacturer of your

* A study done by the National Bureau of Standards discovered that 45 percent of gas-station air gauges are off by at *least* 3 psi (pounds per square inch).

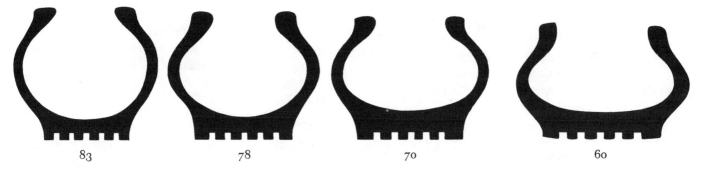

| 83 | 78 | 70 | 60 |

Tire Widths

CONDITION	RAPID WEAR AT SHOULDERS	RAPID WEAR AT CENTER	CRACKED TREADS	WEAR ON ONE SIDE	FEATHERED EDGE	BALD SPOTS	SCALLOPED WEAR
EFFECT	1. / 2. (illustrations)	(illustration)	(illustration)	(illustration)	(illustration)	(illustration)	(illustration)
CAUSE	UNDER-INFLATION OR LACK OF ROTATION	OVER-INFLATION OR LACK OF ROTATION	UNDER-INFLATION OR EXCESSIVE SPEED*	EXCESSIVE CAMBER	INCORRECT TOE	UNBALANCED WHEEL OR TIRE DEFECT *	LACK OF ROTATION OF TIRES OR WORN OR OUT-OF-ALIGNMENT SUSPENSION.
CORRECTION	ADJUST PRESSURE TO SPECIFICATIONS WHEN TIRES ARE COOL ROTATE TIRES			ADJUST CAMBER TO SPECIFICATIONS	ADJUST TOE-IN TO SPECIFICATIONS	DYNAMIC OR STATIC BALANCE WHEELS	ROTATE TIRES AND INSPECT SUSPENSION SEE GROUP 2

*HAVE TIRE INSPECTED FOR FURTHER USE.

Tire Wear Chart. Courtesy of the Chrysler Corporation

auto equips it with when it leaves the factory, that is, original equipment. Original equipment tires are usually of the "78 series" profile and are adequate for normal driving conditions.

TIPS FOR GETTING THE BEST MILEAGE FROM YOUR TIRES Keep your wheels in alignment (align them once a year or 10,000 to 15,000 miles).

Keep your tires inflated at recommended pressure (check weekly). Tires should be cold when checking pressure. (Allow for two or three pounds extra if they heated up on the drive to the gas station.) Bear in mind that temperature affects your tire pressure. Every ten degrees the temperature drops, your tire pressure drops one pound. So, in cold weather you will need to add more air than normally. Tires heat up and pressure builds up after fast driving. DO NOT bleed air from hot tires. Check pressure after they cool. This can save you up to one mile per gallon.

Keep your wheels balanced (balance them once a year or every 10,000 to 15,000 miles).

Avoid:

hard cornering except in emergencies
excessive speed (tires wear five times faster at 80 mph than at 50 mph)
fast starts (spinning your wheels)
unnecessary braking or panic braking (leaving your rubber on the road instead of the tire)
dirt roads, gravelly roads, rough shoulders
curb crashing or scraping

Don't overload your tire's rated weight capacity.

Check tires regularly (particularly before starting out on long trips) for cuts, bruises, bulges, knots, and so on. Keep tires free from stones, nails, glass, pebbles, and other foreign objects embedded in the grooves of the tread.

Store extra tires away from heat and petrochemicals, which destroy rubber.

Keep shock absorbers, brakes, and springs in good repair.

If, for some reason, your tires have worn unevenly, have the cause corrected and then rotate tires to even out the wear.

Buy guaranteed tires from a reputable dealer.

If you travel a lot, buy a brand that has national distribution centers, like Sears or Goodyear, so you can get replacements on the road.

ROTATING YOUR TIRES This is a controversial subject. Some manufacturers recommend it and others don't. Naturally it costs money, or time and effort if you do it yourself. Some contend it isn't worth it, others disagree. The consensus is not to rotate *unless* you have already had uneven wear, then rotate to even out the wear. Rotating radials, belted bias-plies, or studded winter tires is *not recommended* because it may have an adverse effect and break the belts of the tires.

STORING YOUR TIRES Store them flat, away from heat and sun, damp and oil.

FLAT TIRES AND BLOWOUTS See Maintenance, pages 161–162, for changing a flat tire.

TIP: Ask the mechanic who changes your tires to either use a torque wrench to tighten your tire lugs or tighten them by hand instead of with his pneumatic drill. I can never get my tire lugs loose when they have been applied with a pneumatic drill no matter how much I caution the mechanic to take it easy.

If your car suddenly pulls to one side or swerves in the tail, you probably have a flat. Pull off the road as quickly and safely as possible and have a look.

If you have a blowout you'll know it because you'll hear it and your car will violently swerve or pull to one side. AVOID BRAKING, *even though your instinct tells you to brake.* Hang on to the wheel with all your strength until the car slows and lets you steer it off the highway. Don't worry about anything else at that moment but your safe retreat to the side of the road out of harm's way. Don't worry about ruining the tire. It's shot anyway. And even if you have to drive a little way on the rim, better to buy a new rim than get yourself hit by staying in the middle of the road. Secondhand rims are cheap; secondhand limbs aren't!

WHEELS

Unless you are prone to running over curbstones at high speeds or you get into a bad accident, not much has to be said here about wheels except that they should be round, they should be in balance, they should be in line, and they have to be securely fastened to the axle of your car. (And the wheel bearings must be greased periodically.)

If your wheels are out of *balance* you will undoubtedly notice it in one of two ways: (1) the car will start to shake, shimmy, or vibrate at moderate to high speeds, sometimes until your teeth rattle; (2) the tires will have bald spots on them.

Whenever you change a tire or put on a new tire, you should have that tire balanced when it is put on and then checked at about five hundred miles to see if it needs balancing again.

There are two ways to balance a wheel: *statically,*

when the wheel is *not in motion,* and *dynamically,* when the wheel is *moving.*

When a wheel is said to be "out of static balance," that means that for some reason the wheel or tire is heavier in one part than the rest, whether due to excess rubber in one spot or whatever. As a result, the tire or wheel, when allowed to spin freely and seek its own stopping place, will, due to the law of gravity, rest with the heavy part down. This condition is corrected by applying small lead weights to the opposite side of the tire to compensate or to "balance" it so that each part of the tire weighs the same as the rest of the tire.

When the tire or wheel is "dynamically" out of balance, it tends to wobble from side to side when it is moving. To correct this is easy . . . if you have the fancy equipment that it takes to determine where and how many weights of what size should be applied. Most good service stations and garages now have this equipment. The balancing cost varies from two to five dollars a tire. Let your fingers do the walking. Make a few phone calls to service stations and tire dealers in your neighborhood to find where you can get the best deal. Also have them check your front wheel alignment if those tires are showing spotty wear. If they have worn badly in spots you might benefit by rotating those tires to the rear so the wear will even out.

To obtain the best steering quality and longest tire life it is imperative that your wheels be properly *aligned;* the *kingpin angle, caster angle, camber angle,* and *toe-in angle* (see pages 95 and 97) are related not only to each other but to the chassis as well, and therefore must be adjusted from time to time by experts with the proper sophisticated equipment.

A front-end alignment can cost anywhere from twelve dollars up depending on where you take your car and what part of the country you live in. To align the front end, balance your tires, and rotate them is about an hour-and-a-half job if the servicemen know what they are doing and have the right equipment. As always, take the car to a reliable place that guarantees its work so that if after you drive away the shimmies and wobbles and bad wear persist, you can get satisfaction.

5. The Steering System

Steering is probably the one thing that we all knew how to do before we ever learned to drive an automobile — we had all been practicing for years on our kiddy cars and tricycles from the time we were tots. All we had to keep in mind when we took our first driving lessons was to keep our eye on the road and not on the foot pedals or the scenery behind us. The most important part of the steering system is *you,* the driver.

We steer only with the front wheels; the rear wheels simply follow.

There are two types of steering mechanisms in use today: the *rack-and-pinion system* — which is primarily used on small sports cars — and the *recirculating-ball system.* The rack-and-pinion system uses a direct linkage to the wheels and gives extraordinary road feel; the slightest movement the driver makes is transferred directly to the wheels and vice versa. There is very little "play" in the steering wheel. (*Play* refers to the degree you can turn the steering wheel without moving the wheels.) The recirculating-ball (standard) system is the system found on most automobiles, par-

ticularly in America, where cars tend to be much heavier than the average European car.

Because of their weight, cars in this country are manufactured with power steering or power-assisted steering. They utilize power from the motor to help you turn the wheels, again using the principle of hydraulics. The main components are: the pump that pumps the fluid (oil) that gives the power; a valve that limits the amount of fluid; a cylinder/piston arrangement that pushes the fluid. Unfortunately, since power steering is powered by the engine, when the motor stalls, the power goes out of the steering. This can be not only inconvenient but dangerous. When all these newfangled things work, they are fabulous; when they don't, one often wishes they had never been invented in the first place.

Some terms having to do with the steering system:

Toe-in — this concerns the angle at which the front wheels are set; instead of being absolutely parallel, they are made to "pigeon toe" at approximately 3/16" off dead parallel. This tends to compensate for the wheels' natural tendency to head outward.

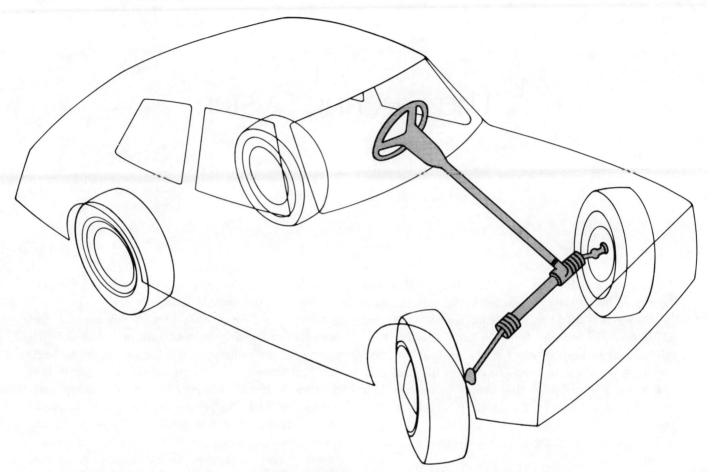

Steering System (Rack-and-Pinion)

Toe-out — the opposite of toe-in. This is sometimes used in front-wheel-drive cars. When they toe-out they look "slew-footed," like my Uncle Walter.

Camber — a term used for the degree of tilt in the wheels. Most cars' front wheels are tilted slightly on their axes; when they are closer together at the top than at the bottom, this is called "negative camber"; when closer at the bottom than at the top, a "positive camber." This makes steering easier. Each front wheel should have the same degree of camber. If camber is out of whack, the tire will wear badly, usually on the outside.

Caster — this is what makes the steering wheel right itself after you have turned a corner. You know what a caster is if you have ever pushed a supermarket cart that had a bad caster; you quickly exchanged it for a good one. If you ever had a tea caddy, you know what a caster is — that funny wheel that is off-center and does things an on-center wheel won't do. An auto has a less accentuated caster to its wheels. If you find your front wheels wobbling like mad they may well be "out of caster."

The steering system is a very precise system. Any problems should be taken care of by experts with the proper equipment for aligning and testing.

6. The Suspension System

Suspension — "something on or by which something else is suspended or hung." Thus, your car is held off, or suspended from, the ground by the suspension system. This system ensures passenger and driver comfort and safety.

The suspension system is essentially comprised of *shock absorbers* and *springs*. Automobiles use two different types of springs, *leaf* springs and *coil* springs.

Leaf springs are the same things that were used on the old buggies of yesteryear, the kind that had a horse in front of them. Most cars have leaf springs in the rear. The more leaves in the springs, the heavier the load capacity.

For the front suspension we have coil springs. Essentially they function the same, to cushion the effects of a bumpy road from the occupants and the car itself so it doesn't bounce apart. They actually act as energy absorbers.

In addition to springs, which are not enough for our not-so-rugged constitutions, we have shock absorbers. Their function is to stop the springs from continuing to bounce up and down. They look and work differently from springs. They are cylindrical and contain fluid (oil) and work on a hydraulic principle incorporating a valve and piston.

As life has gone on, and our own frames become softer and softer, everything in our autos has become more sophisticated. *Torsion bar suspension* was invented, the principle being "opposing stress." If you can picture twisting a pencil around and around in a rubber band and then letting go, you'll see the principle of torsion. Torsion bars can be either round or flat or square, held fast at one end and twisted against the direction of the bounce at the other, thus equalizing the motion.

One more thing has been added on some cars, a *stabilizer bar,* or *antiroll bar,* or *sway bar,* which helps to equalize the car in a turn as it goes over the bumps, lessening the tendency of the car body to roll.

Springs break if you hit a hard bump too fast with a heavy load, as when driving along back roads with an overloaded van. Even without being overloaded, on

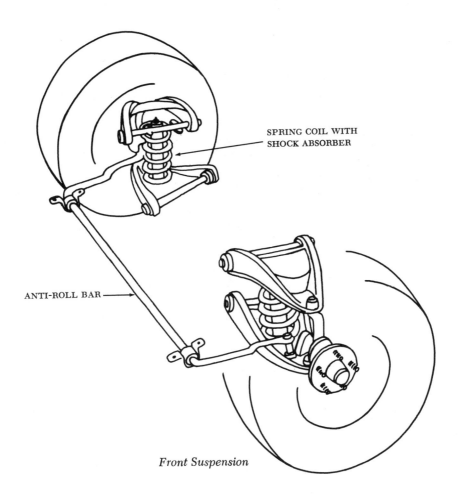

SPRING COIL WITH
SHOCK ABSORBER

ANTI-ROLL BAR

Front Suspension

bad roads you can almost count on breaking a spring. At least springs *can* last the life of your car; shocks are good for between 20,000 and 50,000 miles. Shock absorbers wear out or can jiggle loose.

Suffice it to say that most of the suspension work that must be done on your car is not for beginners. It takes strength and special tools unless it is merely a loose shackle or bolt that needs tightening.

There are several types of shock absorbers available. Most passenger cars have *standard-duty* shocks. They give a soft ride and are not fabricated for hard, bumpy road use with a heavy load.

Heavy-duty shocks are for heavy loads and high speeds and rough roads. As might be expected, they give a harder passenger ride.

Spring-type shock stabilizers tend to self-adjust to

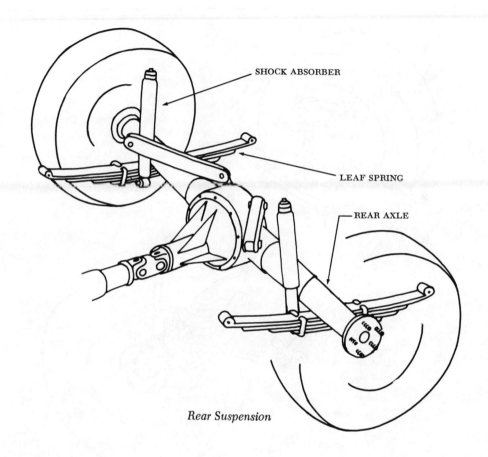

SHOCK ABSORBER

LEAF SPRING

REAR AXLE

Rear Suspension

level the load — perfect for traveling salesmen who carry heavy samples in their trunk during the week and then unload them for the weekend to take a few beach chairs to the seashore.

Special police shocks give excellent cornering stabilization for fast chases but give a harder ride.

7. The Braking System

"A brake is a mechanism to slow or stop a moving vehicle."

Once you get your car started there are four ways it can come to a stop. It can drift to a stop — which requires a considerable amount of time and distance. It can meet up with an immovable object, such as a large truck or mountainside — which can be dangerous and even fatal. More conventionally, *you* can stop it by applying your *foot service brake* or your *emergency brake.*

The foot service brake is activated by a pedal usually located on the floor to the left of the accelerator (gas) pedal on a car with an automatic transmission or between the gas and the clutch pedal on one with a manual transmission. (For the handicapped there are special steering-column "hand" brakes.)

If your conventional service brake fails to work there is an alternative — the *emergency brake,* or *parking brake.* This is either a smaller foot pedal located to the far left of the driver's cockpit or a hand lever also located to the far left on the driver's side — except on some foreign cars where it is located down on the driver's right between the seats. The emergency brake was not designed for an *easy,* smooth stop but to keep the car from moving *after* you have already stopped it with the conventional foot service brake.

PARKING TIPS: When you are parked on an incline you should always put on your emergency brake *in addition to* facing your front wheels *in* to the curb or mountainside and putting the gearshift into the *park* position. With a manual shift, the proper procedure when parked facing down a hill is to put on your emergency brake, face the front wheels toward the curb, and place the gearshift into *reverse.* If parked facing *up* the hill, put on the brake, place the gearshift in *low,* and turn your wheels the opposite direction — so that the *rear* of the front wheels are headed into the curb.

In the mountains during the Depression, when people couldn't afford to get their emergency brakes fixed, they used to carry wood blocks to place behind their wheels to make sure their car would still be there when they returned from shopping.

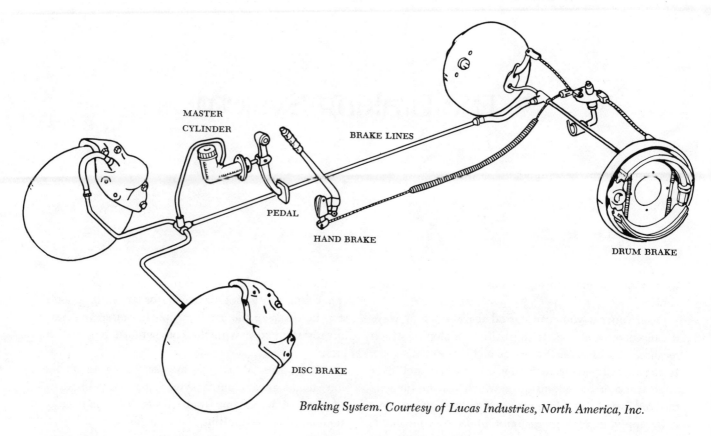

MASTER
CYLINDER

BRAKE LINES

PEDAL

HAND BRAKE

DRUM BRAKE

DISC BRAKE

Braking System. Courtesy of Lucas Industries, North America, Inc.

If you have to use your emergency brake to *come* to a stop, try to keep your head and apply it *gradually* or it will *grab* and throw you and your passengers suddenly forward, possibly through the windshield.

SUGGESTION: Practice every once in a while gradually stopping with your emergency brake so you get the hang of it. Then, when the crisis strikes you will instinctively not slam it on and slam everyone else to the dashboard.

CAUTION: *Do this on a little-traveled road.*

The parking brake is not operated by hydraulic power. The parking brake is mechanical. It is some-times referred to as the *hand brake* because in some cars (like my Dodge van) you apply it by hand. Usually the parking brake has to do with only the rear wheels and operates by pulling on a set of cables leading to each of the rear wheels.

I hadn't had my van a month when one day just before setting out on a long camping trip I girded my strength to pull on the emergency brake and went flying backwards in my seat because it went on without any effort. That's strange, I thought. I tested it by starting the car and gently setting it rolling and pulled on the hand brake. Nothing happened. The car kept on rolling. I stopped it with the foot brake, shifted the gears into park, and got out. I crept carefully under the rear of the van and, lo and behold, the parking brake cable was swinging merrily in the breeze. It had somewhere along the way lost one of the clips that hold it taut, to the side of the undercarriage. I drove to my service station. They put the van up on the hydraulic lift. My van has a large, high, fiberglass top that makes it over eight feet high. Luckily I was there to watch, because the mechanic had no sooner put it on the lift and pushed the lift button than the phone rang. He turned his back to answer it while I watched the van rise and rise and rise. I don't know how many seconds it took me to realize that the lift was going to crush the van's fiberglass top against the ceiling of the garage. I screamed. He dropped the phone and stopped it within millimeters of the ceiling.

After that crisis had passed we got down to the business at hand, fixing the loose brake cable. He looked underneath, looked at his watch, and shook his head. "You'll have to come back tomorrow when I can get a clip from the Dodge people."

I looked at the other clips and said, "Can't I get something at the hardware store that would do the trick?"

"Like what?" he asked, as though I was crazy. "Like a little turnbuckle with an open end," I replied.

He thought for a minute and said, "Yeah, I guess you could."

Ten minutes later I was on my way, for eighty-nine cents. He was so embarrassed he hadn't thought of the turnbuckle that he didn't charge me for installing it.

How the Braking System Works

Brakes work by *friction*. From our dealings with disagreeable people we have learned that friction makes heat. To give you an idea of how much heat your brakes make — to stop an average-sized American car traveling 70 mph, your brakes generate over 800 BTU of heat, equivalent to lighting over a thousand matches.

When you apply your foot to the service brake pedal you mechanically activate the *master brake cylinder,* which pushes a piston that forces fluid past a check valve through the brake lines (steel tubes) to each of the pistons in the *slave cylinders* in each wheel assembly. In your wheel assembly you will find either *disc*-type brakes or *drum*-type brakes.

NOTE: If your car was built after 1967 you will find two (*dual*) pistons in your master brake cylinder with two sets for the rear wheels. This was done as a safety measure so that if one set develops a leak or has a fault, at least you have another for a backup. Although the backup system has only half the braking power, it's a darn sight better than none.

Brakes are hydraulically (using a fluid) powered. A Frenchman named Pascal discovered that "pressure exerted on a confined liquid is transmitted undiminished." Unlike air, fluid cannot be compressed, that is, made smaller in volume. If it could, the water wouldn't rise when you sat down in a tubful of it. Instead, it would squeeze together.

CLUE: If you spring a leak in one half of your brake system it will show up in your brake pedal — which will travel farther to the floor than usual. Many cars have warning lights that are triggered by this reduction in pressure.

Your brake lines (tubes) are specially constructed. They are made of double-thickness steel tubing that is both lead-coated and copperplated to prevent corrosion and rust. The flexible hose connection at the wheels is also specially designed to withstand high pressures. Be extremely careful that your repair shop

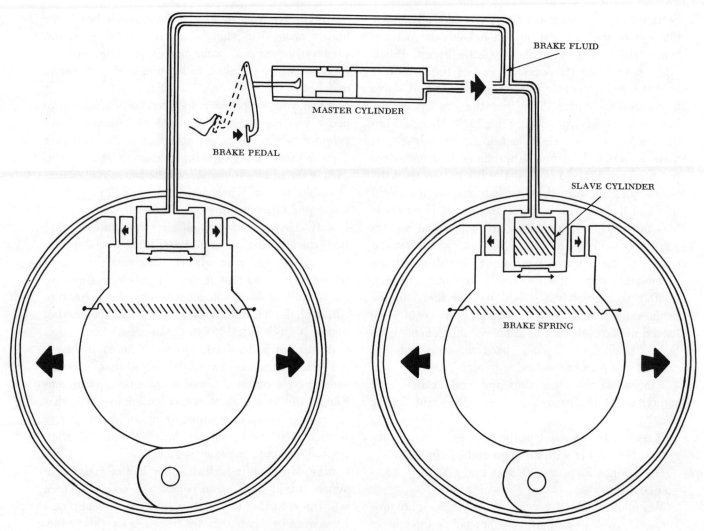

BRAKE FLUID

MASTER CYLINDER

BRAKE PEDAL

SLAVE CYLINDER

BRAKE SPRING

Hydraulic Brake System

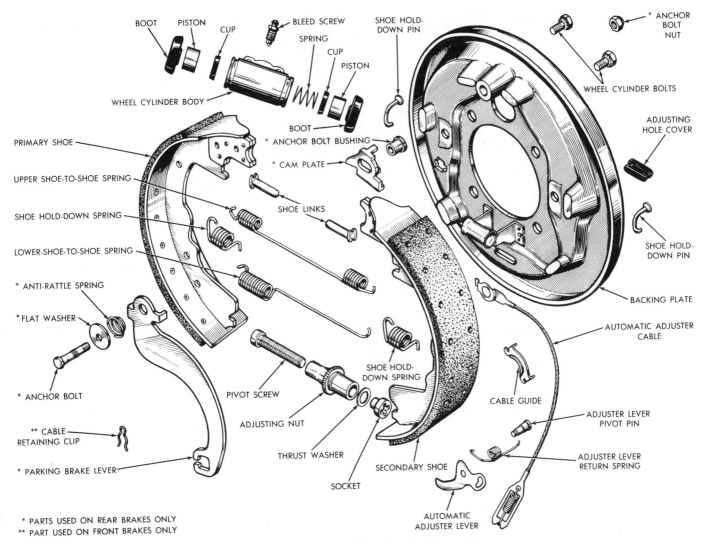

BOOT PISTON CUP BLEED SCREW SHOE HOLD-DOWN PIN * ANCHOR BOLT NUT

SPRING

CUP

PISTON

WHEEL CYLINDER BODY

WHEEL CYLINDER BOLTS

BOOT

PRIMARY SHOE

* ANCHOR BOLT BUSHING

ADJUSTING HOLE COVER

UPPER SHOE-TO-SHOE SPRING

* CAM PLATE

SHOE LINKS

SHOE HOLD-DOWN SPRING

LOWER-SHOE-TO-SHOE SPRING

SHOE HOLD-DOWN PIN

* ANTI-RATTLE SPRING

BACKING PLATE

* FLAT WASHER

AUTOMATIC ADJUSTER CABLE

* ANCHOR BOLT

SHOE HOLD-DOWN SPRING

** CABLE RETAINING CLIP

PIVOT SCREW

CABLE GUIDE

ADJUSTER LEVER PIVOT PIN

* PARKING BRAKE LEVER

ADJUSTING NUT

THRUST WASHER

SECONDARY SHOE

ADJUSTER LEVER RETURN SPRING

SOCKET

AUTOMATIC ADJUSTER LEVER

* PARTS USED ON REAR BRAKES ONLY
** PART USED ON FRONT BRAKES ONLY

Drum Brakes. Courtesy of the Chrysler Corporation

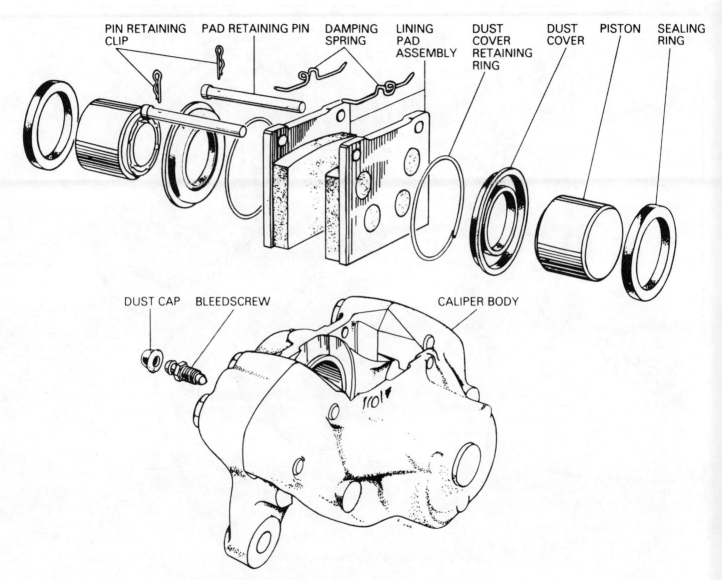

PIN RETAINING CLIP PAD RETAINING PIN DAMPING SPRING LINING PAD ASSEMBLY DUST COVER RETAINING RING DUST COVER PISTON SEALING RING

DUST CAP BLEEDSCREW CALIPER BODY

Disc Brake Unit. Courtesy of Lucas Industries, North America, Inc.

uses only high-quality material when working on your brakes. A cheap brake job makes as much sense as a cheap heart transplant.

The principle of drum brakes is this: the pistons in the slave cylinder push it outward against the brake shoe. Imagine you put your hands together and started your hat spinning around on them. If you wanted to stop it, you would spread your hands outward.

Disc brakes work on a slightly different principle. They employ a clamping or pincerlike movement that grabs the wheel disc on both sides. Most of today's bicycles use disc brakes. Imagine you are rolling a nickel or dime across the table between your fingers. When you want to stop it from rolling you merely squeeze your fingers together against the sides of the coin and it stops or slows down as you wish.

In power-assisted or power-boosted hydraulic brakes, you have at your disposal a power potential of almost a thousand pounds of pressure on each wheel to stop it, if necessary. This power comes from a vacuum created by the motor. That is some improvement over the old cars.

Unless you have a high-powered, high-performance car it is unlikely that you will find disc brakes on all four wheels. Usually you will have all drum brakes, or disc brakes in front and drum brakes in the rear, which is ideal as the front brakes do most of the work.

Although disc brakes are initially more expensive, they have several advantages over drum brakes. They tend to heat up less, be less affected by water, and are easier and less expensive to reline.

TIP: Immediately after you have plowed through a deep puddle of water, gently pump your brakes. That creates heat and "squeezes" the water out of the brake linings. Soggy brake linings work like a soggy handkerchief, not well or not at all.

ANOTHER TIP: In snowy climes, don't leave your emergency brake on in freezing temperatures unless it is absolutely necessary, because it can freeze quite solidly to the wheel drum.

When your brakes are subjected to excessive heat they are adversely affected. They tend to fade, that is, not function at full capacity. The hotter they get the worse they get. Therefore, it behooves the driver to give them time to cool off whenever possible. That is why you should downshift on a steep hill, that is, go into a lower gear that will tend to hold the car back rather than relying solely upon your brakes. Heavy trucks often go into first gear on steep grades for that reason. If you make a habit of downshifting on steep hills, you will not only be driving safely but be saving a lot of wear and tear on your brakes.

Another big factor in saving brakes is to decelerate sooner. When you see a stoplight or stop sign ahead, don't keep your foot on the gas until the last minute and then brake. Try to time it so you won't have to brake or will brake just a little. It saves gas too. Only bad drivers use their brakes a lot. The next time you're in a chauffeur-driven limousine, notice how smooth the ride is — that's because the driver isn't constantly speeding up and braking quickly to a stop. It's all nice and easy.

Brake Fluid

All brakes in today's automobiles are hydraulically powered. That means they use a fluid (liquid), a synthetic petrochemical composition that has special qualities such as an extremely high boiling point (550° F for disc brakes). You should *check in your owner's manual for the proper fluid for your particular car* and NEVER USE ANYTHING ELSE. Even in a pinch do not substitute a more available fluid like whiskey or

Clorox or gasoline. High-grade brake fluid is blue-green; cheap fluid is amber in color. Clean fluid is clear; dirty fluid looks muddy. Drum-brake fluid should say "Super Heavy Duty" on the can. It may say "Meets or Surpasses SAE Specifications J-1703 and 70R3." Take nothing less.

Another quality that your brake fluid has is that it won't hurt the rubber parts of the brake system, such as the diaphragm in the master cylinder or the hose linkages that tie in the brake-line tubes with the wheel assembly. In other words, these intricate systems were not planned willy-nilly at the factory — they took into consideration all the endurance factors and properties of each component and the stress it would be under, so don't take it upon yourself to switch-hit on this item.

Consider the brake fluid to be the blood of the system. As low blood pressure is a no-no, low brake pressure is a no-no. That is why you or someone you can trust should look into the master cylinder twice a year on general principles just to make sure the fluid level is perfect. (See Maintenance, page 158, for further information on this.)

BRAKE LININGS (DISC PADS)

Brake linings and disc pads are attached to the brake shoe. The linings get the wear, the friction; they are what rubs against the brake drum, causing it to stop or slow down. Remember the analogy of your hands stopping the spinning hat. Well, if your fingertips stopped enough hats from spinning they would wear right through to the bone. That's what happens with your brake linings, they wear right on through to the brake shoe — then you have metal rubbing on metal and that means trouble.

All brake-lining composition contains asbestos to handle the extreme heat buildup. Brake linings can be affected by many things. They get wet when you drive through water; then they don't work well. Sometimes they get grease on them and then they don't work well. They wear out at anywhere from 15,000 miles to 75,000 miles, depending on any number of factors — the size and design of the car; the quality of the lining to begin with; the care taken by the driver.

I read in a Chilton's auto manual about two guys who drove from Detroit to L.A. without ever touching their brakes! That's really planning ahead. Two thousand miles worth. Try seeing how far you can drive without touching yours! Some drivers can get double or triple the amount of mileage from a set of linings than other drivers under the same driving conditions. However, on the average, brake linings last about 20,000 to 30,000 miles. The front brakes usually wear out first because they do most of the work.

Brake linings are either riveted to the brake shoe or bonded with a superadhesive. Most heavy-duty vehicles such as trucks have riveted linings.

Excessive heat sometimes glazes the linings, rendering them too smooth to do their friction job properly. This can be found on cars that are only driven at low speeds for city driving when you normally don't have to jam your brakes on, but use them frequently and repeatedly but not hard. This can sometimes be remedied by taking the car for a spin on the highway and braking hard a few times to remove the glaze.

The *brake pedal is certainly an important part of the system,* not only because it activates the braking procedure but because it is oftentimes the indicator of impending trouble. When you put your foot on the pedal and push as far as it will go there should be *at least* two inches of *pedal reserve*. Preferably three inches. If there is less, have the system checked out. *Anytime* the brake pedal feels different than it usually does, there may be trouble somewhere in the system. Have it looked after at once. (See Troubleshooting, page 184.)

Repairing the intricate hydraulic brake system is not a job recommended for amateurs since its proper functioning is a life-and-death matter at all times. However, if you want to learn how to repair your own brakes, an excellently illustrated and reasonably simplified instruction book I recommend is *How to Service and Repair Your Own Car,* a Popular Science book by Richard Day.

CAUTION: Never "ride" your brake pedal, that is, never *rest* your foot on it unless you intend to apply your brakes. Riding the pedal causes excessive heat and can wear your brakes down in no time.

TIP: If you are buying a used car that shows only a few thousand miles on the odometer, take a close look at the brake pedal. If the rubber is worn down you can rest assured that the car has plenty of mileage on it.

8. Fuels and Lubricants and Additives

GASOLINE

In the old days you just drove up to the gas station of your choice and ordered regular or premium. As time has gone on and more sophisticated carburetors, fuel injection, and emission-control systems have hit the market, the petroleum industry has had to make many revisions and offer a greater variety of products to fit these needs.

Most cars manufactured today require unleaded gasoline to cut down on noxious emissions into the atmosphere. (Naturally, unleaded gasoline costs the consumer more than leaded regular.) Most 1975 and later models call for a gasoline classification number 2, which has a minimum "antiknock index" of 87 octane. To confuse or unconfuse you, let me explain that there are *RON*, or Research Octane Number, and *MON*, meaning Motor Octane Number. They are simply two different ways of measuring the octane quotient of your gas. The *Anti-Knock Index* averages out the two and that is the one that should be posted on your dealer's gas tank. You should be using gasoline of the quality that allows your engine to run knock-free (ping-free). In other words, don't use any higher octane than necessary. Try a lower and lower grade until your engine starts to ping. Then move back up that one step to where it didn't ping. (*Continuous knocking will ruin your pistons.*) There is no point in buying a gas any more expensive than you need. The higher the octane, the more it costs. The true test is to accelerate while going uphill. I shop around for gasoline and usually buy from one of the discount stations, and over a period of a year save myself a bundle. They buy their gas from Shell or Gulf or from one of the other big suppliers.

Lead in gasoline acts as a lubricant. However, my Mercedes worked better without lead in the gas, because of the fuel injection. Lead deposits tended to form if I used leaded gas. It is better to use the gasoline recommended in your owner's manual for trouble-free performance.

Oil

Oil is classified into four different categories: mineral, vegetable, animal, and synthetic. Mineral oil is derived from crude petroleum. The crude oil is fractionated into several different products. For instance, from 100 gallons of crude oil you get about 44 gallons of gasoline; the rest becomes different grades of other fuels, such as kerosene, and other lubricants, paraffins, asphalt, and bitumen. Ninety percent of the gasoline you buy is fuel while the other 10 percent is lubricant, which serves the engine walls, rings, and valves.

Animal oils (such as sperm-whale oil) have excellent lubricating qualities under extreme pressures.

Synthetic oils are not very good for extreme pressures but are used in solvents, hydraulics, and cosmetics.

Viscosity is the rate at which oil will pass through an opening, like your ketchup's viscosity coming from the bottle; that is, the thickness or "flowability."

Grade is the range of viscosity at certain temperatures.

Oxidation is an oil killer. Oxidated oil becomes sludge. Heat causes oxidation over a period of time. That is why it is necessary to be meticulous, fastidious about changing your oil and oil filters at the recommended intervals, if not sooner, depending upon your driving conditions. Clean oil is the lifeblood of your car. Treat it as such. Buy a premium-grade oil that is recommended for your temperature range. *Don't add additives to a fine oil.* The oil-company engineers and chemists know what they are doing. You will only muck it up by adding things to it. Good-quality oils have detergents already added, like phosphates or sulfonates. Don't mix your oils. If you change oils, change filters. Don't use oils not made for *your*

engine, like racing oils. They are only made to last a day, the day of the race.

And most important, don't rev your engine until it has warmed up and the oil has had a chance to get to all the places it has to go.

Lubricants

Oil. Light machine oil such as 3-in-1 can be used to protect things from rusting — like your tools and chrome trim — as well as for oiling hinges, small motors, and so on. The motor oil used in your engine can be used for heavy-duty motors and heavy moving parts. When you are buying oil you might purchase a small oilcan that facilitates dropping oil in small quantities in the right places.

Penetrating oil — used for unlocking nuts and bolts that are rusted tight. The longer you leave it on the more it penetrates. There are several good ones on the market. The one I prefer is CRC, which is used a lot in marine work because it does the job. CRC and like products also "displace" water and moisture and are good for coating surfaces to protect from rust and moisture damage. (When I bought my new electric typewriter I happened to be living in Florida by the sea. I immediately gave the works a shot of CRC to protect it from the sea moisture and rust.) In the winter it is wise to give your door and trunk locks a shot of this to keep the moisture out. There is nothing more annoying than being locked out of your car in a blizzard because your door locks have frozen solid. Also highly recommend for keeping the moving parts of your tools in shape, such as the worm drive on your adjustable wrenches.

White grease — a lubricant that comes either in a

can or, easier to use, in stick form, used for greasing your door hinges, latches, and strikers. Also your hood hinges and trunk hinges and strikers.

Belt lubricant. Nothing is more grating on the nerves than a squeaky fan belt. A few drops of this on the inside edge will sometimes eliminate the problem.

Speedometer-cable lubricant — as the name implies, to eliminate squeaky speedometer cable. Some speedometers are sealed units to discourage used-car salesmen from tampering with them.

Silicone lubricants — good for window grooves that squeak and groan when you roll the windows up and down.

Adhesives

There are many different adhesive products for use in various places on your auto to perform different jobs.

Silicone rubber sealant — a liquid rubber that comes in black, white, aluminum color, and clear. Can be used to seal leaky windshields and weather stripping.

Gasket cement. If you are going to be involved in changing gaskets you need gasket cement to keep them from slipping and to create a tight fit between the metal parts and the gasket.

Trim cement — a specially made adhesive that bonds almost anything, like rubber or plastic, to metal, and to itself. Can be used to seal joints in radiator hoses as well.

Exhaust-system sealer — made to withstand the heat of exhaust pipes. Used for sealing pipe joints.

Ignition sealer. If you are troubled with ignition problems in wet weather, this may solve them. Spray it on your electrical wires, distributor cap, spark-plug wires and caps.

Lock-nut — a terrific substance that locks your nuts and bolts securely but still allows you to unbolt them when necessary. Good for use on bolts that take a lot of vibrations and tend to work loose. You just pour some on the threads of the nut or bolt before you screw it in. It hardens forty-five minutes to an hour later.

Cleaners and Solvents

There are several hand cleaners on the market that do the job of getting the grease off and still leave some skin on your pinkies.

Naval jelly — the greatest boon to mankind since the Water Pik. Brush it on rust, leave it on for five minutes or so, wash it off, and voilà! the rust washes off with it. Coca-Cola, believe it or not, also does a good job on rust.

Degreaser or *degunker* — any one of several good ones that are used to clean off accumulated grease, which is a fire hazard, from your engine. Simply spray it on, taking care to cover carburetor and distributor with a plastic bag, then spray the garden hose on it to wash off the grease and grime. Also terrific for getting grease out of your clothing, any kind. Not recommended for your body.

Carburetor cleaner — great for keeping your carburetor in tip-top shape.

Automatic-choke cleaner — great for keeping your choke linkages free and moving easily, which is necessary for good gas mileage.

Protectors — of your own hands from grease. The first one to hit the market way back when and still one of the best is put out by du Pont and called Protek. You simply apply a coating to your hands *before* you start to work on your car (or painting your apartment). When you are finished, the grease and paint wash off like plain old mud.

MULTIPURPOSE ITEM

Bal-Chip additive is a Philippine product, wonderful as a decarbonizer and rust inhibitor, and for freeing rusted bolts. As a gas additive, it improves mileage. It also improves the life of crankcase oil, and is an effective water displacer (spray in wet distributor to dry it out) — but it's hard to find in stores.

9. Warranties and Guarantees—Is There a Difference?

According to my dictionary, a warranty is a written guarantee. According to my Dodge's "Limited Warranty," Chrysler Corporation assures me that "for the first 12 months of use or 12,000 miles, whichever occurs first, any Chrysler, Plymouth or Dodge dealer will fix without charge for *parts* or *labor*, any part of this vehicle we supply (except tires) which proves defective in normal use."

They extend that warranty in regard to the battery, which is unconditionally guaranteed for the first 12 months or 12,000 miles. After that, the battery is guaranteed pro rata for a total period of 36 months. That means that if your battery goes dead after you have owned the car 24 months, you have used it for 24/36, or ⅔, of its natural life and they will give you credit on a new battery for the remaining 12/36, or ⅓.

The Chrysler warranty does *not* specify that I have to take it in to a Chrysler dealership for periodic checkups for the warranty to be effective. Many other manufacturers' warranties do. For example, my VW van had a 24-month or 24,000-mile warranty *but* it was valid only if I had the van checked out every so many months at an authorized VW dealer. Well, these checkups ran anywhere from twelve to fifty dollars, depending upon which part of the country I happened to be in at the time and also upon how many miles the van had traveled. That is, an 18,000-mile checkup costs a lot more than a 3,000-mile checkup. It took me about three checkups before I got wise that the so-called warranty was costing me a hell of a lot of money. So bear that in mind if a manufacturer offers a very long warranty period. In the long run it may cost you rather than save you.

In the pre–Ralph Nader days I once purchased a new Ford convertible. I hadn't driven it fifty miles away from the dealer before the hood flew up in my face, and the doors flew open every time I rounded a sharp corner. The car had a three-month guarantee against such things. Every other weekend or so I would drive the car back to the dealer to get these problems fixed. Every time I picked the car up they assured me they had repaired it. Finally the three-month guarantee was up and the defects were still not fixed. "Tough luck," said the dealer. "Your three-month guarantee is no longer effective." I still have a file full of correspondence with Henry Ford and Company. I should have saved my stamps for all the satisfaction I got from them. Eight years later, with the hood still wired down and the doors wired shut, I junked the car, including the little doll in the trunk that had a remarkable resemblance to Henry Ford, with a bolt through its heart.

A word of caution about having special equipment installed in your auto. This may abrogate the dealer's warranty. Make sure that whoever installs the equipment gives you their warranty in case something goes wrong and be sure they are a reputable and financially stable outfit.

For instance, I had some special electrical equip-ment installed on my van, a refrigerator, inside lights, and so on. I had an electrical fire and Dodge was not liable because they had not done the work but had farmed it out to a subcontractor. Had the van com-pletely burned up, the subcontractor would not have been financially stable enough to cover the damage, so I would have been up the well-known creek.

We still have a long way to go in the area of both dealer and manufacturer accountability but in the past twenty years there has been considerable progress made, thanks to the efforts of Nader *et al.* Choose your congressmen wisely and even more progress may come *your* way, instead of government's favoring big business and profits. The legislative emphasis should go toward safety and the public welfare.

~~warranty~~

Warranties:
- condition you have to follow
- special equiptment installed.

10. Tools and Fasteners

Tool — a contrivance or fabrication held in or worked by the hand for assisting the work of mechanics. . . .

Which comes first, the chicken or the egg? Which comes first, the screws, nuts, bolts, studs, lugs, cotter pins, washers, spring clips, and so on, which we call *fasteners,* or the variety of pliers, wrenches, ratchets and sockets, and screwdrivers that we use on the various fasteners to secure, tighten, loosen, or remove them? Suffice it to say we can't have one without the other.

FASTENERS

Let's start with fasteners. They come in all shapes and sizes and are made from a variety of materials; their purpose in life is to fasten one object to another.

In America, bolts, studs, and screws have *threads* and are measured in *inches* (or fractions thereof). *Screws* have slots for screwdrivers to fit into. Screws can be flat or pointed on the opposite end from the slot. The ones with pointed ends are either wood screws or sheet-metal screws. The ones with flat ends are called flat screws. A flat screw is usually married to a *nut* that will enable it to be tightened and held secure.

NOTE: Most screws, studs, nuts, and bolts have right-hand threads. That means you turn to the *right* to tighten (clockwise) and to the *left* to loosen (counterclockwise). If you find that hard to remember, try L = L, left to *loosen*. Right to tight.

The only exceptions you are likely to find to that rule are your wheel lugs, where the opposite may apply. The theory is that if the wheel is going around clockwise it will tend to loosen the lugs with a right-hand thread so that you could lose a wheel. If that is the case on your car, the lug will be marked clearly with an "L" on the end of the stud, meaning that it is a *left-hand* thread. Therefore you would turn right to loosen and left to tighten . . . but *only* if it is marked with an "L."

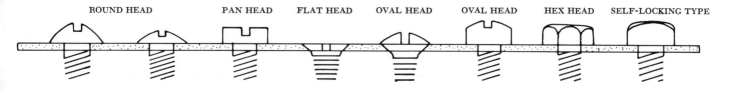

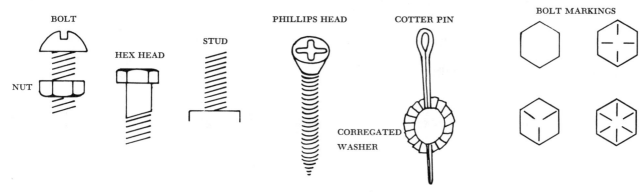

Screws, Nuts, and Bolts

Threaded nuts, bolts, and studs are measured in two ways: first by the diameter of the threaded part, so you fit the right-size fastener into the right-size hole, and second by the number of threads per inch. The variations of the threads have to do with their specific use; for instance, bolts that have fewer but deeper threads are better for soft metals and cast iron. "Finer" threaded (or more threads per inch) screws are used for electrical work.

Naturally life is complicated. Just as we don't have one language or one currency for the entire world, we don't use the same-sized fasteners or matching wrenches and sockets all over the world. At present in Great Britain and America we measure them by the inch or fraction thereof, and in Europe they are sized by the metric system.* Therefore, if you have one European car and one American car you need two completely different sets of tools, one metric and one in inches, because not only are the diameters different but the threads and pitches of the threads are different.

In addition to sizing we also have to deal with *strength* of certain bolts and screws. This is indicated by a marking on the top of the bolt. No markings mean average (medium) strength — three, four, five or six lines mean the more lines, the stronger the material the bolt is made of. That also tells you how hard you can turn it — its "torque" strength, or the amount of turning or twisting pressure it will withstand before the head breaks off the bolt.

* In England cars made before 1951 used "Whitworth" measurement. Eventually the entire civilized world will be metric.

WRENCHES

My first what you could call reasonably new (three years old) car happened to be a Nash Rambler convertible. At the time I was working as a timekeeper on a construction gang. My boss was a car freak and was always tinkering with his big four-holer (had four vent holes on each side of the hood) Roadmaster Buick. I hadn't had my Rambler but a few days when one lunch hour he was fooling around his car and I borrowed his ratchet and socket. I started tightening the studs on my motor block. I had never used a ratchet before and therefore was not used to the torque power. In no time flat, with, it seemed, very little strength on my part, I had sheared the top of the bolt right off. Not knowing much about engines, I was terrified I had ruined the car. My boss laughed and said I hadn't ruined it but I would have to take it to a garage and have them "reverse" drill it out and replace it with a new bolt. That was my first lesson in the torque, or twisting, power of ratchet wrenches.

The important nuts and bolts on your car have torque settings, meaning how many pounds pressure they will stand without shearing off. Conversely, if

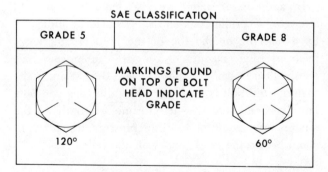

Bolt Markings for Torque Values. Courtesy of the Chrysler Corporation

BOLT TORQUE

Size	GRADE 5		GRADE 8	
	Ft. Lbs.	newton metres	Ft. Lbs.	newton metres
1/4-20	95 In. Lbs.	10.7	125 In. Lbs.	14.1
5/16-18	95 In. Lbs.	10.7	150 In. Lbs.	16.9
1/4-28	200 In. Lbs.	22.6	270 In. Lbs.	31.2
5/16-24	20	27.1	25	33.9
3/8-16	30	40.7	40	54.2
3/8-24	35	47.5	45	61.0
7/16-14	50	67.8	65	88.1
7/16-20	55	74.6	70	95.0
1/2-13	75	101.7	100	135.6
1/2-20	85	115.2	110	149.1
9/16-12	105	142.4	135	183.0
9/16-18	150	156.0	150	203.4
5/8-11	115	203.4	195	264.4
5/8-18	160	217.0	210	284.7
3/4-16	175	237.3	225	305.1

Bolt Torque. Courtesy of the Chrysler Corporation

the bolt isn't tightened enough it may work loose and allow some important item to drop off completely. So in order for us to be able to have it "just tight enough" they invented the torque wrench.

Torque wrenches can be used with sockets for the different-sized bolts and nuts. Some of them have pointers that show the exact pressure you are using. Others can be preset and when the desired pressure is met will automatically turn off and cease to exert more pressure. They vary in price, anywhere from $10 to $150, depending upon their quality and capabilities. If you don't want to buy one you can sometimes rent or borrow one. Your car's manual tells you the different torques of each major nut and bolt in your auto.

Guy, my instructor, said, "God, how much money, time and trouble I could have saved myself over the years with even a cheap torque wrench."

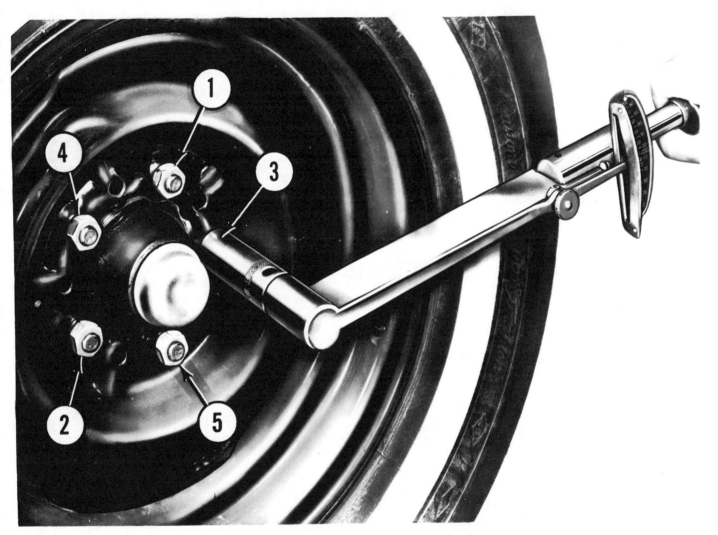

Order in Which Bolts Are Tightened. Courtesy of the Chrysler Corporation

hexagon-shaped indented setscrews that screw against or into something to hold it fast. For instance, the knob on the windshield-wiper switch of my Dodge van had worked loose and fell on the floor. What held it tight in the first place? — an Allen screw set right into the knob. I had to buy a set of Allen wrenches to tighten it back on. You are likely to find that many accessories, such as door handles, are attached with Allen screws. Sometimes you can make a regular screwdriver work in these hexagonal openings instead of an Allen wrench and sometimes you can't.

My dad was always after my brother and me about having the proper tools to do the job well. Don't use pliers instead of a wrench. Don't use a good screwdriver to open your paint can or pry loose a rock. He was a nut about keeping his tools in good shape.

When I bought my house in Spain the man from the electric company came to install a meter. He had on a business suit and no tool kit, just the meter. He reached in his pocket and pulled out a small pair of scissors with which he poked four starter holes in the softwood meter board. Then he withdrew four nails from his pocket, stepped outside the door, picked up a rock, and hammered the nails in. He smiled the smile of a man with a job well done, replaced the

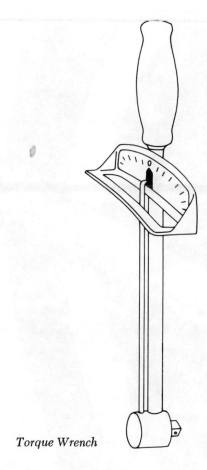

Torque Wrench

NOTE: Never replace a bolt in your car with a bolt of lesser torque rating, that is, of lower quality.

Not all bolts have nuts (and vice versa). Some screws or bolts merely screw into the part or engine. Sometimes they employ a washer or lock washer to keep them from working loose.

In addition to these more conventional and familiar types of tools and fasteners there is something called an *Allen wrench* or *key*. These L-shaped keys have hexagon-shaped ends of varying size and fit into

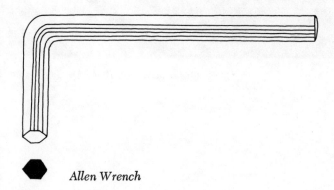

Allen Wrench

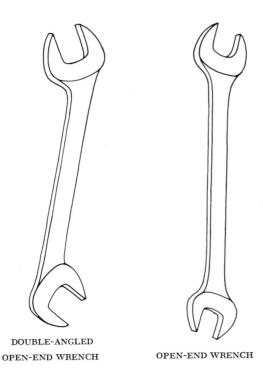

DOUBLE-ANGLED
OPEN-END WRENCH OPEN-END WRENCH

parallel jaws, one pair 1/16″ farther apart than the other.

A set of wrenches may go from ⅜″ to ¾″. If you are on your toes you will note that there are only six sizes instead of a possible twelve, allowing two ends to each of the six wrenches. That is because many times you will need two jaws of one size when working on an auto part — one to hold the nut fast while you are unscrewing the bolt with the other wrench. They therefore repeat on a graduated scale.

Another type of wrench is the *box*, or *ring*, wrench.

scissors in his breast pocket, threw the rock out the door, and left!

The moral: there are ways and ways of getting a job done. It's nice when you have the right tools but if you don't you can sometimes improvise.

Wrenches come in different shapes and sizes and angles and combinations.

The most common wrench is the *open-end* wrench. If you can afford only one set or even only a couple of wrenches you should get the open-end type. They can be used on bolt heads, square heads, and even hex-headed studs or bolts or nuts. They can be used in places where socket and box-ended wrenches cannot. The purpose of the wrench is to tighten, loosen, or hold fast while you are working on another part, a nut or bolt. At each end of the wrench are two

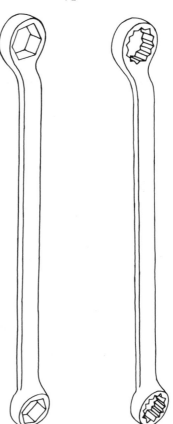

SIX POINT TWELVE POINT *Box-End Wrenches*

These perform the same function as the open-end wrench except they are stronger and lighter and allow for less slippage and shearing off of corners. They can be purchased with offset heads for ease of working. They can also be purchased with ratchets in them so that you needn't remove and replace them with each full motion; that is, you can rock them back and forth without removing them from the bolt head to either tighten or loosen, speeding up your work considerably by the facility of motion.

CAUTION: The ratchet-type box wrench is not to be used for loosening tight nuts or bolts. Use your regular open-end or conventional box wrench for that, then switch to your ratchet for *running* — rapid loosening or tightening.

TIP: Twelve-point box wrenches and sockets are better than six-point. They afford greater facility in tight spots. Six-point sockets are used where the socket strength is a consideration.

However, there is one disadvantage to the box wrench. In certain cases, there isn't room to fit it onto the nut or bolt — that's when you have to use the open-end wrench.

You will find the sizes you use the most will be in both open-end and box — 7/16″, ½″, 9/16″, and ⅝″ — so if you can only afford a couple, get those. (Metric sizes — 10 mm, 11 mm, 12 mm, 13 mm, and 14 mm.)

A *combination wrench* is a wrench with an open-end on one end and a box-end on the other end, generally of the same size.

If you don't have complete sets of wrenches it is advisable to have an adjustable open-end wrench that you can adjust to whatever size (within a certain range) you need. These are also handy for use on nuts and bolts that may be slightly worn so that your fixed-size regular wrench may slip on them.

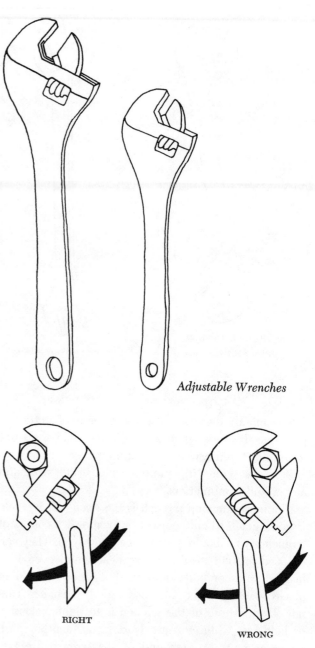

Adjustable Wrenches

RIGHT

WRONG

Proper Use of Adjustable Wrench

NOTE: The size of the jaw determines the length of the handle. That is done for a reason — so you don't apply more force than the handle can deliver, because the amount of torque for the size of the nut or bolt was taken into consideration in the tool's design. So don't tighten any more than you can under your own power — don't bang the wrench with a sledgehammer or slip a pipe over the end of it to give yourself more torque or you'll probably break off the bolt or nut.

Remember, when you're working with wrenches, always try to pull instead of push. Then if the wrench breaks loose you'll save yourself many a banged knuckle. If you must push, wrap your paddies in a heavy cloth or glove.

A *socket ratchet wrench* set is a must if you are going to do much work on your car. As with box wrenches, get twelve-point sockets. These sets come with extension bars to reach difficult places as well as universal-joint fittings that allow for screwing and unscrewing in tight spots. The sockets and extra fittings snap on and off the ratchet handle easily. There are sockets for every size nut and bolt in your car, even an especially deep one for your spark plugs.

The wrench shaft is called the *drive*. Drives come in different sizes (each requiring its own sockets or adapters), ¼″, ⅜″, ½″, or ¾″ drive. The ½″ and ¾″ are for heavy-duty repairs on autos and trucks respectively, the ¼″ and ⅜″ for the smaller stuff. Besides the ratchet handle they come with swivel handles or crank handles for tough tightening and loosening jobs.

Preferred order of choice for attacking nuts and bolts:

1. socket set
2. box-end wrench

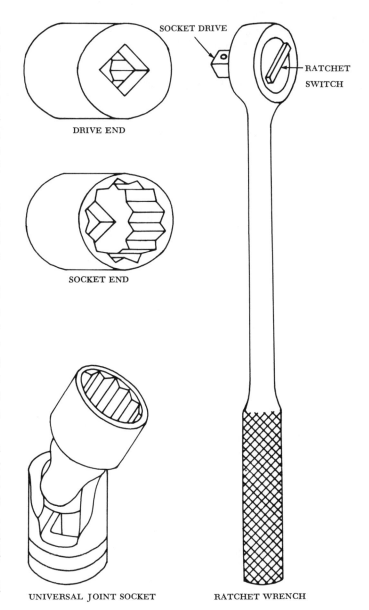

DRIVE END

SOCKET END

SOCKET DRIVE

RATCHET SWITCH

UNIVERSAL JOINT SOCKET

RATCHET WRENCH

3. open-end wrench
4. adjustable wrench
5. vise grip and large hammer and
   select choice of words

TIP: These same sockets can fit on your torque wrench. A ⅜″ set is the most useful.

OTHER TOOLS

Vise-grip, or *lock-on, pliers* — a great invention. You squeeze the two handles together on the nut or bolt or whatever you want to hold fast; then you screw the little bolt that protrudes from one end of the pliers'

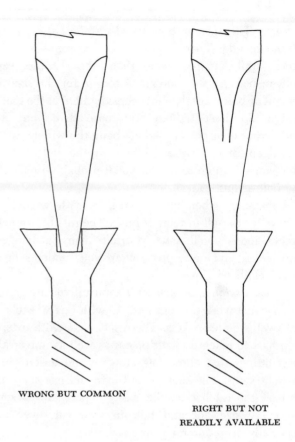

WRONG BUT COMMON

RIGHT BUT NOT
READILY AVAILABLE

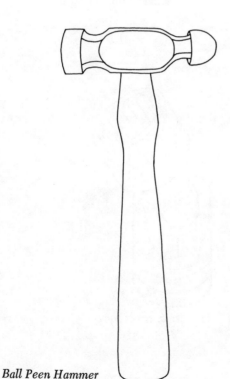

Ball Peen Hammer

handle and locks the pliers shut, holding fast the object to which it is attached until you press the release lever. A handy, versatile supplementary tool that no amateur or professional should be without. Used properly it can serve as a third hand for the mechanic.

TIP: Not to be used for turning nuts or bolts except in emergency, as these pliers can strip the corners off with their serrated edges.

Regular slip-joint pliers — another versatile tool no mechanic should be without. They are the standard "gripping" tool or "steel fingers" for the mechanic. A good useful size is 8 inches long. Not to be used on nuts and bolts as they round off the edges.

Needle-nose pliers perform the same gripping function but because of their elongated shape can get into small places and hold more delicate objects. A must for your toolbox. Great for picking up small parts, gripping cotter pins, bending spring ends, and so on. Easier for the delicate jobs than regular pliers.

Phillips Head Screwdriver

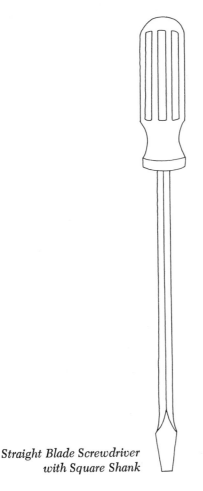

*Straight Blade Screwdriver
with Square Shank*

It is really important to buy a high-quality needle-nose.

Channel pliers — yet another variation of the regular pliers but instead of just two adjustments to expand the jaws there are several "channels" to vary the jaws' opening. Be sure the jaws are parallel to ensure a good grip.

TIP: Never use pliers on nuts or bolts. Use a wrench of the proper size. Pliers chew off the corners and eventually render them difficult if not impossible to get off. If it's an emergency, use vise-grip pliers.

Offset screwdrivers — handy for those places that allow no room to work with your long-handled screwdrivers or even a stubby one by the time you include the size of your hand. If you are starting your tool kit from scratch, it is cheaper to buy screwdrivers by the set. Specify square shanks, because you can employ a wrench for better leverage.

1 ¾ -pound ball peen hammer
1 oilcan
1 wire-cutting pliers, unless your regular pliers have wire cutters
1 small hacksaw for cutting hoses, etc.
1 ½" cold chisel for slicing off rivet heads, etc.
1 test light for checking out electrical circuits and connections (with needle probe)
1 flashlight for tiny places and emergencies

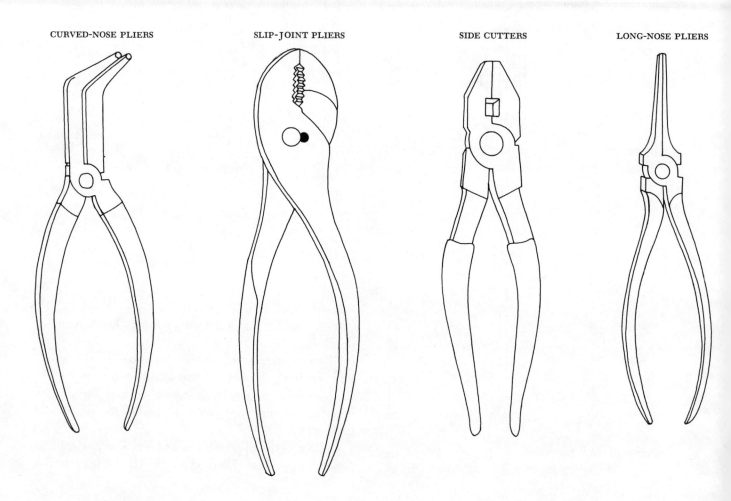

CURVED-NOSE PLIERS   SLIP-JOINT PLIERS   SIDE CUTTERS   LONG-NOSE PLIERS

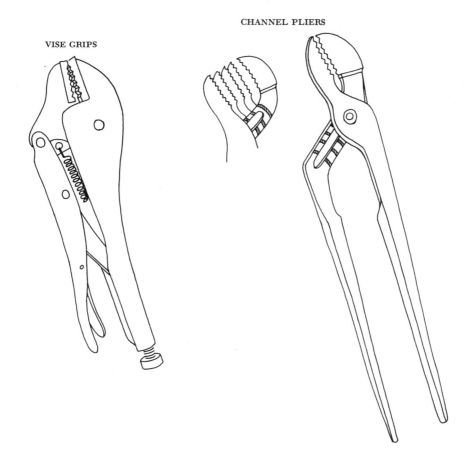

VISE GRIPS

CHANNEL PLIERS

1 grease gun if you intend to do your own grease jobs
1 penknife, for a million reasons
1 work light if you are going to be working anywhere on your car
1 6′ to 8′ set of jumper leads with alligator clips for bypassing defective circuits
1 oil-filter wrench, and a pan for draining the old oil. These things you can buy in a change-your-oil set for under five dollars.
1 set of thickness (or feeler) gauges for setting your

spark-plug gap and breaker points. CAUTION: If you have an electronic ignition system, make sure your gauges are nonmagnetic (copper or bronze) or you'll blow the works.
1 fire extinguisher. A good one that works under 32° F (in freezing temperatures) and on all types of fires *including* electrical.
1 set of battery jumper cables to carry in the car at all times
1 tire gauge

1 good jack that you can work and trust — preferably a scissors jack

1 good lug wrench (crossbar) that works, if you are going to do your own tire changing

1 timing light (not neon bulb — they don't produce enough light)

1 compression tester — screw-in type with cable is best

1 cam/dwell-tachometer

1 tune-up kit containing:
    set of spark plugs
    condenser
    points (or reluctor)
    rotor
    distributor cap

CAUTION: Never get *under* a car that is elevated by a bumper jack or scissors jack without first blocking up the wheels with wheel chocks.

A *jack* is that tool you have to carry with you at all times in case of a flat tire. It is the instrument with which you raise your car high enough off the ground to enable you to remove the flat tire and replace it with an inflated one.

I once traveled all through northern Morocco with another girl in a Volkswagen van without a jack. We were plagued with flat tires. Not only didn't we have a jack, we didn't have a lug wrench. Each time we had a flat (three of them) we had to stop carloads of Arabs, who would pool their tools to get the lugs off the car. Then three or four of them would get on each bumper and lift the car up by hand while the others quickly changed the tires! I strongly *don't* advise following that example. Granted it was terribly dangerous in Morocco for two women but at least there they accommodated us. Here, good luck having carloads of people stop and lift your car up for you.

The best kind of jack for you is the one you can most easily use, as long as it is safe and can support the weight of your car. Some people prefer *bumper jacks,* others *scissors jacks,* and still others *hydraulic jacks.*

I heartily suggest that *before* you find yourself with a flat tire out in the country on a dirt road with no one else in sight you do a dry run with your jack and see if you can use it to get your car's wheel off the ground. If you can't handle your jack, get a type that you can use with some facility and safety. Any auto-supply store or Sears auto-department salesman will show you how to use it properly.

CHEMICAL TOOLS

What's a *chemical* tool? Something that assists the mechanic in his work by means of chemicals. Remember the du Pont slogan, "Better things for better living through chemistry"?

Modern chemistry has given us some fabulous things to help us in our work, particularly in the auto mechanics field. Some that you will find helpful in maintaining and repairing your car are discussed on pages 111–113. They come in a variety of containers. Remember that aerosol cans not only cost more but are bad for the atmosphere and stratosphere.

11. Checkpoints for Buying a Used Car

Used cars have a purpose. They cost less money *at the outset* to buy. Sometimes they cost more in the long run and sometimes they save you money. If you must buy a used car, try to make sure it wasn't an *abused* car. Like abused children, they tend to seek revenge for their deprivation of love on the next people they meet.

Here are some quite simple things you should look for when shopping for a used car.

Check with your Better Business Bureau *before you buy* from a used-car dealer. They are second on the national list of complaints of the BBB. The used-car industry has had such a bad reputation over the years that the used-car salesman has become a national joke when you are referring to someone of shady business practices. So Caveat Emptor all the way. Watch the dealer like a hawk and don't sign anything without fully reading and understanding it. If *you* don't understand it, take it to your banker or lawyer or someone who does. Get an unconditional guarantee. But bear in mind that a guarantee isn't worth the paper it's written on if you try to return the car and the place where you bought it has turned into a vacant lot with the proprietor out on a long lunch, say five or ten years.

As I mentioned earlier, most U.S. cars are programmed to wear out at around 10 years / 100,000 miles, whichever occurs first, unless they have had extraordinary care and were damn good cars to begin with. As the old used-car-salesman joke says, "owned by two old spinsters who kept it garaged except when they drove to church on Sundays."

Strangely enough, in my vast experience with automobiles over the past thirty-five or forty years, the only really good cars, cars that caused me no trouble, were used, second- or third- or even fourthhand. All that implies is that the people who owned them before me had all the wrongs righted before I got the car and probably a great many of the worn-out parts replaced. But I consider myself just as lucky with used cars as I have been unlucky with new ones.

Considering the 10-year/100,000-mile factor, you have to prorate how old (and how much mileage) the car you are contemplating buying is against those figures, that is, if the car is nine years old, you can figure that a lot of things are going to be wrong with it and that it will cost you a considerable amount of money to put it to rights. Unless you plan on doing most of the repairs yourself, I wouldn't recommend buying it.

Automobiles depreciate most the first year, some up to 20 percent of their original value. The second and third years also take a heap of the total depreciation. Therefore, a car that is older than three years is considered the best bet to take advantage of those statistics. Bearing those facts in mind, it is now up to you to check out the individual car as well as you can. Some cars five years old are in better shape than others only two or three, depending upon how they were taken care of, how they were driven, the conditions under which they were driven, and so forth. Cars driven over dirt roads for three years will be pretty well shot. Cars driven around salt water have terrible rust problems, some so bad they won't pass inspection because of rusted-out places. I've seen cars in Florida that looked like fancy lacework they were so rusted through.

The average driver puts about 10,000 miles per year on a car. If there is much more than that (2 years, 20,000, and so on) the car has had heavy use and should cost commensurately less. On the other hand, if you have a choice between two models, one having 50,000 miles put on it in one year and the other having 50,000 miles put on it in five years, choose the one with the fast mileage, the first one, because fast mileage doesn't take as much out of a car as age plus miles, all other things being equal.

TIP: There is in the auto industry such a thing as "The Blue Book," which every salesman has. It is put out every year and lists three values for each used car: one if it's in good condition, one for medium condi-

tion, and the third for poor condition. Ask the salesman to see that book and locate the car you are thinking of buying and compare those values with the price he is charging. If he won't show it to you, go elsewhere, for he is probably trying to charge more than the market value of the car.

The used-car classified section of your local Sunday newspaper is a good place to get a reasonable "ball park" idea of how much a particular make and model is worth on the open market. Bear in mind that a reputable dealer has to charge more than a private seller if he is going to offer you a guarantee, probably anywhere from two to five hundred dollars more.

If you buy from a private owner, usually he will let you take the car to your mechanic for a quick checkup to make sure it is in good condition. Or take your mechanic with you when you go to see the car.

VISUAL CHECKS

Get out your magnifying glass and inspect carefully the following items.

Look at the finish of the paint. If the finish is mottled and "thin"-looking, and even though the dealer has polished it up you can see that that is probably the first polish it has had in years, forget it. Usually people who care about their cars keep the outside up as well as the motor. On cars that have had consistent polishing and waxing the paint job looks heavy and shiny, not just skin-deep.

Have the car put up on a lift and check underneath, in the wheel wells, in seams and cracks for rust. Particularly check around door bottoms, sills, and sides. Tap suspected areas with a screwdriver or penknife from underneath. Heavily rusted areas will sound different from those with good metal. Look under carpets for floor rust. Lightly rusted chrome can be expected on older cars. Paint bubbles or blisters usually indicate rust.

Look around the door jambs and under the hood to see if the car has been repainted. If it has, chances are it may have been in an accident and you should avoid it at all costs. Most cars aren't worth a damn after a bad accident. That's why people trade them in. Likewise look for "ripples" or "crinkles" in the body. That also indicates an accident.

Open and close all doors to see if they latch properly. Same with hood and trunk. Roll all the windows up and down to see if they work. Try the roof window or convertible top to make sure it functions easily.

Check out every accessory you can find. Push and pull every knob in sight to make sure all are in working order — headlights, turn signals, brake lights, dimmer, heater, defroster, air conditioner, blower, horn, windshield wipers, windshield washer.

CHECKLIST

OK	*Need repair*	
—	————————	headlights, high and low beam
—	————————	turn signals
—	————————	brake lights
—	————————	dimmer
—	————————	heater
—	————————	air conditioner
—	————————	blower
—	————————	defroster
—	————————	horn
—	————————	windshield wipers
—	————————	windshield washers

DASHBOARD LIGHTS AND GAUGES

— ———————— OIL-PRESSURE LIGHT. When you turn on the ignition and the engine starts, the oil-pressure light should go out. If no light goes on at all, that should be checked out too. Perhaps it's just a bulb but perhaps it's something more. Don't drive without its being fixed.

— ———————— GENERATOR/ALTERNATOR LIGHT. This should go on when you start the car and go off when the engine is running.

— ———————— BRAKE LIGHT. Should go off when you release the emergency brake.

— ———————— COOLING SYSTEM. Check the hoses under the hood. They should not be too hard or too soft. Check closely at the connections for signs of leaks. Check radiator for signs of leaks. Look for red (or blue-green) antifreeze discolorations.

— ———————— EXHAUST SYSTEM. Preferably when the car is jacked up or on a lift, check the muffler and pipes for corrosion and looseness.

— ———————— WIRING. Look for cracked or frayed wires, or dangling unconnected wires.

OK   *Need repair*

—   —————————

—   —————————

front —   —————————
rear   —   —————————
hood   —   —————————
trunk —   —————————
left   —   —————————
right —   —————————

l.f.   —   —————————
r.f.   —   —————————
l.r.   —   —————————
r.r.   —   —————————
sp.   —   —————————

—   —————————

—   —————————

BATTERY. Battery should be clean with no corrosion around terminals. There should be no signs of swelling sides or top, which indicate you will soon need a new battery.

SUSPENSION SYSTEM. Put your entire body weight on each end of the car, in turn. Press down or jump down on the fender. The car should bounce up, down, and then return to original position. If it keeps on bouncing, it probably needs new shock absorbers.

LATCHES AND LOCKS. Check each door latch to see if it holds fast. Try the key in all the locks and try the inside locks to make sure they work properly.

FRONT WHEELS. Jack up each in turn. With the wheel completely off the ground, grab the top with your right hand, the bottom with your left hand, and push back and forth. If there is more than 1/16″ play in the wheel it bears further looking into as it probably needs bearings, kingpins, or tie-rods.

TIRES. Make sure all the tires are worn evenly and that they have some tread left on them. If they are not worn evenly they are probably out of line, out of balance, or both. See Tires and Wheels, pages 89–94, for further details. Check tires for cuts; run your hand around the inside as well. Make sure they are all the same breed, that is, all belted or all radial, and all the same size.

STEERING. Have the car on a level with wheels pointing straight. Turn steering wheel slowly. If there is much play before the wheels start to turn, it probably indicates excessive wear and calls for either adjustment or new parts.

BRAKES. Push down on the brake pedal. It should go to within a few inches of the floorboard, no farther. It should feel firm, not spongy. Visually check the brake pedal. If it appears worn, that usually means there is a heck of a lot of mileage on the car, regardless of what shows on the odometer.

THE TEST DRIVE

In the final analysis, all the other checks are secondary to this test. Don't buy a used car (or a new car) that you can't test drive. First, before you take it on the highway, ascertain that the dealer is insured, just in case the brakes don't work and you clobber someone.

If you don't know *anything* about cars and engines, try to take someone with you who does. (Maybe your service-station attendant would go with you or some kid down the block who tinkers with his own engine.)

1. The car should start easily.

2. Look out the back and make sure no bright blue or black smoke is coming from the exhaust. That is definitely a no-no.

3. Let the engine warm up. When it is warmed up it should sound even and purring, when idling or when you accelerate, and should not make any funny noises.

4. If it is a manual shift, the clutch pedal should come up evenly, taking hold about one inch after it leaves the floorboard. If the engine revs after you reach that inch and you don't start moving forward, the clutch is probably worn and slipping. That is also a no-no.

5. *Check behind you before you do this.* When you are rolling, hit the brakes at about 30 mph. The car should not swerve but come surely and firmly to a stop. If you hear any strange shuddering sound, the brakes will need repairs.

6. Take the car to a hill and see how it makes the grade.

7. Run the car on the flat at *your* normal top speed and see how you like its performance. Try it on a sharp curve to see how it corners.

MAINTENANCE

12. Battery, Spark Plugs, Cooling System, and Body

Strictly adhere to the manufacturer's bible, the *owner's manual,* for the suggested maintenance schedule for your automobile. I cannot stress this too strongly, because *they* know what they put in your car and what is required to keep it in working condition. Granted, they hope that you will take it to their designated garages for all this work to be done, but no matter where you take it or if you do the work yourself, maintenance *must* be done to ensure a trouble-free car.

It is important that you establish some sort of good relationship with a mechanic or particular garage if you want conscientious work done on your vehicle. Many, many garages either overlook the maintenance procedures or simply charge you for them and do not do the work. If you are having your oil changed, check the condition (color) of your oil before you drop off the car, then check it before you drive it away. The color should be different. The new oil should be clear and amber-colored. If you are having your car greased (which you ordinarily have done at the same time you have your oil changed), make sure they have an in-struction manual for your car; otherwise, leave them yours (which is usually located in the back of your service manual), particularly if you happen to own an "off-beat" model or foreign or vintage car.

BATTERY AND SPARK-PLUG MAINTENANCE

BATTERIES ARE DANGEROUS. The electrolyte (sulfuric acid solution) in the battery is a very powerful acid that can blind you if it gets into your eyes; it can eat a hole right through your clothing if it happens to fall on you. I inadvertently rubbed my ankle against a battery several years ago and ignored it. *When I woke up the next day the acid had eaten a hole* right through my skin to the anklebone. If it gets on you, wash immediately with a lot of water and then bathe with a solution of baking soda and water. GET TO A DOCTOR AT ONCE IF IT GETS IN YOUR EYES.

BATTERIES CAN ALSO EXPLODE. They give off a highly explosive gas, so don't expose them to fire or sparks — if they explode the acid flies all over.

If you are going to be carrying batteries from place to place very often, I suggest you invest in a battery carrier.

HOW TO TEST YOUR BATTERY I bought a hydrometer at an AID auto-supply store for seventy-five cents. The directions read:

1. Insert tube into battery cell.
2. Squeeze bulb and release slightly until solution reaches three-quarter level.
3. Tap lightly to dislodge air bubbles.
4. Observe the number of floating balls with tube upright.
5. Refer to chart (below) to determine condition of charge.
6. Return solution to battery cell and repeat steps in all battery cells.
7. Rinse tube in clear water to prevent accidental harm to clothing or person.

CONDITION OF BATTERY USING A BATTERY CHECKER

Count the Floating Balls

balls floating	battery charge
(0)	DEAD
(1)	25% charged
(2)	50% charged
(3)	75% charged
(4)	100% charged
(5)	OVERCHARGED

If your battery is dead it has to be charged or replaced. Check out your charging system. If the battery is overcharged, check out your voltage regulator.

HOW TO REPLACE YOUR SPARK PLUGS Removing spark plugs may or may not be easy, depending on where they are located and how tightly they are screwed in.

You will need: a ⅜″ ratchet wrench, an extension, a spark-plug socket, and a universal joint that swivels and makes your life a lot nicer because it allows you to maneuver at all angles.

Do one spark plug at a time and get in the habit of working in some kind of order. Like starting at #1 plug and following down the line on one side; then at #2 plug and following down the line on the other side if you have a V-type engine. If you have a straight-type engine, always start at the same place, either front working back or back working toward the front. It makes life simpler in the long run. Always start on the same side. If one is more difficult than the other, I always do the hard side first while I still have my strength and patience.

Remove the rubber boot gently. Clean off dirt around spark plugs. Place the socket over the plug, holding your hand firmly on the universal joint, and give a *quick* tug (or push) to loosen it. Remember to do it counterclockwise to loosen it. Once it is sufficiently loose you can complete unscrewing it by hand-holding the socket. Once it is out, read it.

A good mechanic can read your spark plugs like other people read a book and can tell you a lot about what's going on with your car just by looking at the condition of your plugs. By familiarizing yourself with this chart you too will be able to read your plugs and decide what to do about what their condition indicates. When you remove each plug, read it and record what cylinder it came from and govern yourself accordingly.

If it looks all right then it should be cleaned before you regap and reinstall it. If your service-station guys are nice, they may clean your plugs for you for nothing in their sandblasting machine.

Even though your set of new plugs should have

TOO RICH OR RETARDED

SOOTY

GOOD

BROWN OR GRAY

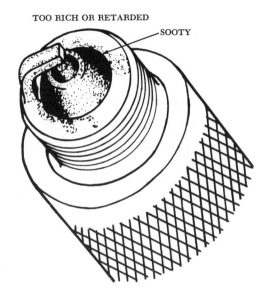

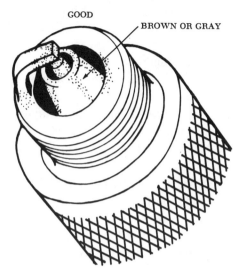

OIL FOULED

TOO LEAN OR ADVANCED

WHITE OR BLISTERED

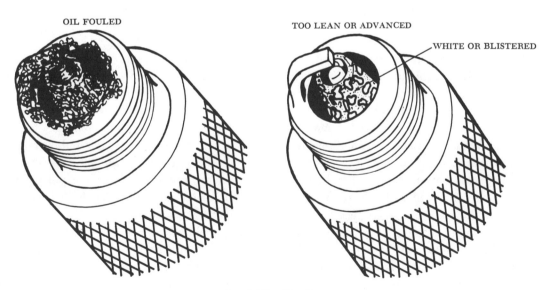

Spark-Plug Readings

been pregapped at the factory, check each one yourself to make sure they are gapped according to your car's specs. If not, get your spark-plug-gapping gauge and change the gap accordingly.

Slip the feeler in the gap at the bottom of the plug, between the electrode that protrudes from the base of the plug and the electrode wire that comes around from the side. There should be just a tease of a grip between the two. Don't force the feeler gauge if the opening is too small. Use the special tool on the gauge to bend the electrodes apart slightly and retest. If you have bent them too far apart, bend them back again slightly until you have it just right. Just right is when you can slip the gauge through and feel just the slightest amount of friction, like a fleeting kiss. Then it is just right.

Now you are ready to install the new plug. Get the special spark-plug socket out of your ratchet set, insert the plug all the way in the socket (electrode and threads showing), apply a few drops of graphite or penetrating oil to the threads for easy screwing, then insert plug into the engine block and screw it in *by hand* as far as you can. If it doesn't screw in easily the first few turns, you have probably got it in wrong (crooked). Remove by hand, wipe it off, oil it, and start over. It should screw in with no resistance until the last few turns, when it is getting well down into the engine block. *Then* attach the ratchet and give it a half turn. DO NOT OVERTIGHTEN. If you have a torque wrench, of course use that instead, and tighten to proper foot/pound setting, which should be listed in your manual (or in the spark-plug box specs).

Repeat the process until all plugs have been gapped and replaced in engine block and tightened.

TIP: To give you some idea of how many turns it should take to seat the plug, run your fingernail downward across the threads and count the clicks. That will tell you approximately how many full turns it should take to screw it all the way in.

COOLING-SYSTEM MAINTENANCE

WATER PUMP Some water pumps are fitted with a grease nipple and require periodic lubrication. Chrysler recommends every 6 months or 10,000 miles. (And, they caution, do not use a high-pressure grease gun.) Water pumps are good for four or five years; don't be shocked if at any time after that you need a new one.

Other water pumps do not require maintenance, because they are permanently packed and sealed at the factory.

RADIATOR You should do a monthly or bimonthly look-see into your radiator. If it needs topping off with coolant (half water, half ethylene-glycol antifreeze), it should be filled enough to cover the honeycomb of fins that you see when you peer down into it. Leave at least an inch and a half room at the top.

CAUTION: All radiator and cooling-system work should ideally be done when the engine is cool. If the engine is hot, be extremely careful if you have to remove the filler cap. In fact, wait several minutes for it to cool down. I have seen caps blow sky-high and boiling water spew over everything and everyone. *Boiling water in the face and on the hands is no fun.* Always have a heavy rag to unscrew the cap if you even *think* it might be hot, and do it slowly to let the steam escape a little at a time.

Most cooling systems today have an overflow, or surge, tank that has an "add coolant" line that is visible without opening the radiator cap. Never overfill. Heated water needs room for expansion. Some say that if you don't flush your radiator at least every three years you can count on replacing it the fourth year.

The radiator filler cap is specially constructed to withstand pressure. It therefore has rubber sealing gaskets that should be in good condition, as should the rubber sealer in the neck of the radiator. If these look worn or damaged, replace them at once with a cap of the same size and pressure rating. Check your manual.

The radiator needs to be clean to function properly — free of bugs and road dust on the outside and free of rust and corrosion on the inside. To clean the outside, you can sometimes hose the bugs off or blow them off with a pressure hose at the gas station; blow the hose from back to front lest you blow all the bugs into the engine compartment. A whisk broom or brush will help with the more persistent bugs.

Most manufacturers recommend that the inside of your radiator be flushed out and new coolant added every two years. That is quite sufficient. Don't let the service manager talk you into changing every year; it isn't necessary unless it says so in your manual, but you can add a can of rust inhibitor once a year.

HOSES The hoses are an important part of this system. Do not neglect to inspect them every six months or so. They clog up inside. Squeeze them hard to make sure there is passage space. Check for bubbles or holes or slits, and for faulty connections. Replace if necessary with the same size hose. Certain pinch-type hose clamps can be a chore to remove and replace unless you have a hose-clamp pliers. I suggest using instead a worm-drive clamp, available at any hardware or auto-supply store.

Hardened, cracked, swollen, or restricted hoses should be replaced. One thing you should remember about hoses: if *one* is shot, they probably all need replacing. They are good for only about three years, give or take a couple. Always replace with good-quality hoses with the same internal diameter. And if your hoses need replacing, it is about time to replace the thermostat too. (Some V-8 models have two thermostats.) See page 161 for replacing hoses and thermostats.

Naturally, if you are going to have to replace hoses, you will have to drain the system. But, if you are only replacing the top hoses, you need drain only enough fluid so that the coolant level is below the hose you intend to replace.

AIR-COOLED ENGINES Simply because your engine is air-cooled instead of water-cooled doesn't mean that it is trouble-free. Air-cooled engines also overheat if the air channels are clogged or not receiving enough air to cool the engine. This used to happen on the old Volkswagen vans. You will notice on the highway many of them with homemade air vents fashioned out of tin to catch more airflow because their engines were running hot. In the later models VW moved the air ducts to the top of the vans to rectify this problem.

Body and Interior Maintenance

If you want to keep what's on your chassis classy you have to periodically do certain things. Maintaining your car's body not only keeps it looking its best when you are driving it but also greatly enhances its trade-in value.

The most important thing you can do for your car's appearance is to keep it clean and well polished with a good wax, such as Simonize, which protects it from rust and damaging chemicals in the air. The wax coating should be thick enough so that it repels water, that is, water should sit in droplets on a well-waxed finish. Depending upon your climate and atmosphere, a good wax job should last at least six months, sometimes a year. Between wax jobs I use a Kozak cloth to wipe down my car every week and that saves me a lot of washes.

Dents and small pits in the paint should be attended to immediately, *before* rust starts. If you live in a cold climate where salt is used on the roads, try to wash off the underbody of the car as well as the top, as salt rapidly corrodes metal. If you live by the sea, try to keep your car washed with fresh water as much as possible and certainly well waxed at all times.

If you take your car on a ferry across salt water, try to have the car put in the hold rather than on deck. If it does go on deck, wash it as soon as you can after going ashore.

Take your car to one of those car washes that has a high-pressure hose and spray it at the hard-to-get-to places under the car, like the wheel wells, where mud and grime tend to collect. Spray till the water runs clean. Spray down the air intake in front of your windshield and watch the water run out the bottom of the chassis. If it doesn't, the holes underneath are plugged up. Unplug them with a stick or your pocketknife until they run free.

During perishingly cold weather, when the slush and salty water freeze under your car, do not try to clean it off, since it is only when it begins to thaw that the salt does its damage. Wait till the weather warms up and then take the hose to it.

For those tiny nicks where the paint has come off, rub the rust off with a piece of emery paper and then get a small container of paint from your dealer the same color as your car and cover the nick with a few very thin coats of paint. Some manufacturers sell little vials of paint with a brush right in the top, like a bottle of nail polish.

Shop around for your major body repairs. There can be as much as 200 percent difference in price. Usually an independent body shop is much cheaper than your dealer, who more often than not farms the work out to a body shop. In fact, I have found that almost any reliable independent shop is cheaper than your dealer for any repair, unless it is something that is strangely indigenous to your model.

I keep a plastic spray bottle of vinegar-and-water mix in my car to clean the windows, and a spray bottle of Fantastic to keep the interior trim, dashboard, door interior, and so on, clean. I have mats to keep the carpeting clean. And about once every two or three months I vacuum (in good weather).

When I'm held up waiting for a freight train or for whatever reason, I pick up my dust cloth and polish. It keeps my nerves calm and keeps the car clean at the same time. It's called "never waste a minute."

If window stripping comes loose, you can buy a rubber glue in the auto-supply store.

It is usually much less expensive to fix whatever starts to go wrong immediately rather than to wait, because the longer you wait to repair the problem, the worse it gets and the more it costs.

Most manufacturers advise lubricating the following every six months, to keep them in smooth working order:

> hood hinges — oil (heavy weight)
> door hinges — oil (heavy weight)
> door lock — graphite
> tailgate door (on station wagons) —
>   oil (heavy weight)
> fuel access door hinge — oil (heavy weight)

13. The Tune-up

GETTING READY FOR THE TUNE-UP

1. Read your owner's manual and follow all the recommended safety rules carefully.

2. BEFORE starting your engine, place gear in *neutral* if you have a manual transmission; in *park* if you have an automatic transmission.

3. Unless you are working outdoors, make sure your garage is well ventilated or you have vented your exhaust via a leakproof hose connection to the outside of the building. Carbon monoxide is highly poisonous and is difficult to detect as it is odorless. If you want to play it really safe, try the old coal-miner's trick . . . get a canary to stay with you. When the canary stops singing and drops over dead you know there is a leak in the hose somewhere and it's time to get some fresh air.

4. DO NOT SMOKE or permit sparks or flame around the carburetor, fuel lines, fuel pump, filter, or other sources of gasoline or gasoline vapors. Flame or fire will follow gasoline vapors borne on the wind right back to the source, the gasoline supply, and boom, you won't need a tune-up, at least not on that car. Exercise the same caution around your charging battery. Electrolyte is highly explosive.

5. When working around your battery, remember:

a. Avoid contact with battery acid. It will eat holes in your clothing, your eyes, and your skin. If you spill it, wash the area down at once with a mixture of baking soda and water, lots of water, and then apply more baking soda to the area to neutralize the acid. If it gets in your eyes, get to a hospital or doctor at once or even to the nearest pharmacy.

b. The battery is the storehouse for the car's electricity and is capable of producing high current, so exercise care when working around the battery to avoid sending the current through you instead of the car. You won't get electrocuted (unless perhaps you're standing in a pool of water) but you can get enough of a shock to smart a bit.

c. Do not touch any part of the battery post adapter to ground when making a connection to the positive battery terminal as this will short out the battery. Then you would have to have the battery recharged.

6. Dress (or undress) for the job. Remove all jewelry, such as loose beads or long earrings, scarves, neckties, loose clothing, and so forth, and tie back long hair or anything that could conceivably get caught up in a moving fan belt, fan blade, or whatever. Those blades can slice up a salami in a hurry. Likewise, keep your testing-equipment wires well away from the blades and belts.

7. DO NOT puncture your spark-plug wires to hook up testing equipment. Use proper adapters.

8. Avoid touching hot exhaust-manifold tubes, radiator, high-voltage wires, or ignition-coil terminals (when the engine is running). Just jerking away from the shock might result in hitting something else that would injure you.

9. Do not hang your face or hands directly over the throat of the carburetor while the engine is running or cranking. A sudden engine backfire can cause serious burns.

10. Don't remove the radiator cap from a hot radiator. You can burn your hand, and the hot coolant can spew out and burn your face and body.

11. When jacking up your car, do not crawl under the car with only your jack holding it up. They are notoriously untrustworthy. ALWAYS employ additional blocks and wheel chocks to ensure that the car *stays* up.

Tools and Supplies You Should Have Before You Start

1 feeler gauge set for breaker-point gap (or air gap) NOTE: If your car has an electronic ignition system be sure to use nonmagnetic feeler gauges (copper or brass).

1 spark-plug gap gauge (wire, no blades)

3 straight-blade screwdrivers — various sizes. At least *one* with a long shaft. Depending upon where your carburetor is located, you may need a stubby one or one with a flexible shaft for adjusting difficult-to-get-at idle screws and mixture screws.

1 holding-screw-type screwdriver so you don't drop the screws down into the bowels of the distributor or engine

1 long-nose (needle-nose) pliers for bending points if they need alignment, etc.

1 ⅜″ ratchet wrench with extension, universal joint, and spark-plug socket

1 ¾″ adjustable wrench

1 tube of high-temperature "cam" lubricant

1 mechanic's troubleshooting light

1 penknife to scrape electrical connections

1 old blanket to throw over fender. Keeps *you* clean, keeps *car* from scratches (remember to remove belt buckle or move it sideways).

1 dwell-tachometer

1 spring-type clothespin (for handling spark-plug leads so you don't get shocked)

1 compression gauge with flexible tubing

1 timing light (not neon-tube-type)

1 set of tune-up specifications for your model and year. If you can't get one from your car dealer, auto-supply stores carry good ones by Petersen or Chilton for a few dollars.

The following five items must be specifically made for your auto's make, model, and year:

1 complete set of spark plugs

1 set of breaker points (or reluctor, if you have electronic ignition system that requires replacement)

1 condenser

1 rotor
1 distributor cap

Pre-Tune-up Checkout

1. Check manufacturer's specifications and procedures for tune-up of your car. They should tell you how to set up for each of the tests necessary. For example: Air cleaner on *or* off? Transmission in *which* gear? Lights or accessories on *or* disconnected? Idle speed, fast idle, and idle mixture settings? Rpm settings for idle, dwell (point gap), timing, mixture adjustments, vacuum advance connected or disconnected? Emission-control adjustments and tolerances?

NOTE: On late-model cars you will probably find a sticker somewhere on your engine block or in the engine compartment as well as in your manual that looks something like this:

2. Check and record present idle speed and breaker-point dwell with dwell-tachometer.

3. Check and record present ignition timing with stroboscopic timing light.

Dwell/Timing Relationship

There is a direct relationship between dwell and timing. However, it is only a one-way relationship. If you change the dwell angle of the breaker points, you will automatically change the timing of the ignition. Changing the timing, though, has no effect on the dwell angle. For this reason, it is important to recheck the timing whenever the dwell angle has been adjusted.

When the dwell angle is increased, the timing is retarded. Conversely, when the dwell angle is decreased, the timing is advanced. In fact, there is a

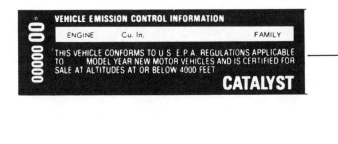

Vehicle Emission Control Information Label (Typical of Federal). Courtesy of the Chrysler Corporation

one-to-one ratio between dwell and timing; for every one degree change in dwell, there is a corresponding one degree change in timing. If, for example, you wish to advance the timing two degrees, it can be done by reducing the dwell angle two degrees. Of course, in making such adjustments, the dwell angle should not be moved out of its specified range.

Due to wear of the rubbing block, the normal tendency is for the dwell angle to increase. This causes the timing to become retarded and results in a loss of power and economy. If the engine was properly tuned initially, restoring the dwell angle to its original setting will restore the timing to its original setting, but the timing sould be checked.

Hookup for Point, Dwell, and Rpm Tests on Standard Ignition Systems

NOTE: For hookup to nonstandard ignition systems, see owner's manual.

1. Connect *red* clip to the distributor (negative) terminal of the ignition coil.
2. Connect *black* clip to a good ground on the engine.
3. Set the *cylinder-selector switch* to the 4, 6, or 8 position, according to the number of cylinders in the vehicle to be tested.

NOTE: Reverse test leads for positive-ground cars. Negative-ground cars have battery's negative (−) post attached to the metal frame of the car. Positive-ground cars have battery's positive (+) post attached to the frame of the car.

Dwell Test
(to see if your point gap is correct)

1. Put function-selector switch on dwell-tachometer to "dwell" position.

2a. Disconnect and plug up (use a pencil or piece of tape) vacuum-advance hose(s) at the distributor because on some distributors the dwell changes when the vacuum advance operates.
b. If your car is equipped with an advance/retard solenoid, disconnect solenoid wire at the carburetor end.
3. Start engine (engine should be at normal operating temperature for this test). Let engine operate at idle rpm.
4. Read "dwell" scale on meter and record it. It should agree with your manufacturer's or it will need adjustment.

STOP — DON'T DISCONNECT ANYTHING YET UNTIL THE NEXT TEST, ENGINE TIMING.

How to Check the Timing

1. Stop engine.
2. Set dwell-tachometer on "tach" setting. (The vacuum-advance hose should still be disconnected and plugged up.)
3a. Hook up timing light. There should be three leads coming from your light. (Only the right kind has three leads.)
CAUTION: Keep wires clear of fan and fan belts. Do not puncture spark-plug lead wires with hookup pincer.
b. Attach red lead to positive (+) battery terminal.
c. Attach black lead to negative (−) side of battery.
d. Attach remaining lead to #1 spark plug (see manufacturer's specs).
4. Start engine. (Engine should be warm and operating at normal idle speed, about 700 rpm, maybe 800 if you have air conditioning. Check specs.)
5. Shine light down on crankshaft pulley until you lo-

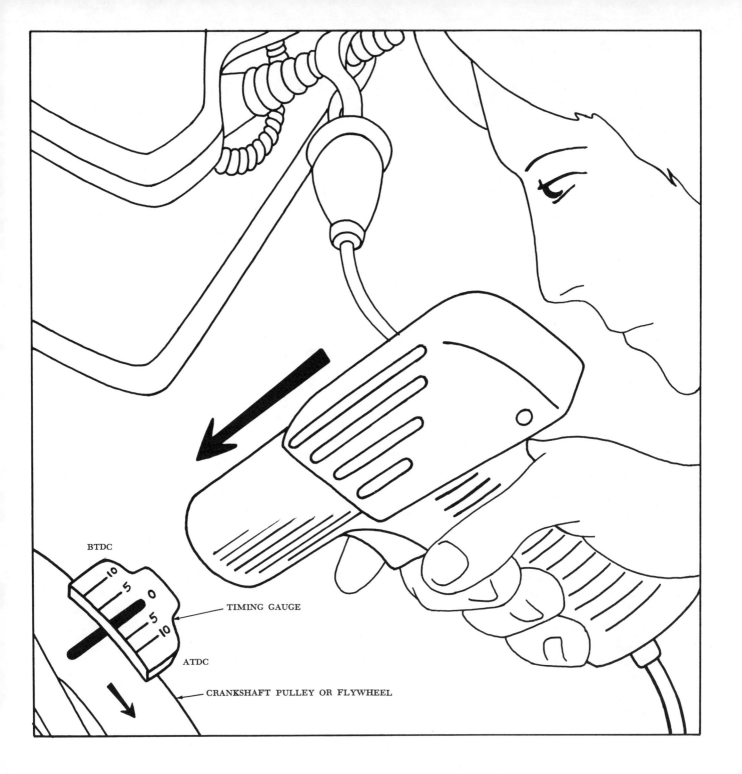

BTDC

TIMING GAUGE

ATDC

CRANKSHAFT PULLEY OR FLYWHEEL

cate markings. Read the markings as the light flashes on and record what the pointer indicates. Check this with your manufacturer's specs. If they agree, super. If they don't, you will have to adjust the timing *after* you do some other things in the tune-up procedure.

6. *Scribe future reference mark* on distributor cap and engine block for existing timing. That way you will be able to align it properly when you put it back together.

TESTING ENGINE COMPRESSION

All good tune-ups include checking the compression of the cylinders. Poor compression results in poor engine performance. Therefore, there is not much point in proceeding with the rest of the tune-up if your compression in each cylinder it not up to snuff.

1. To test compression the engine must be warm. Run it at least five to ten minutes or until it reaches operating temperature (shortly after hot water is running through both your radiator hoses). Turn off engine. Place gear in neutral.

2. Gently and carefully remove high-tension leads to spark plugs from center of distributor cap and ground it on the engine block. (Damage to ignition system could possibly result if this step is not taken.) Don't jerk; don't yank or twist or bend them or you could cause an *internal* break that wouldn't necessarily show on the outside. Grasp the plug wire *at the nipple*, twist gently to loosen it, then pull it off. Number each wire as you remove it with masking tape so you can replace it properly. You may find this is more easily done with a pair of spark-plug-wire forceps (about $2.50) that were designed especially for this. Since the engine is hot this can be a tricky job, and the forceps enable you to accomplish your task without risk of burning your hands or getting a shock.

3. Wipe away all dirt and grime from around plugs before removing them. Wipe area clean. You don't want dirt falling down in your engine when you remove the plugs.

Now, either you have borrowed or purchased a remote starter or you will need a partner to complete this test.

4. If you haven't a partner, then connect the remote starter switch per manufacturer's directions (not all cars can be started remotely).

5. Now remove one spark plug.

6. Insert compression gauge into spark-plug hole firmly. Crank engine over (with gas pedal floored). Record pressure — for example, #1 plug, 100 psi. Release pressure from gauge back to zero.

7. Repeat procedure for each cylinder and record same.

8. Read your results. Consult your owner's manual or shop manual for the proper compression pressure for your particular engine. The higher-compression engines produce higher pressures, ranging from 100 psi (pounds per square inch) to 175 psi or more. However, between any two cylinders there should be no more variation than 25 psi. No cylinder should read less than 100 psi.

EVALUATING THE RESULTS

1. Readings satisfactory. Breathe freely again.

2. If one or more of the cylinders did not register enough pressure there is yet another test — the *wet* test. Pour about 1 teaspoon of engine oil in each of the faulty cylinders and retest the compression with the gauge.

3. If the cylinders that were faulty in the initial test were improved by the wet test, your pistons, piston

rings, and/or cylinder bores are probably worn. This is a major repair job and could run into big money.

4. If two cylinders right next to each other had similar low readings and were not improved by the wet test they probably share a common cause — a head-gasket leak. This is sometimes a difficult repair job and *could* cost.

5. Usually, if an engine is working properly the pressure on the gauge will rise uniformly and then level off. If instead the pressure on any one cylinder rises jerkily, more on one engine stroke than on another, it probably indicates a sticky or leaky valve. This is a major repair job.

Tuning Up the Distributor

1a. Remove distributor cap. This is held in place either by two metal clips or by two screws. To remove the clips, slip the end of your screwdriver under the the clip and pry open. If the cap is screwed on, it is not necessary to remove the screws completely; merely press down and turn or loosen them until they are free from the base, then while they are still in the cap, remove cap and tape screws in so they don't get lost.

b. Carefully inspect the inside of the cap for flashover (indicated by black line on inside of cap); cracking of center carbon button; crack in cap; burned, worn, or grooved terminals. If you find any of the above conditions the cap should be replaced. Some ignition kits come complete with distributor caps. If you don't need it now, save it till the next tune-up and buy the next kit without a cap.

c. If you have an electronic distributor, inspect the connector that goes to the control module for a firm connection.

This is a good time to check the spark-plug cables at the distributor end to make sure they are seated well. DON'T *remove them unless the nipples show damage.* (If there is not enough slack in the plug wires to allow you to remove the cap, you will have to remove the wires from the cap. BE SURE TO NUMBER THEM EACH WITH MASKING TAPE; *this is necessary so that you will be able to replace them in their proper order.* VERY IMPORTANT.)

d. If the cap has grease or dirt or powderlike stuff on it, wash it off with warm water and Joy or any light kitchen detergent and wipe dry with a soft cloth. If you detect a light scaling on the terminals, scrape clean with your trusty scout knife. If there is a heavy scaling, get a new cap.

2a. Unscrew and lift off the rotor. BE CAREFUL NOT TO MASH SPRING CONTACT. Inspect for burned tip, lack of tension on spring terminal, and hairline cracks. If any of these are present, get a new rotor. If you detect a light scaling on the tip, that too can be scraped off with a knife; but if the scaling is heavy, replace the rotor before you put the distributor back together.

b. Now as you look down you should be able to see the points, the condenser, and the plate that holds them. Here is where you should make a little drawing showing the direction that all these parts are headed and the way the wires are headed and attached so that you can get it all back together the same way. (On cars that have Delco distributors you may find a two-piece plastic cap that needs to come off at this point. This is a radio-noise-suppression unit. Just unscrew the hold-down screws and remove it.)

3. Remove condenser, unscrew condenser-bracket hold-down screw. Note that a wire leads from the

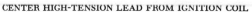

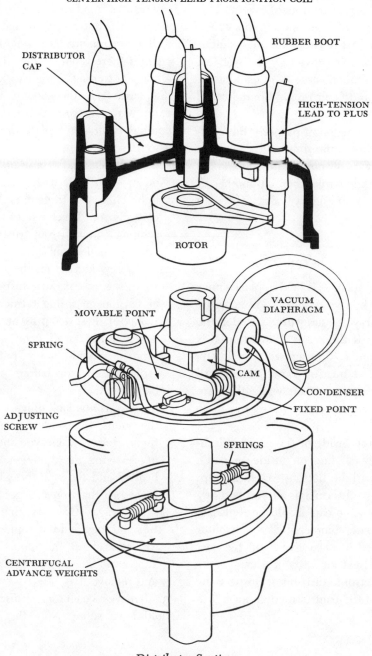

CENTER HIGH-TENSION LEAD FROM IGNITION COIL

DISTRIBUTOR CAP

RUBBER BOOT

HIGH-TENSION LEAD TO PLUS

ROTOR

MOVABLE POINT

SPRING

VACUUM DIAPHRAGM

CAM

CONDENSER

FIXED POINT

ADJUSTING SCREW

SPRINGS

CENTRIFUGAL ADVANCE WEIGHTS

Distributor Sections

condenser. This must be removed also. Either it is attached with a "quick disconnect" that allows you to just pry it out or on some models you must unscrew a screw or loosen a nut that allows you to release it from its connection.

4. Remove the old points. (Every mechanic I know recommends replacing points *and* condenser each tune-up time. Don't reuse the old ones.) One or two screws hold the point assembly to the breaker plate. Remove them and lift the old points out. BE CAREFUL YOU DON'T DROP THE SCREWS DOWN INTO THE DISTRIBUTOR.

5. Now is the time, with all the parts out, to lubricate the distributor parts. This requires a special, high-temperature lubricant, "cam lubricant." Apply a drop

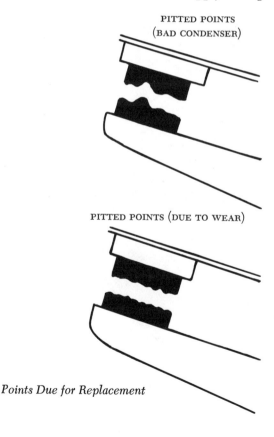

PITTED POINTS
(BAD CONDENSER)

PITTED POINTS (DUE TO WEAR)

Points Due for Replacement

on your fingertip and spread it evenly around the bottom of the cam lobe. Notice a hole in the breaker plate marked "oil." Place a drop in there. DO NOT OVERLUBRICATE. *Wipe off clean any excess you might have dropped on the plate.*

6a. Place the new condenser into the bracket correctly, screw it back down, and insert new electrical leads into the connection.

TIP: It doesn't matter in which order you remove and replace the condenser and the points. What does matter is that if you are going to replace either, you should replace both. They tend to marry, once they start functioning together, and do not react well, one without the other, if they get separated, even though one part may seem all right when the other has worn out.

b. Now, holding a can of lightweight motor oil (SAE 20), look in the distributor shaft. If it has a wick or felt washer, give that 2 or 3 drops of oil (no more, or it will fly on your new points and cause them to burn). Also put a drop on the pivot post of the vacuum arm and on the pivot post of the breaker points and the moving parts of the centrifugal-weight advances if you have them on your car and they are accessible. Wipe the entire area clean of excess oil and dirt before replacing the parts. If necessary, a few drops of solvent on the rag will help. Also, wash or clean your hands thoroughly before installing new parts, to remove any oil. (Before replacing your points, pull a piece of paper through them to remove any oil.)

7. Replace your points. Put the new points over the pivot post. Most points are slotted so they can go back only one way, the right way. Slip them around until the tangs fit into the slots. Once they are seated properly, *look at them.* Are the two round ends aligned perfectly, flat nose to flat nose? Dead on center, no over-

lapping? If not, gently bend the *stationary* arm until they fit against each other perfectly flat and on target. DO NOT BEND THE MOVABLE ARM (or you get forty lashes). Now insert the hold-down screw(s). Here you may find it to your advantage to use that specially built screwdriver that holds the screw securely in its clutches so you don't drop it into the abyss. Tighten slightly.

On Delco distributors eliminate steps 8, 9, and 10.

8. Check your owner's manual and find out what dwell (gap) setting is specified for your points and extract that particular feeler gauge from your set.

9. Points must be set when they are *all the way open*. This is done by getting the rubbing block on each point together with the high spot of the cam lobe. Unless you're extremely lucky and happened to stop your motor at just that precise moment when this phenomenon occurred, *you* will have to *cause* it to occur. This can be accomplished in one of two ways. Either you "bump" your motor while you watch (with your

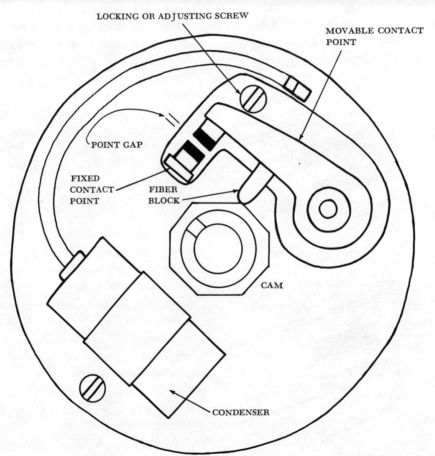

partner's assistance or with your remote starter switch) until the cam lobe does stop right on the point's rubbing block (which can be a tiresome and tedious procedure sometimes), or you loosen the hold-down nut that fastened the distributor tight in its housing. For this you will need (usually) a 1/2″ or 9/16″ wrench, to loosen just enough to enable you to turn it that fraction of an inch by hand until the high spot of the cam lobe is hitting on the points' rubbing block, causing them to open fully. Do not retighten the distributor hold-down nut completely at this juncture.

10a. Now you are ready to adjust the point gap (if necessary). Stick your feeler gauge through the point gap straight on, not at an angle. It should feel as if both points are just brushing it or touching it equally on both sides, gripping it ever so gently.

b. If that is not the case, get two screwdrivers. Place one in the point assembly hold-down screw. Tighten this screw just until the point moves when you move the screwdriver, *no tighter*. Now, depending upon the type of distributor you have, next to the hold-down screw there may be notches or a hole. Insert your second screwdriver in here and twist until the gap you want is reached. Then tighten the hold-down screw (not permanently, just enough for now until you check the gap after you remove the screwdrivers), trying not to move the point again as you do so (otherwise you will have to repeat the procedure).

c. In GM cars it is much simpler to do this gap adjustment. In the distributor is a small window into which you insert the proper-size Allen wrench. With the motor running you can simply turn this wrench and adjust the dwell by using your dwell-tachometer and taking the readings.

d. Recheck gap with your feeler gauge. If you are satisfied it is the correct opening, tighten hold-down screw.

11. Rotate distributor body back to its original position and *slightly* tighten distributor hold-down nut. (The original position can be found by lining up the score marks you made before you started.)

12. Replace rotor. Some rotors have slots that fit only in one position. Be sure you have it in its slot and well seated.

13. Check to be sure you have replaced all wires and that they are not interfering with any moving parts.

14. Replace distributor cap. Turn it until you feel it slip into its seat. (Look for score marks again.)

CHECKING THE IDLE SPEED Now you are ready to test the results of your work with the dwell-tachometer. First check the idle speed:

1. Remove hose from vacuum-advance mechanism. This looks like a metal muffin sticking out of the side of the distributor. Plug hose with pencil.

2. Hook up dwell-tachometer per directions. Here is the way most of them work:

a. Set meter on "tach" setting.

b. Connect *red* clip to the *negative* terminal of the coil. (You can find that wire terminal because the other end leads to the distributor.)

c. Connect the *black* clip to a good ground on the engine — a metal bolt will do.

d. Turn cylinder-selector switch to the number of cylinders your car has.

e. Start engine, and allow it to reach normal operating temperature.

f. Adjust curb-idle speed to manufacturer's specifications by turning idle screw on carburetor clockwise for faster, counterclockwise for slower. When the needle on your tachometer shows the right rpm for your car, your idle speed will be correctly adjusted.

CHECKING POINT ADJUSTMENT Now you are ready to dynamically check to see if your points are properly adjusted. Cross your fingers and hope.

1. Change dwell-tachometer selector to "dwell." (Motor still running.)
2. The reading on your dwell-tachometer should now fall within your manufacturer's specifications (plus or minus tolerance). If not, you have to go back to square one.

   a. Stop engine, and disconnect meter.
   b. Remove distributor cap and rotor.
   c. Move distributor body until points are fully open.
   d. Reset points for proper gap.
   e. Rotate distributor body to original position; tighten nut.
   f. Replace rotor and distributor cap.
   g. Reconnect meter.
   h. Start engine.
   i. Recheck dwell again and repeat steps a through i if necessary.

3. Again, if you have a GM car that has a window in the distributor and your dwell isn't correct, merely insert your Allen wrench into the little window and turn left or right until the dwell reads to manufacturer's specifications. This may be done while the engine is running.

CHECKING THE TIMING Now you must check the engine's timing. This is important because it determines the exact moment the spark is delivered to the cylinder: too soon — advanced spark — no good; too late — retarded spark — no good. For this test we need the timing light again, to know if we must advance or retard the spark exactly to the manufacturer's specifications, so many degrees before or after *top dead center* (TDC).

1. Stop engine. Check manufacturer's specifications for timing.
2. Set meter selector on "tach."
3. Remove vacuum hose (as before) and plug with pencil.
4. Hook up timing light. KEEP WIRES AWAY FROM RADIATOR FAN.

   a. Attach light per directions to #1 spark plug. *Do not puncture spark-plug wires.* The timing light that works from your car battery will have three leads.
   b. The *red* lead attaches to the positive side of your battery terminal.
   c. The *black* lead attaches to the *negative* side of your battery terminal.
   d. The remaining lead attaches to your #1 plug.
   e. The theory: A timing light attached to the #1 spark plug lights up every time the plug fires. At that moment the mark on the vibration damper should align with the degree mark that the manufacturer specifies on the timing cover. (See illustration page 147.) If it doesn't, if it lines up two or more degrees off, your timing is off. Your timing is adjusted by loosening the hold-down nut and turning the distributor one way or the other. (That is why we didn't tighten it all the way before — because now we may need to move the distributor to correct the timing.) On my car the manufacturer gives me a four-point leeway; the specs read "TDC±2°," meaning it's okay if the timing is set anywhere between 2 degrees before (+) top dead center to 2 degrees after (−).

CAUTION: Be sure you are reading the timing marks from a "front-on" position. A sideways look can give you a wrong reading, just like looking cockeyed at your watch — parallax error.

5. Check timing with light. If necessary, adjust to manufacturer's specifications by rotating distributor body after loosening distributor hold-down nut.

6. After correcting timing, tighten that hold-down nut firmly.

7. Recheck timing with light. If incorrect, loosen distributor body, correct alignment, and repeat steps as necessary.

8. If timing is correct, give yourself a treat and a pat on the back.

9. Shut off engine.

You can now disconnect the timing light, but leave the tachometer connected.

Adjusting the Idle

1. Check your manufacturer's specifications and procedure.

2. Use your service manual to locate:

curb-idle screw
idle-mixture screw
fast-idle screw
curb-idle solenoid (on late-model cars only)

3. Adjust curb idle to specifications (using your tachometer; see pages 153–154) by turning curb-idle screw + (right) or − (left). If your car has both a curb-idle screw and a curb-idle solenoid, adjust the curb-idle solenoid first per manufacturer's specifications and directions, and then disconnect its single wire before adjusting the curb-idle screw to obtain lower idle speed. Reconnect solenoid wire before proceeding.

4. To set correct air-fuel mixture at curb idle, turn the idle-mixture screw clockwise until the engine starts to slow up or idle roughly from too lean a mixture. Make a mental note of that position. Then screw counterclockwise until the engine starts to speed (from too rich a mixture). Somewhere about halfway in between should be the right setting. Observe the following:

a. Turn screws only ⅛ of a turn at a time and wait 30 seconds for engine to react before turning again.

b. If you have a two-barrel carburetor, complete adjustment on one side before starting on the other (each barrel has its own adjustment screws).

c. On cars with emission controls you may run into plastic limiter tabs (some are colored) over the screw heads. In that case turn the idle screw until smoothest idle is obtained.

d. On some late-model cars further steps may be necessary due to emission-control systems. Consult your manual.

e. If the above adjustments do not affect the performance of your engine — see your mechanic.

5. Recheck curb idle with tachometer. Correct if necessary.

6. Locate fast-idle screw. It usually rests against a stepped cam. Rotate the cam until it rests at the step your manual calls for, usually the top or second-highest one. Turn the fast-idle screw until it shows the correct speed on the tachometer — generally about twice the slow-idle speed. Open the throttle (by pushing on the gas-pedal linkage) to release the cam and return to curb-idle speed.

7. Checkout for cars with an *antistall dashpot*: open throttle (step down on gas pedal) and release suddenly. If engine stalls or nearly stalls that means the

antistall dashpot needs adjustment. With engine running:

a. Loosen dashpot locknut.

b. Turn dashpot by hand until its plunger allows the throttle lever to close gently to curb-idle speed without stalling.

c. Check tachometer to be sure engine slows down to proper idle speed. If it does not, slowly screw dashpot away from the throttle lever until it does.

d. Tighten locknut on dashpot.

e. Disconnect tachometer and replace hoses as necessary.

14. How-to Recipes

How to Change Engine Oil*

1. Start car and run engine until it reaches operating temperature. Park on level surface or use lift.

2. Place large pan beneath sump (4 quarts is usual capacity of American cars).

3. Remove oil-pan drain plug and let oil drain out. Remove top filler cap to facilitate draining. (Drain plug will usually have to be fished out of pan.)

4. Examine and replace drain-plug gasket if cracked or brittle.

5. Reinstall drain plug snugly. This is a step you will forget only once! (Never, never run engine without oil!)

6. Before pouring new oil through the filler opening into the engine, it is best to install a new oil filter, despite the fact that it is not required by most manufacturers at every oil change.

7. After refilling with correct quantity of oil (for most cars add one extra quart when changing filter), start engine and check for leaks at drain plug and oil filter. Tighten if necessary.

HOW TO SELECT ENGINE OIL Most new cars should use SE-quality oil. This replaces the old SAE MS rating. Older cars (before 1970) may use SD.

Cars that burn oil can use SC oil. See accompany-

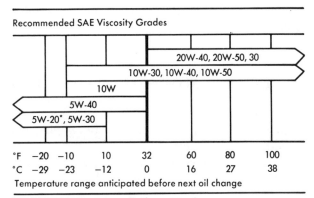

Recommended SAE Viscosity Grades

| | 20W-40, 20W-50, 30 |
| 10W-30, 10W-40, 10W-50 |
| 10W |
| 5W-40 |
| 5W-20*, 5W-30 |

| °F | −20 | −10 | 10 | 32 | 60 | 80 | 100 |
| °C | −29 | −23 | −12 | 0 | 16 | 27 | 38 |

Temperature range anticipated before next oil change

*SAE 5W-20 Not recommended for sustained high speed vehicle operation.

Oil Viscosity Chart. Courtesy of the Chrysler Corporation

---

* Other fluid levels that should be checked and replenished at this time are: transmission, brake master cylinder, steering, differential, radiator, and battery.

ing oil-temperature chart for correct viscosity (page 157).

Multiweight oils such as SAE 10W–40 will serve in temperature ranges from −10° F to +90° F. However, single-weight oils give better service where temperatures are expected to remain constant for the length of time the oil is to be in the engine.

How to Check Automatic-Transmission Fluid

1. Drive car to bring transmission to operating temperature.
2. Park on level surface.
3. Check owner's manual to determine if transmission should be in neutral or park and whether engine should be idling or shut off for fluid check.
4. Withdraw automatic-transmission dipstick from tube (generally located in rear of engine compartment) and read level.
5. If level is low, add transmission fluid recommended by manufacturer to bring to "full" mark.

CAUTION: Do not overfill! Transmission damage may result.

How to Check Manual-Transmission Fluid

1. Park on level surface.
2. Remove filler plug from gearbox after wiping plug and surrounding area clean.
3. Check fluid level visually or with probe. Fluid level should come up to bottom of filler-plug hole.
4. Add type of gearbox oil recommended by manufacturer.
5. Reinstall filler plug.

How to Check Brake Fluid

NOTE: Some master cylinders are screw-type (with or without a dipstick) while others are held on by a bolt or spring clip.
1. Clean off cover of master cylinder and remove.
2. If fluid is not within ½″ of top of cylinder, add type of brake fluid recommended by manufacturer.
3. Check condition of rubber gasket. It should not be cracked, pitted, or overstretched. If it is, replace it.
4. Reinstall cover.

How to Check Manual-Steering Fluid

1. Car should be parked on level surface. Wipe plug and surrounding area clean.
2. Remove plug and check fluid level.
3. Add gear oil as recommended by manufacturer until level reaches bottom of plug hole.
4. Reinstall plug.

How to Check Power-Steering Fluid

1. Car should be parked on level surface. Warm up engine and let it idle.
2. Turn steering wheel full right and left several times — do not hold at extreme positions.
3. Shut off engine.
4. Clean cap and surrounding area.
5. Add type of fluid recommended by manufacturer to bring level to "full" mark on power-steering dipstick.
6. Reinstall cap.

How to Check the Differential Fluid Level

1. Wipe filler plug and surrounding area clean.
2. Remove filler plug.
3. Insert probe or finger in hole. Fluid should come up to bottom of plug hole.
4. Add fluid as recommended by manufacturer. A squeeze bottle or pressure gun helps here.
   NOTE: Conventional differentials take one kind of fluid, limited-slip differentials another.
5. Reinstall filler plug.

How to Check the Radiator

1. Park car on level surface. Engine should be cold.
2. Remove radiator pressure cap. If car has coolant recovery system, check by viewing level in see-through plastic tanks.
3. With engine running, bring coolant level to about 1½″ below top of filler neck or to mark on see-through tank with a mixture of ethylene glycol (antifreeze) and water. See label on antifreeze for proper proportions.
4. Reinstall radiator cap.
   CAUTION: Do not overfill.

How to Check the Battery

1. For maximum battery life, use distilled water, as tap water generally contains some minerals that will contaminate the battery.
2. Wipe top of battery clean. If white or green powdery deposits are observed, wash battery down with a mixture of baking soda and water (1:1 ratio).
3. Remove cell covers. Check level of electrolyte.
4. Add water until level reaches bottom of filler holes or level marks on battery.
5. Reinstall covers.

How to Change an Oil Filter

1. Loosen filter with oil-filter cylindrical wrench or spanner as required.
2. Unseat by hand. Keep top of oil filter *up* to prevent spilling.
3. Smear thin coat of clean oil on new oil filter's gasket.
4. Tighten new filter by hand (it should go on easily) until new gasket just begins to compress; then give it another one-half to three-quarter turn by hand.
   CAUTION: Tightening a new oil filter with a wrench will generally overcompress the gasket and ruin its leak-sealing capacity, as well as possibly damaging the threads and causing an oil leak and future installation difficulties.

How to Replace Fuel Filters

CAUTION: *Do not smoke.*

In-line and integral fuel filters are the most common. The in-line filter sometimes has a replaceable bronze, paper, foam, or ceramic element. Although it is generally located between the fuel pump and the carburetor, it may also be found between the gas tank and the fuel pump. If it is located below the fuel tank, a method must be devised to clamp the supply line closed or fuel will spill everywhere! Also note the arrow on in-line fuel filters. It denotes the direction of fuel flow.

Integral fuel filters are located in the carburetor inlet.

CAUTION: Metal fuel lines are very soft. Great care and good wrenches must be used to prevent bending and crimping.

REPLACING AN IN-LINE FUEL FILTER

1. Keep engine cold.
2. Clean holding clips and surrounding areas.
3. Release clamps holding filter — use rag to catch fuel spillage.
4. Pull filter off.
5. Install new filter (note arrows) and secure clamps.

REPLACING AN INTEGRAL FUEL FILTER

1. Keep engine cold.
2. Disconnect fuel-line connection (small nut) at fuel-filter nut (large nut).
3. Remove fuel-filter nut.
4. Remove filter and spring.
5. Blow on filter's fuel-inlet end.
6. Replace filter if air does not pass easily. Bronze filter may be cleaned in solvent.
7. Reinstall in opposite order of disassembly.
8. Check for leaks with engine running.

HOW TO REPLACE AND ADJUST A BELT

1. Loosen nut that secures the alternator* bracket.
2. Push alternator toward engine. Remove old belt.
3. Thread new belt on pulleys.
4. Pry back alternator until belt play is ¼" to ½".
   CAUTION: Pry against engine block and alternator center casting. Placing pry bar against alternator end plates is likely to cause damage to alternator.
5. To secure alternator tighten nut while holding alternator in place with pry bar.
6. Recheck new-belt tension after 100 miles.

* Also applies to air-conditioner, power-steering, air-injection, etc., belts.

HOW TO SERVICE CARBURETOR AIR CLEANERS

There are several types: (1) paper filter (most cars use this type); (2) metal mesh wetted with oil; (3) foam over wire screen; (4) oil bath with metal mesh.

1. Unscrew top holding nut on carburetor air cleaner.
2. Remove air-cleaner element.
   a. Paper filter (type 1) may be examined by holding light on inside and viewing from outside. If light can be seen, filter is still good and may be cleaned by rapping sharply on the ground several times to dislodge dirt, or by blowing out with compressed air from inside the paper element. Replace paper element if light is not seen.
   b. Types 2, 3, and 4 are cleaned in solvent, blown dry with compressed air, and lightly wetted with heavy-weight (SAE 40) oil. Excess oil should be blown or spun off, as it will interfere with the fuel/air ratio.
3. Refit filter element.
4. Replace cover and tighten by hand.
   CAUTION: Overtightening of cover nut will likely warp carburetor body and cause choke operating problems and other difficulties.

HOW TO INSPECT DRIVE BELTS

1. Visually examine for: cracks and frays on inside and outside of belt, glazing on inside (pulley side) of belt. If any of these conditions are present, replace belt.
2. Press belt midway between pulleys. It should move ¼" to ½". Adjust belt tension if there is more slack than that.

HOW TO TEST HOSES

1. Visually examine hose clamp for white, green, or rust-colored deposits that indicate a leak. Tighten

clamp or replace clamp and/or hose as necessary. Usually if one hose in the system is shot, then all need replacing.

2. Squeeze hose and replace it if it cracks along the surface, is soft and mushy, or is very hard and brittle.

How to Replace a Hose

1. Remove old hose and clamps. This may require a special tool — hose-clamp pliers.
2. Wire-brush pipe connections and wipe clean.
3. Coat pipe connections with water-resistant sealing compound.
4. Slide clamps on new hose and seat hose solidly on pipe connections. Old clamps may be reused if in good condition. Saliva freely applied to the inside part of the hose acts as a lubricant and facilitates installation here.
5. Place clamps at least ⅛″ from ends of hose and tighten securely.
6. Start engine and check for leaks.
7. Top up system as necessary.

How to Test a PCV Valve

1. Let engine idle.
2. Pull PCV valve from rocker cover.
3. Place finger over valve. If valve is operating properly, you will feel a strong vacuum pull and you will hear hissing with finger off valve.
4. Shake valve — good valves will click.
5. Replace valves that do not pass these tests.

How to Replace a Thermostat

1. Keep engine cold.
2. Drain coolant to below thermostat level. This usu-

ally is the large hose on top of the radiator, although in some cars it is the lower hose.

3. Remove one end of hose from thermostat housing if necessary.
4. Unbolt thermostat housing.
5. Remove thermostat housing.
6. Remove thermostat from seat.
7. Install new thermostat according to manufacturer's specifications.
8. Install new gasket!

CAUTION: If a new gasket is not installed, leaks are sure to ensue.

9. Reinstall thermostat housing, hoses, and clamps.
10. Start engine and check for leaks.

How to Change a Tire

1. Place car in *park* with automatic transmission. Place car in *gear* with manual transmission.
2. Apply hand or service brake.
3. Place a wood block or rock in front and in back of wheels to remain on ground. This will prevent car from rolling.
4. Place jack according to owner's manual. A small plank of wood under base of jack will help if ground is soft.
5. Pry off wheel cover (hubcap).
6. *Slightly* loosen nuts (lugs) that hold wheel.

CAUTION: On some cars — notably Chrysler and Pontiac cars as well as some foreign makes — nuts are loosened by turning them *clockwise*. This usually occurs on the left side of the vehicle and sometimes is identified with an "L" to indicate left-hand thread.

NOTE: If wheel nuts were tightened with an air wrench at your service station, the wrench supplied by the manufacturer for changing tires will probably not be up to the task. A 16″ four-way crossbar lug wrench is the tool to use. Trucks usually carry one.

7. Jack up car so that wheel clears ground.

CAUTION: Never crawl beneath a car that is held up by a jack.

8. Unscrew nuts (place in hubcap).

9. Remove wheel and replace with spare. (It may be necessary to raise car further.)

10. Replace nuts (tapered conical side toward wheel).

11. Hand tighten in crisscross (opposite-nut) fashion, working on all nuts a bit at a time (see illustration page 119).

12. When nuts are hand tight, let car down and finish tightening with lug wrench.

13. Replace hubcap. A rubber mallet helps here.

14. Have flat tire fixed immediately!

TROUBLESHOOTING

The important thing is to proceed *with one thing at a time* and to keep your wits about you. Do the easy things first!

Your eyes are your most important tool. Many troubles are visually ascertainable.

If you must use a jumper wire to bypass a switch or solenoid, you will have to know the location of that device. Locations are found in manufacturers' service manuals.

If the remedy says remove and replace, that sometimes means that the unit cannot be tested on the car except with very sophisticated equipment. If replacing a unit "cures" the problem you can be 98 percent sure you found the problem. The other 2 percent is given over to units that fail because other units are bad. Replace cheap units first.

Sometimes a good kick will effect a "temporary" cure.

All the tasks in the following tables are easy except as noted:

H = Hard (sometimes this means really messy)
P = Professional

The best way to ensure that you don't develop starting or engine-performance problems is to keep your motor "in tune." In the event difficulties are encountered, work through the chart by the process of elimination.

Carburetor problems generally are not easily ascertainable. Therefore, suspect the carburetor last. Usually it must be disassembled to determine what is wrong with it. (P)

STARTING SYSTEM

Condition	Possible Causes	How to Check	Remedy
Engine does not start. Starter motor does not turn over. Headlights dim. (Make sure gear selector is in park or neutral and seat belts properly fastened.)	Battery is partially or completely discharged. (A partially discharged battery will often cause the starter solenoid to chatter.)	(1) Turn on bright lights and sound horn. A weak-sounding horn indicates that there is not enough juice coming from the battery.	Charge battery or jump start or replace.
	Loose or corroded battery cables.	(2) Test as above. Lift hood and check cable connections.	Loose cables should be tightened. Corrosion may be cleaned with a 1:1 mixture of baking soda and warm water.
Engine does not start. Starter motor does not turn over. Headlights bright.	Defective starter solenoid.	If battery is known to be fully charged and cables tight, a defective solenoid will click or chatter.	Remove and replace. (Sometimes the solenoid is built into the starter motor.)
	Defective starter motor.	Same as above or starter whines.	Same as above.
	Defective starter (key) switch.	Bypass switch with jumper wire. (H)	Remove and replace. (H)
	Defective neutral switch.	Bypass switch with jumper wire. (H)	Remove and replace. Easy to hard depending on location.
Engine turns slowly but will not start.	Battery charge is low or battery cable loose.	Same as (1) and (2) above.	Charge battery or jump start.
	Cold weather: engine oil too thick.	See viscosity chart, p. 157.	Wait for warmer weather. Jump start with a strong battery. Replace oil with that of proper viscosity after oil is warm.
	Defective starter-motor connections.	Visually and with gentle tugs.	Tighten.
	Defective starter motor.	If it's none of the above and the engine is not frozen or seized.	Remove and replace.
Engine turns normally but does not start (and you have gas in the tank!).	Ignition-system fault.	Remove spark-plug lead and insert screwdriver into cap. Hold screwdriver by handle with metal shank of screwdriver 1/4" to 1/8" away from	A bright blue spark indicates an ignition system in good order — proceed to fuel system. If the fuel system checks out okay, the timing should be

Condition	Possible Causes	How to Check	Remedy
Engine turns normally but does not start.		metal part of engine. Crank engine and look for spark to jump gap. A bright blue spark indicates good ignition; however, timing may be incorrect or spark plug may be bad.	checked. If the timing is correct, then try replacing the spark plugs. If that doesn't work, you've overlooked something.
		If no spark or a weak yellow spark is present, the ignition system is at fault and must be checked out piece by piece.	Start with the secondary system first (it's easier), although it's more likely to be the primary system that's at fault.
	Secondary ignition system fault.	Check for spark from ignition coil by removing center lead from distributor and inserting screwdriver into ignition-coil-wire cap. Hold screwdriver by handle $\frac{1}{4}''$ to $\frac{1}{8}''$ away from metal part of engine. Crank engine and observe spark. If bright blue spark — see Remedy. No spark or a weak yellow spark indicates a defective primary ignition system or a bad ignition coil (coils do not go bad very often).	A bright blue spark indicates a good ignition system up to the distributor cap. The rotor may be worn — replace; the cap may be cracked or dirty — clean or replace. The spark-plug leads may be defective — replace. Wet weather will sometimes cause the secondary system to leak. In an emergency, spray cap and leads with a water-displacement spray.
	Primary system fault.	Remove distributor cap.	The business card will open points so they are not grounded. Visually examine system for grounding out and short circuits.
	If you have electronic ignition, special tools are required to perform tests. If the primary system is bad in an electronic system, it must be replaced.	A test light is required to determine that circuit is not grounded out. Slip a business card between points. Clip one side of test light to ground; touch point of probe to $+$ (battery) side of ignition coil. Bulb will light if ignition (key) switch is good and wire from battery is good and ballast resistor is good.	If bulb does not light: Bad condenser — replace. Bad lead from battery — replace. Bad ballast — replace. Bad ignition switch — replace.
		Take pointed probe to $-$ (distributor) side of ignition coil. Bulb should light if primary part of coil is good.	If bulb does not light: Bad condenser — replace. Bad ignition coil — replace.

Condition	Possible Causes	How to Check	Remedy
Engine turns normally but does not start.	Primary system fault.	Take pointed probe to junction of lead from ignition coil, condenser, and spring contact of points. Bulb should light if lead from coil is good, condenser is good, and movable contact is not grounded.	If bulb does not light: Bad condenser — replace. Bad lead from coil — replace. Movable contact grounded — repair or replace.
		If bulb lights it indicates: Dirty points — check visually.	Slip card back and forth to clean.
		Pitted points — check visually.	Replace, gap, and check timing.
		Worn points — check visually.	Replace, gap, and check timing.
		Misaligned points — check visually.	Bend fixed point to align.
		Incorrect gap — check with feeler gauge.	Regap and check timing.
		Bad condenser — replace with one known to be good.	Replace.
		Bad coil (secondary) — check with oscilloscope. (P)	Replace.
	Timing incorrect. Backfiring through carburetor usually means timing is advanced; through muffler, that it is retarded.	Strobe timing light needed.	Reset timing. Refer to tune-up section.
	Spark plugs fouled.	Remove and examine.	Replace, or sandblast. (P)
	Spark-plug gap incorrect.	Remove and check with feeler gauge.	Regap and replace.
	Spark plug shorted out.	Oscilloscope. (P)	Replace.

Warning Lights and Gauges

Condition	Possible Causes	How to Check	Remedy
Oil warning light stays on, or gauge reads low. (This is very serious. Running an engine that has insufficient oil pressure leads to excessive engine wear and you will soon have to consult section on engine noises — an expensive section.)	Lack of oil.	Stop engine and check oil.	Add oil.
	Oil warning circuit defective.	Remove wire from sensing device on engine. If light stays on, fault is in wiring.	Repair wire or socket, or replace.
		If light goes out, fault may lie in sensing device.	Remove and replace.
	Oil pump defective.	Remove valve cover — see if oil is pumped up with engine running (very messy).	Replace oil pump.
	Oil lines blocked.	Remove valve cover and sump. Check for sludge.	Flush engine.
Oil warning light goes out or gauge pressure increases only when engine speed is increased.	Lack of oil.	Stop engine and check oil.	Add oil.
	Inadequate oil pressure at low speeds.		Seek expert help.
Alternator charging light stays on or Ammeter reads discharge, above idle speed. CAUTION: Alternators are very delicate. Service should be left to a professional.	Broken fan belt, or fan belt slipping.	Lift hood to observe.	Tighten or replace.
	Loose or disconnected wires.	Lift hood and make visual check.	Stop engine before reconnecting wires. CAUTION: If you put the wrong wire in the right place, you may ruin the alternator or voltage regulator.
	Voltage regulator defective.	Professional test equipment.	Remove and replace.
	Alternator defective.	Professional test equipment.	Remove and replace.

FUEL SYSTEM

Condition	Possible Causes	How to Check	Remedy
Engine turns normally but does not start (and you have gas in the tank!). NOTE: Carburetor problems are generally difficult to test without special equipment and tools. The professional mechanic usually replaces the carburetor — rather than rebuild it — when carburetor problems are suspected. Fortunately carburetors — compared to ignition systems — are relatively trouble-free.	Fuel to carburetor — if ignition checks out but engine does not start.	Remove air cleaner. Look down carburetor barrel to see if mist is present. If it is, fuel is reaching the carburetor. Pump throttle once or twice to see if fuel squirts down carburetor barrel. CAUTION: Never attempt to start car while looking down barrel of carburetor. It may backfire and burn your face or hands. If fuel is reaching carburetor, see Possible Causes below.	If fuel is reaching carburetor and you have not overlooked troubles in the ignition system, suspect the spark plugs (replace) or that the carburetor is dirty or jammed (it must be disassembled for proper cleaning). (P) CAUTION: Fool not with carburetor settings. They are very delicate and you are sure to muck it up.
	Flooded.	Smell. Also, spark plugs will be wet. CAUTION: Be careful about running battery down — it's better to go away for a cup of coffee.	Hold choke plate open. Hold throttle in full open position (do not pump!). Try to start car every few minutes with brief starting bursts.
	Choke not operating properly.	See if choke plate is in correct position — closed for cold and open for warm — and moves freely. Check for binding in throttle linkage.	A choke and carburetor cleaning spray.
	Air leakage.	Visually check hoses and gaskets.	Tighten or replace.
	Carburetor out of adjustment.	Exhaust gas analyzer. (P)	Set to specifications. (P)
	Fuel reaches carburetor but does not eject into barrel.	Disconnect fuel line to carburetor. Crank engine while emptying fuel line into container. (H) If fuel is pumped out, fuel pump is good and lines are not restricted.	Carburetor must be disassembled and cleaned out by compressed air. (P) Do not use wire to clean passages for it may change the diameters of the calibrated holes and jets.
	Fuel not reaching carburetor.	Test as above.	Trace fuel line back to restrictions or fuel pump not working.

Condition	Possible Causes	How to Check	Remedy
Engine turns normally but does not start.	Restrictions in fuel line.	Test as above. Step-by-step elimination of parts.	Clean or replace.
	Fuel pump not working.	As above.	Remove and replace.
Engine backfires repeatedly through carburetor.	Ignition timing incorrect — probably too far advanced — or Distributor cap and/or spark-plug leads wet.	Timing light. Look for stray sparks in dim light.	Check and reset timing. Dry thoroughly. Also check firing order.
Engine fires but does not keep running.	Ignition-system or fuel-system problem.	Treat as if engine will not start.	Run through tests for "Engine turns normally but does not start."

Engine Performance

Condition	Possible Causes	How to Check	Remedy
Engine stalls at idle speed when cold.	Choke not operating properly.	Remove air cleaner and observe operation. Choke plate should be closed when cold and open slowly as engine heats up. Look for binding.	A carburetor spray cleaner and lubricator should solve the problem. If it does not, the carburetor may be warped due to overtightening (replace), or choke may be defective (replace).
	Choke out of adjustment.	Erratic starting behavior with changes in weather.	Readjust; a trial-and-error procedure.
	Emission controls not working properly.	Look for leaks, pinched hoses, misplaced hoses, blocked valves, etc.	Clean or replace. Due to variety of types, a service manual is a must.
Engine stalls when idling at normal operating temperature or Rough idle at normal operating temperature.	Idle speed set too low.	By sound or with a tachometer.	Readjust.
	Carburetor idle-circuit fuel mixture improperly set.	By sound, or exhaust-gas analyzer. (P)	Readjust.
	Choke plate jammed.	Remove air cleaner for observation.	Clean with carburetor cleaner and lubricator.
	Contact-breaker points worn, pitted, or incorrectly gapped.	Remove distributor cap and check visually and with feeler gauge. Or check with dwell-tachometer.	Readjust or replace. NOTE: Readjusting dwell will require readjusting timing.
	Ignition timing incorrect.	Timing light.	Readjust.
	Fouled or incorrectly gapped spark plugs.	Remove to check.	Clean or replace.
	Intake vacuum leak.	Listen for hissing sounds. Squirt oil in joints to see if it is sucked in. May be checked with vacuum gauge.	Tighten and/or replace gaskets or hoses.
	Internal carburetor malfunction.	Disassemble. (P)	Rebuild (P) or replace.
Engine stalls on acceleration.	Choke not working properly.	Remove air cleaner.	Clean or readjust or replace.
	Air cleaner dirty.	Visually.	Clean or replace.

Condition	Possible Causes	How to Check	Remedy
Engine stalls on acceleration.	Carburetor accelerator pump not working properly.	Disassemble. (P)	Rebuild (P) or replace.
	Carburetor dirty or passages blocked.	Disassemble. (P)	Rebuild (P) or replace.
Engine has poor acceleration or Engine seems to have less power.	Incorrect timing.	Timing light.	Readjust.
	Intake vacuum leak.	Listen for hissing sounds. Spray oil on joints to see if it's sucked in. May be checked with vacuum gauge.	Tighten and/or replace gaskets or hoses.
	Distributor automatic-advance unit binding or worn, or springs broken or worn out.	Timing light and tachometer. Check specifications and observe timing advance relative to engine speed.	Replace springs or advance unit.
	Accelerator linkage out of adjustment or binding.	With engine off, air cleaner removed, choke open, look down carburetor barrel to determine if full throttle at pedal is full throttle at carburetor (a two-person job).	Adjust or replace linkage.
	Engine compression low.	Remove center lead to distributor and ground to engine. Remove spark plug and fit compression gauge. Crank engine with full throttle and record reading. Check all cylinders. Check against engine specifications.	(1) Tighten head gasket; use torque wrench. (2) Set valve clearances to specifications if they are not hydraulic. (P) (3) Replace head gasket if damaged or leaking. (P) (4) Valve and ring job. (P)
	Fuel starvation.	Check fuel supply to carburetor; disassemble carburetor to clean. (P)	Rebuild (P) or replace. NOTE: Fuel starvation may be caused by a faulty fuel pump. Replace.
Engine stalls when coming to a stop. Performs normally other times.	Idle speed set too low.	By sound or with tachometer.	Readjust throttle stop screw.
	Intake manifold or vacuum leaks.	Listen for hissing sounds. Spray oil on joints to see if it is sucked in. May be checked with vacuum gauge.	Tighten and/or replace gaskets or hoses.

Condition	Possible Causes	How to Check	Remedy
Engine stalls when coming to a stop. Performs normally other times.	Carburetor idle circuit dirty.	Disassemble. (P)	Clean and rebuild (P) or replace.
Engine misses or surges.	Ignition system defective.	See "Engine turns normally but does not start." May be checked with an oscilloscope to pinpoint problem. (P)	Replace defective part.
	Intake vacuum and manifold leaks.	Listen for hissing sounds. Spray oil on joints to see if it is sucked in. May be checked with vacuum gauge.	Tighten and/or replace gaskets or hoses.
	Water in fuel, carburetor dirty or flooding. Carburetor out of adjustment.	Disassemble. (P)	Clean and rebuild (P) or replace.
Engine misses at high speed — high engine rpm. (See "Engine misses" above.)	Loose electrical connections.	Visually.	Tighten or replace.
	Air cleaner dirty.	Remove and check.	Clean and/or replace.
	Spark plugs faulty.	May be checked with an oscilloscope. (P)	Replace.
	Contact points worn, dirty, pitted, or incorrectly set.	Visually and with dwell-tachometer.	Replace.
	Contact points "floating" at high speeds or distributor shaft worn.	Timing light. Timing mark will appear to fluctuate or bounce as engine speed is increased.	Replace points. Replace distributor. (P)
	Valve clearance incorrect (engines not fitted with hydraulic lifters).	Vacuum gauge; or remove valve cover and check clearances. (H)	Reset to specifications. (H)
Engine falters and stops when hot in stop-and-go traffic. Restarts after pause.	Vaporization in carburetor or fuel line.	By traffic and weather conditions.	Allow time for fuel system to cool. An antivaporization additive may help.
Engine "runs on" when switched off.	Engine overheating due to incorrect timing.	Timing light. Check automatic-advance operation.	Set to specifications. See "Engine seems to have less power."
	Engine overheating due to cooling-system malfunction.	See Cooling System.	See Cooling System.
	Vacuum leak causing fuel/air ratio to lean out.	Listen for hissing sounds. Check with vacuum gauge.	Tighten and/or replace gaskets or hoses.

Condition	Possible Causes	How to Check	Remedy
Engine "runs on" when switched off.	Spark plugs overheating.	Check spark-plug insulator cone. If white or blistered and timing is correct and fuel/air ratio is correct, color indicates spark plug is too hot.	Replace with next-cooler spark plug.
	Valve clearances incorrect (engines not fitted with hydraulic lifters).	Vacuum gauge; or remove valve cover and check clearances. (H)	Reset to specifications. (H)
	Emission controls.	Cause engines to run hot even when not faulty due to very lean air/fuel ratios.	(1) Try higher-octane fuel. (2) Seek expert help. (3) Learn to live with it — experts can't fix it either.
	Hot spots in combustion chamber.	Process of elimination — dismantle engine to verify. (P)	Decarbonize and reassemble. (P)
Engine "pings" or knocks, especially on acceleration.	Low-octane fuel.	The first and easiest thing to do . . .	Try higher-octane fuel.
	Engine overheating.	See Cooling System.	See Cooling System.
	Ignition timing too advanced.	Timing light.	Set to specifications. If that doesn't work, try retarding timing an additional 2°.
	Defective centrifugal automatic-advance unit.	Timing light and tachometer; check full advance against engine speed. Refer to specifications.	Replace springs and/or advance unit.
	Spark plugs too hot.	Check spark-plug insulator cone for blistering and white color.	Replace with next cooler plug.
	Excessive carbon deposits in combustion chamber.	By process of elimination the last on the list. Dismantle engine. (P)	Remove carbon and reassemble. (P)

COOLING SYSTEM

Condition	Possible Causes	How to Check	Remedy
Engine does not reach normal operating temperature.	Thermostat stuck in open position or is of the wrong temperature range.	Replace with one known to be good and of the proper heat range.	Replace.
	Temperature-sensing unit defective.	Remove and replace with a new unit.	Replace.
	Temperature gauge or bulb defective.	Remove and replace with a new unit.	Replace.
Engine overheats.	Ignition timing incorrect.	Timing light check.	Adjust to specifications.
	Lack of coolant.	Wait for engine to cool down. Check for leaks and proper coolant level.	Add coolant.
	Defective or incorrect pressure cap.	When engine is cool, remove cap and check condition of gasket. Also check specifications for correct type of cap.	Replace.
	Loose fan belt.	Check play in belt; it should be ½″ to ¾″.	Adjust.
	Radiator air passages blocked.	Visually.	Clean with degreaser and water. Scraping may damage radiator fins.
	Thermostat defective.	Remove and replace.	Replace.
	Cooling system clogged.	Flush cooling system.	Flush cooling system.
	Water pump faulty or leaking.	Check visually for leaks.	Replace.
Loud squealing noise when starting.	Fan belt glazed or loose.	Visually check for glaze. Check fan-belt play.	Replace. Adjust.
	Water-pump bearings require lubrication.		Oil or grease. Use water additives if recommended by manufacturer.
	Generator bearings require lubrication.		Oil.

Condition	Possible Causes	How to Check	Remedy
Loud squealing noise when starting.	Power-steering unit defective.		Seek professional help.
Radiator continually requires water but shows no signs of leaks.	Leakage into engine.	Check dipstick for excessive reading. Check oil for contamination or color change.	A terrible thing. Indicates a cracked block. Engine may be rebuilt but you are likely to require a new one. An expensive problem.

LUBRICATION

Condition	Possible Causes	How to Check	Remedy
Engine burns oil — requires addition of more than 1 quart per 1,000 miles of driving. Blue or black exhaust smoke.	Valve guides worn or valves not seating properly.	Take compression test. If cylinder(s) show low compression, squirt a few drops of oil into combustion chamber through spark-plug hole. If compression readings do not rise, valve problems are the probable cause.	If valve guides are worn, they may be replaced without removing cylinder head. If valves are not seating properly, cylinder head must be removed. Also known as — a valve job. (P)
	Worn cylinder barrels; or worn or broken piston rings.	Same as above except that compression readings will rise. NOTE: This test is not highly reliable but it is better than taking the engine apart.	Pistons must be removed, cylinders honed, and new piston rings (sometimes pistons as well) installed. (P) NOTE: If either a ring job or a valve job is necessary, it is generally good practice to do both as long as the engine must be taken apart anyway.
Engine requires oil frequently but does not seem to be burning oil.	Oil leaks.	Clean engine thoroughly. Run engine at normal operating temperature and look for leaks.	Tighten or replace gaskets. If that proves ineffective, seek expert help, as excessive oil pressure may be the cause.

The following charts are intended to guide the reader in determining which repairs are related to various symptoms. The "How to Check" column is eliminated, as most of the repairs and testing procedures require the use of special tools and professional testing equipment. While many of the defects can be seen visually, you must know what to look for. Other defects will yield to the substitution method.

Suspension System

Condition	Possible Causes	Remedy
All suspension problems.	Incorrect tire pressure.	Adjust.
	Weak springs.	Replace. (P)
	Defective or worn shock absorbers.	Replace. (P)
	Broken springs.	Replace. (P)
	Car unevenly loaded.	Redistribute weight.
	Loose or broken antisway bar.	Tighten or replace. (P)
	Frame damaged or bent.	Repair (P) or replace (buy new car).

Identifying Engine Noises

Modern engines tend to be very quiet and therefore require periodic hood lifting so that they may be listened to. Each engine type has its own particular sound and even engines of the same type may sound different. It is very difficult to pinpoint the source of a particular noise even with stethoscope devices. The following chart is intended as a salve for your peace of mind. Engine noises that don't belong are usually located by tearing apart the engine to discover their source. It is important to attend to this work promptly, as the noise won't go away by itself if ignored, and it will only cost more to fix later.

Condition	Possible Causes	Remedy
Excessive mechanical noise. Knock when accelerating.	Piston slaps against cylinder wall due to excessive clearance.	Rebuild. (P)
	Piston pins worn.	Rebuild. (P)
Engine knocks when accelerating or coasting.	Excessive clearance front and back of crankshaft (end play).	Rebuild. (P)
	Excessive clearance in bearings that hold crankshaft in place (main bearings).	Rebuild. (P)
	Excessive play in connecting-rod bearings (big end bearings).	Rebuild. (P)
Engine rumble.	Loose crankshaft main bearings.	Rebuild. (P)
Clicking noise — regular, changes with engine speed. May disappear as engine speed is increased.	Valve–rocker arm clearance excessive.	Adjust. (P)
Clicking noise after valves adjusted.	Worn crankshaft bearings.	Replace. (P)
	Worn valves.	Rebuild. (P)
	Worn rocker arms.	Replace. (P)
	Worn crankshaft.	Replace. (P)
Irregular clicking noise.	Broken piston ring.	Replace. (P)

ELECTRICAL ACCESSORIES

Condition	Possible Causes	Remedy
All electrical malfunctions.	Dead battery.	Charge or replace.
	Loose connections.	Tighten.
	Dirty or corroded connections.	Clean.
	Short circuit.	Repair. (H)
	Blown fuse.	Replace.
	Faulty switch.	Replace. (H)
	Faulty relay.	Replace. (H)
	Defective horn, bulb, motor, etc.	Replace.

DRIVE-TRAIN SYSTEM

Condition	Possible Causes	Remedy
Engine runs but car does not move when in gear.	Drive shaft or its universal couplings defective.	Replace. (P)
Engine runs but car does not move when in gear (drive shaft turns).	Rear axle defective.	Replace. (P)
	Differential jammed.	Replace. (P)
Engine runs but car does not move. Drive shaft does not turn but is otherwise okay.	Clutch slipping or defective.	Replace. (P)
	Automatic transmission defective.	Adjust (P) or rebuild. (P)
Transmission noisy in forward gears.	Oil level low.	Top up.
	Transmission misaligned.	Adjust. (P)
	Transmission defective or out of adjustment.	Adjust (P) or rebuild. (P)
Transmission noisy in reverse.	Reverse idler shaft worn or defective.	Replace. (P)
Gears grind when shifting (car not moving).	Engine idle speed too high.	Adjust.
	Linkage misaligned.	Adjust (H) or replace.
Gears grind when shifting, car moving.	Clutch not operating correctly.	Adjust. (H)
	Worn transmission.	Rebuild. (P)
	Worn selector forks.	Replace. (P)
Jumps out of gear selected.	Linkage faulty.	Adjust (H) or replace. (H)
	Worn transmission.	Rebuild. (P)
Difficulty in shifting gears.	Changeover speed too high.	Adjust. (P)
	Clutch does not disengage fully.	Adjust. (H)
	Clutch defective.	Replace. (P)
	Transmission overheated.	Allow to cool, check lubrication.

Condition	Possible Causes	Remedy
Difficulty in shifting gears.	Oil very old and turned to varnish and sludge.	Flush (H) and replace.
	Transmission defective.	Rebuild. (P)
Clutch shudders.	Clutch misaligned with engine.	Align. (P)
	Clutch plate or pressure plate(s) warped.	Replace clutch assembly. (P)
Clutch noisy. Noise goes away when pedal is depressed.	Linkage out of adjustment.	Adjust. (H)
	Clutch throw-out bearing worn.	Replace. (P)
Little increase in speed when accelerator is depressed (especially uphill) although engine rpm increases.	Clutch slipping.	Adjust. (H)
Clutch slips.	Not enough free play.	Adjust. (H)
	Oil or grease on clutch plates.	Rebuild. (P)
	Clutch plate worn smooth.	Rebuild. (P)

BRAKING SYSTEM

Condition	Possible Causes	Remedy
Too much pedal play before brakes engage.	Brake linings worn.	Adjust or replace. (P)
	Not enough fluid in master cylinder.	Top up — check for leaks.
	Master cylinder worn.	Adjust or replace. (P)
Pedal feels "spongy," pumping brake helps.	Air in system.	Bleed system. (P)
	Slight leak.	Correct. (P)
	Master cylinder worn.	Rebuild or replace. (P)
Pedal or brakes shudder.	Loose mountings.	Tighten.
	Drums warped.	Regrind. (P)
	Discs warped.	Replace. (P)
	Brake linings damaged.	Replace. (P)
	Drum or disc cracked.	Replace. (P)
Unusual effort required to operate brakes.	Brake linings worn out.	Replace. (P)
	Slave cylinders seized.	Replace. (P)
	Power-brake unit not operating (where fitted).	Rebuild or replace. (P)
Brakes drag or do not release.	Brake pads or shoes adjusted too close, causing binding.	Adjust. (P)
	Shoe-return springs weak or broken.	Replace. (P)
	Slave cylinder seized in "on" position.	Replace. (P)
	Pedal out of adjustment or is binding.	Adjust. (P)
Brakes smoking, noisy, or fading.	Shoes binding (excessive use of brakes).	Adjust. (P)
Brakes suddenly fail.	Broken cables or leak in hydraulic system.	Rebuild. (P)

Steering System

Condition	Possible Causes	Remedy
Car wanders or pulls to one side.	Incorrect tire pressure.	Adjust.
	Brakes binding.	Adjust. (P)
	Car unevenly loaded.	Redistribute weight.
	Tires worn unevenly.	Replace.
	Front wheels out of alignment.	Align. (P)
	Steering linkage defective.	Replace. (P)
	Front wheel bearings too tight or loose.	Adjust. (P)
	Broken or weak springs.	Replace. (P)
	Rear axle loose.	Tighten. (P)
	Frame bent.	Buy new car.
Steering wheel hard to turn.	Incorrect tire pressure.	Adjust.
	Lack of lubrication.	Lubricate. (P)
	Incorrect front-wheel alignment.	Adjust. (P)
	Steering box or linkage binding.	Repair (P) or replace.
	Kingpins seized.	Replace. (P)
Excessive play in steering.	Worn steering linkage.	Replace parts as required. (P)
	Suspension ball joints or kingpins worn.	Replace. (P)

BIBLIOGRAPHY
INDEX

Bibliography

AA Book of the Car. London, England: Drive Publications, 1970.

Alland, Guy, Miron Wiskiw, and Tony Hiss. *Know-How.* Boston: Little, Brown, 1975.

Bricker, Frederick. *Automobile Guide.* Indianapolis: Theodore Audel, 1971.

Car Owning Made Easier. Ford Motor Company, Dearborn, Mich.

Chilton's Auto Trouble Shooting Guide. Radnor, Pa.: Chilton, 1973.

Chrysler-Plymouth Service Manuals. Chrysler Motor Corporation, Detroit, Mich.

Darack, Arthur. *Repair Your Own Car.* Chicago: Consumer's Digest, 1974.

Day, Richard. *How to Service and Repair Your Own Car.* New York: A Popular Science Book, Harper and Row, 1973.

Dodge Truck Service Manual, 1976, 1977. Chrysler Corporation, Detroit, Mich.

Family Book of the Car. New York: Time-Life Books, 1973.

Goings, Leslie F., and Edward D. Spicer. *Automotive Maintenance and Trouble Shooting.* 4th ed. Chicago: American Technical Society, n.d.

Handbook for Automotive Maintenance. New York: The Automotive Information Council.

Judy, Stephanie. *Everything I Know About Cars Would Just About Fill a Book.* New York: A Berkeley-Windover Book, Berkeley, 1975.

Muir, John. *How to Keep Your VW Alive.* Santa Fe: John Muir Publishing Company, 1969.

Petersen's How to Tune Your Car. Los Angeles: Petersen Publishing Company, 1973.

Stapley, Ray. *The Car Owner's Handbook.* Garden City, N.Y.: Doubleday, 1973.

Stockel, Martin W. *Auto Mechanics Fundamentals.* South Holland, Ill.: Goodheart-Wilcox Company, 1974.

Weiers, Ronald. *More Miles Per Gallon.* Radnor, Pa.: Chilton, 1974.

Weissler, Paul. *Auto Repairs You Can Make.* New York: Arco, 1971.

Index

Buck